Reconstructing the Landscapes of Slavery

Reconstructing the Landscapes of Slavery

A VISUAL HISTORY OF THE PLANTATION IN THE NINETEENTH-CENTURY ATLANTIC WORLD

DALE W. TOMICH

RAFAEL DE BIVAR MARQUESE

REINALDO FUNES MONZOTE

CARLOS VENEGAS FORNIAS

THE UNIVERSITY OF NORTH CAROLINA PRESS

CHAPEL HILL

Publication of this book was aided by the generous support of Binghamton University.

Designed by Richard Hendel
Set in Sentinel and Antique No 6
by Tseng Information Systems, Inc.
Manufactured in the United States of America

The University of North Carolina Press has been a member of the Green Press Initiative since 2003.

Cover illustration: Johann Georg Grimm, *Fazendo Calçado em São José do Rio Preto* (1879), óleo sobre tela 56.4 × 75.7 cm., Fundação Maria Luísa e Oscar Americano, São Paulo SP (fotografia de Vicente de Mello). Published in Fernando Tasso Fragoso Pires, *Antigas fazendas de café da província fluminense* (Rio de Janeiro: Editora Nova Fronteira, 1980), 11.

Library of Congress Cataloging-in-Publication Data
Names: Tomich, Dale W., 1946– author. | Marquese, Rafael de Bivar, 1972– author. | Funes Monzote, Reinaldo, 1969– author. | Venegas Fornias, Carlos, 1946– author.
Title: Reconstructing the landscapes of slavery : a visual history of the plantation in the nineteenth-century Atlantic world / Dale W. Tomich, Rafael de Bivar Marquese, Reinaldo Funes Monzote, Carlos Venegas Fornias.
Description: Chapel Hill : The University of North Carolina Press, 2021. | Includes bibliographical references and index.
Identifiers: LCCN 2020044270 | ISBN 9781469663111 (cloth) | ISBN 9781469663128 (paperback ; alk. paper) | ISBN 9781469663135 (ebook)
Subjects: LCSH: Plantations—Mississippi River Valley—History—19th century. | Plantations—Cuba—History—19th century. | Plantations—Brazil—Paraibuna River Valley—History—19th century. | Plantations—Mississippi River Valley—Pictorial works. | Plantations—Cuba—Pictorial works. | Plantations—Brazil—Paraibuna River Valley—Pictorial works. | Slavery—Economic aspects—Mississippi River Valley. | Slavery—Economic aspects—Cuba. | Slavery—Economic aspects—Brazil—Paraibuna River Valley.
Classification: LCC HD1471.A3 T66 2021 | DDC 306.3/49—dc23
LC record available at https://lccn.loc.gov/2020044270

Contents

Map, Table, and Figures

MAP

TABLE

FIGURES

Acknowledgments

Publication of this book closes a chapter of a collaboration that has involved a marvelous journey across the Americas. The project brought together four different researchers from three different countries, each with distinct institutional affiliations, each at a different stage of his careers. We combined our different interests and areas of expertise to study plantation landscapes in the U.S. South, Cuba, and Brazil. We were interested in what visual sources could tell us about the spatial and material organization of the plantation and how the landscape could help us to better understand the economic and social history of the three most dynamic zones of nineteenth-century slave production. Throughout the course of our research, we were able to travel together extensively. We visited numerous historical plantations that still stand in the Natchez District; the sugar zone in Matanzas, Colón, and Sagua La Grande, Cuba; and Brazil's Paraíba Valley. Archival research in each country complemented research in the field. Walking the land and coming to understand the organization of space and the work that was necessary to produce cotton, sugar, and coffee transformed our understanding of slavery. For us, however, the most important aspect of the project was how it was carried out. From its very beginning, the work was organized cooperatively. The final product is a collective work. At each step of the process there was thorough discussion and an exchange of ideas. The whole was always more developed and stronger than the sum of its parts. Writing the book was the experience of a lifetime for all of us. We are privileged to have had this opportunity.

We soon realized that the project was very ambitious and required us to interpret and analyze a great deal of documentary material from multiple perspectives. Both individually and together, we participated in numerous seminars, conferences, and congresses and gave lectures and taught courses at our own and other institutions. These exchanges with friends, colleagues, and students gave us the opportunity to share our research with others, work through the material, and sort out our ideas. We are grateful to all of them.

Above all, we would like to thank the numerous institutions and individuals in the United States, Cuba, and Brazil who supported our work from the initial formulation of the research project to the realization of the book. First and foremost, we must express our gratitude to the Getty Foundation, which provided a Collaborative Research Grant that made the project possible. The grant provided generous financial support for extended multi-year (2005–9) research in the United States, Cuba, and Brazil. Just as importantly, at the outset the Getty Foundation encouraged us to expand the project to include scholars from all three countries where the research was to be conducted and provided the support necessary to make our collaboration possible. Joan Weinstein, Nancy Micklewright, and Katie Underwood provided administrative, practical, and moral support that helped shape our project and our collaboration in the most productive ways possible and aided us in dealing with the practical and administrative problems that arose in the course of transnational research.

At Binghamton University, the Office of the Provost, the Office of the Vice Provost for Strategic and Fiscal Planning, the Office of the Dean of Harpur College, and the Office of the Vice Provost of International Affairs provided institutional support. Don Nieman, himself a historian, saw the value of the project and was an enthusiastic supporter, first as dean of Harpur College and then as the provost of Binghamton University. He made possible the exhibition *Plantation Places: Coffee, Cotton, Sugar and the Making of Nineteenth-Century Slaveries* in the Binghamton University Art Museum the fall of 2012. The professionalism, expertise, and discerning eye of museum director Diane Butler, along with Jacqueline Hogan and Silvia Vassileva of the museum staff, made sure that the materials were presented in an effective and visually pleasing manner. The contribution of Laura Tomich was indispensable for the selection and arrangement of the images and the preparation of the text. The exhibition played a crucial role in establishing a visual narrative and assessing how the public reacted to our work.

Binghamton University's Fernand Braudel Center for the Study of Economies, Historical Systems, and Civilizations, directed by Richard Lee, provided a home for the project. The center supported a number of international conferences at Binghamton and abroad. It also cosponsored the Joint Research Working Group on "Built Environments of Atlantic Slavery" with the Department of Archeology of the Maxwell School of Citizenship and Public Affairs, Syracuse University (2007–10). Much of the material from these activities was published in the center's journal, *Review*, and in its book series at the SUNY Press, *Fernand Braudel Center Studies in Historical Social Science*. Publication of the results of these activities enabled us to focus the discussion and create the context for the project. Amy Keogh and Katherine Pueschel of the center's staff created the infrastructure that made all of these activities possible.

In Cuba the Antonio Núñez Jiménez Foundation under the direction of President Liliana Nunez Velis organized several conferences where we could discuss our work with Cuban, Spanish, and Brazilian scholars. The foundation also facilitated several marvelous research trips to Matanzas, Colón, Sagua la Grande, and Trinidad. Our visits were hosted by historians Esteban Grau in Matanzas and Eduardo Marrero Cruz in Colón, who took us to various sugar mills and other historical sites. Also in Colón, Eneyda Villegas Zulueta, community activist and creator of the museum dedicated to the memory of the enslaved, received us at the former Álava (now México) sugar mill. Historian Hernán Venegas accompanied us to sugar mills in Sagua la Grande and Trinidad.

At the Bibliotéca Nacional de Cuba José Martí, the late Nancy Machado (former vice director) and Migda Estevez, both specialists in the Cuban map collection, provided indispensable help in locating historical maps and other documents, as did Jorge Macle of the Archivo Nacional. In Trinidad, historian and archivist Bárbara Venegas, sister of Carlos Venegas, also greatly assisted our research.

In Brazil, the Museu Afro Brasil in São Paulo and the Biblioteca Nacional and the Arquivo Nacional in Rio de Janeiro generously cooperated with our research. Olivia Gomes da Cunha of the Laboratorio de Antropólogia e História at the Museu Nacional and Flávio Gomes dos Santos of the Departamento de História of the Universidade Federal de Rio de Janeiro organized the international conference Mares de histórias: Espaço, sociedade e história do Atlântico and later a second conference, Repensando a plantation: Paisagens simbólicas, sociais e materiais. These important forums gave us the opportunity to share our work with Brazilian and international scholars. Also important was the international seminar O século XIX e as novas fronteiras da escravidão e da liberdade, sponsored by Universidade Federal do Estado do Rio De Janeiro and Universidade Severino Sombra (Vassouras, Rio de Janeiro) and organized by Ricardo Salles and Keila Grinberg. The international conference Canavais, engenho e açúcar: História e cultura material in Itu, São Paulo, sponsored by the Museu Paulista, gave us the opportunity to interact with specialists from around the world. A FAPESP research grant enabled Rafael Marquese to travel to Binghamton to work on the project with Dale Tomich.

In Natchez, Mississippi, the Historic Natchez Foundation hosted our research. The generous cooperation of its directors, Ron and Mimi Miller, greatly facilitated our work and led to its successful outcome. Marsha Colson and the Pilgrimage Garden Club, Lyda Jordan, and Mark Coffey graciously assisted our efforts, as did the staff at Hill Memorial Library, Louisiana State University.

At various stages of the project, Kevin Heard of the GIS Core Facility and Ina Brownridge of Multimedia Information Technology Services, both at Binghamton University; Eric Olsen of 3iGraphics, Binghamton, New York; Jim Tomich and the Carlson Company, Madison, Wisconsin; Kelly Doering of Stick People Productions, also of Madison; and Joe Tomich, librarian at the University of Wisconsin–Milwaukee, provided necessary technical assistance of the highest quality. Finally, we would like to express our gratitude to Elaine Maisner and the editorial staff at the University of North Carolina Press for the care and skill with which they produced the book.

Beyond institutional support, we enjoyed the support of a community of friends and colleagues whose generous sharing of ideas shaped the outcome of the project. These include José Antonio Piqueras, Ricardo Salles, Chris DeCorse, Mariana Mauzé, Juan Giusti Cordero, Luis Miguel García Mora, Enrico Dal Lago, Vladimir Benincasa, Leila Vilela Alegrio, Adriano Novaes, Camilla Agostini, Breno Moreno, Maria Cecília Winter, Juan Azevedo, Paulo Roberto Belfort, Roberto Guião de Souza Lima, Richard Steven Street, Ulpiano Toledo Bezerra de Meneses, Paulo Garcez Marins, Carlos Bacellar, Cristina Wissenbach, Robin Blackburn, Ed Baptist, Manuel Barcia, Michaeline Crichlow, Catherine Coquery-Vidrovitch, Olivia da Cunha, Mohammed Wazir, Vicent Sanz, Flávio Gomes, and Michael Zeuske. Sadly, a few friends who greatly influenced the direction of the project—Christopher Schmidt-Nowara, Anthony Kaye, Sidney Mintz, and Stanley Stein—are no longer with us. Nonetheless, their spirit pervades the book.

Reconstructing the Landscapes of Slavery

Figure I.1. *Mural at Fazenda Resgate, Bananal, São Paulo, Brazil. José Maria Villaronga, 1850s. Photograph by Vladimir Benincasa.*

Introduction

COTTON, SUGAR, COFFEE, AND THE MAKING OF NINETEENTH-CENTURY SLAVE PLANTATIONS

The striking trompe l'oeil mural by Catalan artist José Maria Villaronga (figure I.1), painted in the 1850s, adorns the dining room of Resgate, a coffee plantation belonging to Comendador Manoel de Aguiar Vallim, located in the municipality of Bananal in Brazil's Paraíba Valley.[1] Villaronga produced this image at the height of the valley's coffee boom, when the region's planters harnessed the natural environment and the collective labor of enslaved workers to dominate world production and create the world's first mass market for coffee. The image symbolically combines the elements that distinguished the Paraíba Valley's economy in the nineteenth century: coffee, the material source of wealth; the natural environment that made its production possible; money, as the crystallization of that wealth and the link with the world market; and, finally, a caged bird that we may take to be a metaphoric reference to slavery, freedom, and the labor of enslaved Africans.

This book began with our fascination with this image when we first visited Resgate in 2002. Its abstract and highly idealized character, combining realist and symbolic modes of representation, challenged us to understand the ways in which nature and the social relations of slavery were depicted in it and the ways that the depiction might be related to the power and worldview of the slave owners. Is there a politics of representation manifested in the painting? If so, what is it? How do such politics legitimize the authority of the slave owner? These questions led to others. In what further ways might nature and social relations be visually represented and endowed with meaning? How might visual representations document material and social relations? How could such visual evidence contribute to our understanding of the specific historical conditions and practices in which geography and environment, the material processes of coffee production, and the social relations of slavery were combined with one another to create and order the distinctive landscape of the Paraíba Valley coffee frontier? What role might visual representations play in the management of the working landscape and slave labor? What can the image tell us about the linkages that bound this particular historical-geographic complex to the world market and the emerging industrial order? These questions, in turn, led us to consider the connections between historically formed space, material practices, and socioeconomic relations. How did this particular articulation of productive space and slave labor enable Paraíba Valley coffee planters to transform and dominate world coffee production during the first half of the nineteenth century? What can examination of the historical landscape tell us about slavery and coffee in the Paraíba Valley?

The painting at Resgate is the centerpiece of a series of images executed by Villaronga that decorate the elegant neoclassical mansion. The walls of the foyer present a variety of images that are thematically linked to the dining room mural. Facing the entrance and painted above the door leading to the dining room is an emblem of sugarcane stalks and all the tools necessary to cultivate sugar. Opposite it and above the entrance is another emblem representing the basic elements of the slave diet—manioc, corn, and bean plants—and the tools necessary to cultivate them. On the wall to the left is a trompe l'oeil representation of a coffee plant in an urn. On either side are trompe l'oeil portraits of an English country house and the Bracuí harbor on the nearby coast that was notorious for the clandestine landing of enslaved Africans after the slave trade was abolished. On the wall to right of the entrance is a trompe l'oeil reproduction of Jean Auguste Dominique Ingres's *Orangery Villa Borghese* that reproduces the neoclassical elements of the exterior of the great house (*casa grande*) of Resgate and brings them into the interior. Paintings of cotton and tea plants are placed in less prominent positions on the walls. The foyer thus brings together all the material elements of the slave plantation complex and associates them with European cultural traditions going back to the Renaissance and antiquity.[2]

The images in the foyer contextualize Villaronga's allegorical painting in the dining room, which is located at the end of a short corridor. The oversized mural occupies the middle third of the wall and dominates the room. It is flanked by two allegories with Asian themes, suggesting the global context of the plantation. In the main panel the elements of the Paraíba Valley landscape are abstracted from their natural and physical setting and translated into symbols. This allegoric image reworks the themes that are present in the foyer images—the bounty of productive nature, coffee, wealth, an aristocratic tradition of landed property and rural civilization—and presents them as a symbolic landscape. Significantly, in both sets of images there are indirect references to slavery, but slaves themselves are not physically present in the paintings.

The dining room image appears to present the view of the planter's property from the window of the great house, the site of command over the countryside. The focal point of the image is a panorama of hills planted with coffee. The view that it depicts is decidedly not the particular view from this room, but it is nonetheless representative of the surrounding physical landscape and evokes the characteristics of the social and economic geography of the Paraíba Valley coffee frontier. The lower center of the painting illustrates both the landforms and the mode of planting that were typical of the Paraíba Valley during the nineteenth century. The hillsides covered with coffee trees planted in vertical rows stretching to the horizon depict the agricultural practice that at once revolutionized coffee production and bore principal responsibility for the destruction of the valley's physical environment. This vista is framed by iconic representations of the coffee plant, the source of the valley's prosperity, while the window itself is bracketed by Corinthian columns, evoking the culture of classical antiquity and the Renaissance. Sitting on the windowsill, a cashbox with money on top of it signifies both the social and symbolic embodiment of that wealth and the beginning and end of the yearly cycle of commercial agricultural production. The centerpiece of the image is a bird in a cage hanging from the window frame looking at two butterflies that fly free outside of the cage.

Over the past several decades, scholars have been increasingly concerned with the cultural politics of landscape and landscape painting. The conventions of European landscape painting have been associated with property and authority. Various studies have called attention to the relation between landscape, perspective, and power expressed in images such as Villaronga's mural.[3] Such studies emphasize the subjective and representational elements of landscape. They link landscape representation to the technique of linear perspective as a way of ordering and controlling space that has its origins in Renaissance Europe. The single vantage point required by linear perspective is interpreted as a position of command. This position identifies the viewer with the proprietor/patron, who is endowed with the authority to appropriate, define, and order the landscape both visually and physically. Thus, such interpretations assimilate visual perspective to social perspective. The visual language of perspective represents landscape as an ideological projection of the landowner's power, which it serves to legitimize. At the same time, the construction and appreciation of the landscape image validate the taste and sensibility of the privileged observer as these qualities are denied to others who cannot share this unique vantage point. The image thus at once confirms the wealth, status, power, and cultural distinction and discernment of the viewer/proprietor/patron. Not only can this figure afford to have the painting made, but he claims the right to define, order, and represent social space at the expense of others. The landscape image thus freezes a moment of reflexivity: the viewer defines the landscape; the landscape defines the viewer.

Villaronga's trompe l'oeil image presents a sophisticated play with the rules of perspective that gives apparent three-dimensionality to a two-dimensional surface. Like all perspective painting, it establishes a singular vantage point, typically associated with power, from which the visual field is ordered. But here the trompe l'oeil technique breaks down the distinction between the inside and the outside of the great house. The representation of the window orders the gaze of the viewer inside the room and idealizes an imagined nature "outside" the window in order to create a landscape from the perspective of the landowner. At the same time, "external" nature is drawn into the room through the image and becomes part of its decor. The landscape is transformed into an aesthetic object that forms a unity between the big house and the lands of the estate. The painting thus affirms the big house as the focal point of the estate and embellishes the power and prestige of the owner.

While Villaronga's image suggests the physical landscape, the countryside is aestheticized and pacified through its visual reproduction. The painting borrows many of the technical, visual, and social conventions of European landscape painting, but its subject is not pastoral or picturesque. In contrast to European and especially English landscape painting, which conventionally constructs an aesthetic "natural" landscape as against a productive landscape,[4] Villaronga aestheticizes the productive landscape and converts it into a symbolic mode of representation. He presents the countryside as productive "Nature." This civilized Nature is superior to the supposedly savage Nature of the tropical American forest. The abundance of Nature, ordered and improved by (European) Man, is at once the source of visual pleasure and wealth. The rational and quantifiable ordering of endless rows of coffee trees transforms the land into both an aesthetic object and a calculable investment whose arrangement is designed to maximize the return from the world market. This ordered, productive, and profitable countryside is the aesthetically refined and pleasing countryside. (The apparently infinite prospect of orderly rows of coffee trees in Villaronga's mural gives no hint of the destruction of the forest nor of the disorder that followed from this pattern of planting. The Atlantic rainforest was literally destroyed in the course of the nineteenth-century coffee boom, and at the end of the coffee cycle, the land itself was so depleted that it can no longer be cultivated.)[5]

Villaronga's mural thus creates an aesthetic identity between nature and property. Their harmonious relation symbolically orders the landscape and the human relations that derive from it. Notable by its absence is any depiction or representation of the production of the landscape, of the massive expenditure of energy by men and women and beasts that was required to shape the land to the needs of specialized commercial agriculture and to make it bear fruit. The presence of slaves is perhaps evoked by the highly stylized and metaphoric image of the bird in the cage. But this image presents the slave as property, not as worker, and emphasizes the passive role of the viewer/patron as property owner as against his/her active role as manager of slave labor. The absence or de-emphasis of human figures in the landscape eliminates the possibility of other vantage points from which the land may be seen. This absence reinforces the singularity of the perspective from which the image is presented and of the solitary viewer. It is not one of various possible ways of seeing the land and the activity taking place on the land. Rather, it claims exclusivity for itself and, by extension, for the viewer/proprietor. By these means, property is naturalized, while the activity that transformed the natural environment and made possible the wealth of the Paraíba Valley is eliminated from view. Villaronga's plantation landscape thus appears not as produced but as a finished product—a part of the natural order and an object of contemplation. The social and historical tensions embodied in the landscape are obscured behind the facade of property.

Such cultural interpretations of landscape and landscape painting reveal much about the relation of representational strategies to power and to the legitimation of social domination. However, they too often treat the visual domain as conceptually and practically self-enclosed and self-referential. Art historical understandings of landscape, largely derived from painting, have become paradigmatic of landscape as a "way of seeing." Here the "landscape idea" is treated independently from the object that is seen. Landscape images, gardens, parks, and vistas are interpreted in isolation from the material practices and historical relations that transform the practical landscape. Each such representation is presumed to contain its own meaning. The observing eye outside of the landscape image is regarded as the site of its symbolic ordering and cultural meaning. Analysis moves from the image as representation to the social and cultural conditions of its production and circulation and, from there, back again to the representation. Thus, the image as a fixed and closed entity is the constant or repeated point of reference. Both vision and analysis move in a circular path that does not extend beyond its frame.[6]

In such approaches, "landscape," "perspective," and "power" risk becoming formal abstractions, a fixed grid, that can be applied to any particular situation because no element "external" to the image is integral to their formulation and deployment. Consequently, they fail to go beyond, and too often simply repeat, the rhetorics of power and its justifications expressed in the images themselves. Analysis then runs the danger of becoming the continual repetition of the same terms irrespective of any specific material, social, or historical content or context. Historical materials simply illustrate or provide empirical content to already given theoretical categories and do not substantively alter the interpretation. Each representation—whether of a seventeenth-century Italian villa, an eighteenth-century English country house, or a nineteenth-century Brazilian slave plantation—is interpreted as the expression of the domination and authority imputed to the "landscape idea." The historical relations that produce and ground domination and its relation to land and labor are external factors that remain outside the framework of analysis. The analysis of power is, ultimately, analysis of the politics of perspective. Such approaches undermine their own insights and have limited explanatory value. By circumscribing the field of investigation, they leave many questions—indeed, the most important ones—unasked, let alone unanswered.

Raymond Williams has cautioned us that working countrysides are not really landscapes. He stresses that the formal concept of landscape implies detached observation and separation from activity. In contrast, working landscapes are embedded in the social and environmental history of the land and those who work it.[7] They are, in geographer D. W. Meinig's terms, ordinary, lived landscapes that undergo continuous creation and alteration through the routines of daily life as much as through calculated landscape design. Working landscapes are the product of the interaction of historically formed human groups and nature. They are the site of multiple activities and agencies. They are made and continually remade through human activity even as they are formative of that activity.[8] Here, of course, the "historically formed human group" is far from homogeneous and unified. Rather, the "plantation community" is organized through the master-slave relation and sharply divided and mediated by racial, gender, status, and class distinctions. The actors and activities that produce working landscapes overflow the aesthetic conventions of landscape as symbolic object and way of seeing, even as they are consciously de-emphasized or excluded from formal representations. Instead of the solitary gaze expressing the authority of the proprietor, visual practices are integral to the material and social transformation of the land. Power is expressed not merely in the ordered prospect or the facade of the big house but in the physical control over the living activity of human beings and the conscious and purposive reordering of nature. The ordering of the practical landscape may express power and assert a claim to hegemony, but symbolic meanings and cultural interpretations are not confined to formal representation. They permeate material and social practice and are continually contested or negotiated.

Our interest in Villaronga's image and the questions that it raises for us about slavery and coffee production in Brazil led us to also examine visual representations of plantation production in other regions with similar histories. The sites that we chose to investigate were also new zones of slave commodity production during the nineteenth century. Like the Paraíba Valley, the lower Mississippi valley and the broad prairie (*llanura*) to the east of Havana in Cuba offered vast tracts of virtually unoccupied land with low population density and at best rudimentary agriculture. Each zone possessed favorable environmental conditions for the production of its particular crop—cotton in the lower Mississippi valley, sugar in Cuba, and coffee in Brazil. The development of these new "commodity frontiers"[9] was integrally linked to the economic and political restructuring of the capitalist world-economy during the nineteenth century. Cotton, sugar, and coffee became the leading products in world trade as the Industrial Revolution, urbanization, and population growth increased the demand for plantation staples either as industrial raw material or as foodstuffs for the rapidly growing number of middle-class and working-class consumers. Accelerating world demand for these products dramatically expanded the scale of production and contributed to the integration of world markets and the formation of new patterns of mass consumption. Each of these previously marginal geographic zones became the world's leading producer in its respective crop, and together they became key poles of the new industrial world-division of labor.

Atlantic slavery had been embedded in the historical formation of the capitalist world-economy since the sixteenth century.[10] While these new zones of slave production built upon older patterns of slave plantation agriculture, they represented a spatial-temporal rupture with the slave formations that preceded them. Elsewhere we have referred to these new zones of redeployed and reconstituted slavery as the "second slavery" in order to distinguish them from the older colonial slavery and to call attention to their originality and distinctive industrial character. Their emergence challenges conventional views of slavery as incompatible with industrial capitalism and political liberalism and enables us to reinterpret not only slavery but also historical capitalism itself.[11] In these new commodity frontiers, both nature and slave labor were profoundly reconfigured in order to conform to the scale and rhythm of industrial production. Both the zones of commodity production and the plantations themselves were far more extensive than their predecessors. In each zone the concentration of enslaved laborers reached unprecedented levels. In each, the pressures of the world market and the scale of production put the emphasis on productivity—increased output per acre, increased output per slave—and intensified the labor of the enslaved population. The new commodity frontiers formed industrial hinterlands that incorporated new technologies of production and transportation, new strategies of land and crop management, and new work routines and labor discipline that were expressed in the physical organization of the landscape itself. The mass production of these crops transformed the landscape of each particular zone. In each, the crop itself became a powerful symbol of national or regional identity that defined place—the South and cotton, Cuba and sugar, Brazil and coffee. Each symbol viewed in isolation celebrated prosperity, the abundance of a particular nature, and a particular way of life while masking the brutality of plantation slavery.

Analysis of the landscapes of these plantation frontiers requires a broadened focus. Working landscapes cannot be reduced to a singular relationship of vision and power. Rather, they are the result of the practical interrelation of nature and human activity. They are formed through the interactions of definite material, social, and cultural practices that are specific to each particular ecology and each particular crop. Thus, these plantation landscapes form what Meinig refers to as everyday landscapes. However, they are at the same time extraordinary landscapes. In contrast to Meinig's emphasis on the unconscious and routine character of ordinary landscapes, conscious planning and calculation in order to maximize control over land and labor and to increase productivity were decisive elements in the creation of the plantation landscapes under consideration here. The natural environment was systematically subordinated to the specialized production of a single commercial crop destined for the world market. Cotton, sugar, and coffee each grow in a distinct environment and have different physical characteristics. The production of each entails material processes that are peculiar to it. The arrangement of fields, selection of crop varieties, and organization of planting routines were planned to maximize output. Production was forcibly organized through the enslavement of workers. The size and composition of the labor force had to conform to the requirements of the crop. At the same time, the social relations of slavery provided a specific means of organizing labor and of regulating social life on the plantation. The working activity and conditions of life of the enslaved population were organized through the social domination and power of the slave owner and the supervisory staff, but power itself could be exercised only through the material conditions of production and the social relations of slavery.

Viewed in this light, the plantation appears not as a static template that is simply the continual repetition of the same thing[12] but instead may be understood as a fluid and dynamic grammar of space formed from the interactions and mutual conditioning of the world market and division of labor, local environments and geography, the material conditions of crop production, cheap coerced labor, the power and authority of the planter, and the contestation and resistance of the enslaved population.[13] Across space and time, this spatial grammar constructs a modular response to distinct tropical and semitropical environments of the colonized world. It marks them as Western, modern, and capitalist even as it differentiates one from the other.

In contrast to cultural approaches, explanation or interpretation of working landscapes cannot be reduced to all-encompassing discourse or culture. Rather, material, social, and cultural practices each retain their own autonomy even as they are unified through purposive human activity. Working plantation landscapes are formed by the continual interplay of material conditions, forms of social relations of slavery, and historically shaped meanings and modes of symbolic expression, and they embody their interdependence. The interrelation and interaction of these material and social forces—distinguishable but inseparable—transformed the land and created distinctive landscapes that facilitated the mass production of agricultural commodities and enforced labor discipline and social control over enslaved populations residing on the estates as their spatial ordering expressed a symbolic order that legitimated authority.

Thus, we are interested in understanding how the working landscapes and built environments of the American cotton plantation, the Cuban *ingenio,* and the Brazilian *fazenda* at once expressed, ordered, and represented these various relations and processes and how these particular spaces were formed and functioned within the capitalist world-economy. Each plantation frontier was a distinct local response to shared world-economic conditions. In this way, our study of plantation landscapes is an attempt to understand the relation of global political economic processes and local histories, the differentiation and interrelation of zones of slave production, and the diverse ways that slave labor was reconstituted within the specific historical conjuncture of the nineteenth-century world-economy.

This book approaches the history of the working landscapes of slave plantations in Brazil, Cuba, and the lower Mississippi valley during the first part of the nineteenth century through examination of visual documents. It seeks to understand the social, economic, and environmental history of plantation landscapes through the visual record that they have left behind. Landscape representations are inescapably part of the history of agrarian capitalism and its New World slave formations. However, working landscapes cannot be reduced to their formal representations. The turn toward the working landscape registers a shift from a high-culture conception of landscape as an aesthetic "way of seeing"[14] to an anthropological, sociohistorical conception of culture applicable to the visual practice of a collective social subject working the land and, interestingly, to an even older meaning of culture associated with the cultivation of the soil or a cultivated piece of land. Although perspective may indeed embody a visual ideology that necessarily effects representations of geographic space, visual practice is not limited to aesthetic contemplation by the isolated seeing eye. Perspective can be mobilized in many ways to secure visual control over the landscape. There are many ways of seeing, and vision is necessarily part of the laboring activities and social practices that produce the practical working landscape. In the working landscape, vision cannot easily be reduced to a one-to-one relationship between viewer and scene. Rather, it entails diverse ways of seeing by multiple actors engaged in different activities in different locations. Their practices and experiences are not governed by aesthetics.[15]

Thus, we cannot ignore the instrumental uses of perspective entailed in practically ordering the material landscape as well as the role of perspective in the quantification and calculation of spatial relations. Vision and visual practices structure land and labor management. Visual control of the landscape was necessarily part of the day-to-day operation of estates and the processes forming working landscapes. These practices produced visual representations of documentary value. We have drawn upon a variety of such visual sources—including paintings, maps, lithographs, engravings, drawings, and photographs—in order to document, reconstruct, and interpret the social and productive space of nineteenth-century slave plantations. The images that we have selected were produced under varied circumstances and often were intended to serve distinct purposes. Each, in its own way, expresses the permanent tension between representation and practice and imposes constraints on our analysis.

Our focus is on the analysis and interpretation of images as documents of the historical spaces and spatial practices of the second slavery. Thus, we are interested both in the image as representation and in what is represented in the image. Each image is a cultural object that bears the marks of its production. These include the material, technical, and cultural conditions of its production, the purposes of the image's creator, and the visual and technical strategies that were employed to represent its subject matter, as well as the conditions of its circulation and consumption. The image selectively depicts an irreversibly fixed past scene and provides evidence, however partial, of a reality beyond the image. We are concerned with understanding the ways in which these evidentiary traces make legible the spatial order outside of the image.[16] This book is constructed as a visual history. We take as a model and draw inspiration from John Berger's pathbreaking 1972 book, *Ways of Seeing*. The images herein structure the narrative. Through the selection and continual juxtaposition of multiple images, we seek to interpret the working landscape of the plantation and to contribute to the understanding of the material processes and social relations through which the land was transformed. The emphasis is on seeing, reading, and interpreting the relations depicted in each image and the relations between the images. The text is intended to provide the information necessary to illuminate and contextualize the images and to bring out their documentary character. We have ordered their presentation in such a way as to at once point to the conditions common to all three zones and the specific local features of each of them. To avoid repetition, the treatment of each zone emphasizes a particular aspect of its formation—labor for the cotton South, technology for Cuba, and environment for Brazil. Once the reader sees the network of relationships at work in one zone, it is possible to see that the privileged theme is also at work in the other two. Following Berger's example, it is then possible to mentally shift the order of the images around and establish new relationships and construct new narratives.

There are two self-imposed limitations to this study that we would like to draw attention to before we proceed. First, we have focused our attention on the largest, most productive, and wealthiest plantations in each region. We have done so because, in our view, these estates most fully express the forces that formed the new commodity frontiers. They were at the top of hierarchies of production, power, and prestige that characterized each zone. Further, they represented the ideal to which all slaveholders aspired.

Second, the visual documents we have used in this study are generally biased toward the perspective of the slaveholding elites. Landscape images of whatever type naturalize, aestheticize, and pacify the countryside, and, by their very nature, they marginalize and instrumentalize labor and the laboring population.[17] Nonetheless, both labor and violence were necessary aspects of the slave plantation landscape. Labor was secured from the working population through compulsion, and the condition of such compulsion was domination over the life activities of the enslaved. Social domination and labor discipline were expressed in and mediated through the material processes required for each crop, the physical organization of the working landscape, and the built environment of the plantation.[18] The practical, working landscape itself was an instrument of control and regulation. Within its confines and structure, the enslaved population was subject to constant repetitive toil under the strict supervision and discipline of overseers and drivers from sunrise to sunset. At the same time, the plantation landscape was deeply implicated in contestation, negotiation, and day-to-day resistance, punctuated by flight and, at exceptional moments, rebellion by the enslaved. Consequently, there is an irreducible margin of non-correspondence between the various types of landscape representation and the practices and conflicts that shaped the social-material landscape. Most often, the enslaved are not depicted at all. If work is represented, the scale of activity is typically reduced, and the scenes appear to be almost pastoral. Other representations of the enslaved are domesticated and portray an unequal but harmonious community under the benevolent care of the master. Thus, there is an ongoing tension between what is visible and what is invisible in each image. The visually pacified landscape image expresses property, prestige, and power as it masks regulation, exploitation, contestation, negotiation, resistance. In this way, it serves to legitimate a paternalistic social order and agrarian civilization.

The invisibility of the slaves in landscape representations is highly significant, and we have tried to take this bias into account. However, while recognizing the violence inherent in slave relations and the centrality of slave labor and slave resistance, our purpose is to write a visual history of the landscape, not a socioeconomic history of slavery. Although domination, control, violence, and resistance are implicit in different ways in the images that we use, we seek to emphasize their documentary character and to explicate the spatial relations they reveal. To this end, we refrain from treating slave agency and resistance as the explicit or immanent content of the images we discuss.[19] The images themselves are, in a certain sense, instruments of pacification, control, and legitimation. They disclose the infrastructure of social regulation and labor discipline but intentionally exclude as subject matter the explicit acts of conflict and resistance that make such an infrastructure necessary. Further, we use sources outside of the visual record in order to illuminate the images, not to provide a more general account of the plantation or slave relations. To do otherwise risks subordinating the images to the text and reducing them to illustrations. Thus, we have limited ourselves to analyzing the spatial relations of the plantation insofar as we can document them in the visual sources that are available to us. By this means we seek to deepen our understanding of slave commodity production in these new commodity frontiers and to disclose the conditions and constraints placed upon masters and slaves alike by the production and ordering of plantation space.

Part I

Making Landscapes

NEW ATLANTIC COMMODITY FRONTIERS

During the nineteenth century, cotton, sugar, and coffee became commonplace items of everyday consumption for larger and larger segments of the world's population. Industrialization, urbanization, and population growth all contributed to the dramatically increased demand for these products. Cotton, the raw material of the Industrial Revolution, became the leading item in international trade, followed closely by sugar and coffee. Supplying the growing demand for these crops entailed the creation of new productive spaces[1] and the reconstitution of slavery and redeployment of slave labor.[2] In the U.S. South, Cuba, and Brazil, extensive tracts of unexploited land were adapted to the new conditions for the mass production of these crops. The lower Mississippi valley, the broad prairie (*llanura*) of western Cuba, and Brazil's Paraíba Valley emerged as new zones of plantation production on the basis of slave labor. The creation of these zones—the fateful combination of plantation monoculture, mass slavery, and the reordering and transformation of environments—was not simply the result of choices made by local or regional elites. Rather, these zones were the outcome of the complex interaction of world-economic and local relations and processes. Each represents a distinct response to the forces restructuring the nineteenth-century world-economy.

Each of these new zones of slave plantation production formed a distinct "commodity frontier" that offered extremely favorable environmental and geographic conditions for large-scale production of its particular crop[3]—cotton in the lower Mississippi valley, sugar in Cuba, and coffee in the Paraíba Valley. The formation of slave plantation complexes in these new zones was driven by the availability of virtually unlimited tracts of land and the mobility of enslaved labor. Specific ecologies combined with growing world demand to create specialization among the three frontiers. Each zone concentrated on the most appropriate crop for its particular conditions. In each zone, environmental, spatial, and social relations were dramatically restructured and transformed. In each, indigenous populations had been eliminated in one way or another, and there were no groups who could oppose the unrestrained expansion of the plantation system. In each, subordination to the dominant crop reordered and simplified biologically complex ecologies with devastating environmental consequences. In each, concrete, substantive historical slave relations were constituted not only by the form of master-slave relations but also by the material conditions and processes required for the production of each particular crop and additionally by their relative position in the world division of labor and world market. Thus, each slave formation forms a particular historical-geographic complex[4] within the historically changing world division of labor. In each zone, the slave labor process and master-slave relations assumed distinct social and material characteristics that differentiated them from other such slave formations. The formation of these zones expanded the scale of production beyond that of older zones producing the same commodities. These new zones were characterized by more extensive areas under cultivation, more and larger plantations, and greater economies of scale that lowered the costs of production by producing greater volumes of the crop.[5]

We may distinguish a temporal and spatial sequence in the development of commodity frontiers. First was a pioneering phase: abundant land was available, and virgin soils were highly fertile. The labor force was built up, and much of its energy was engaged in clearing the forest, draining the land, constructing buildings and roads, and creating the infrastructure for large-scale commercial agriculture. The pioneer phase was followed by a phase of maturity. The land and labor force were at their peak efficiency, and the crop yield was high. The output of the plantation was at its highest. This phase was followed by a phase of decadence. Soil fertility and plant yield declined, and the slave labor force matured. There were fewer prime workers in the slave population. The gender ratio was more equal between men and women, and there were more children and elderly. These temporal phases coexisted in space and translated into three distinct zones in any commodity frontier.[6]

The formation of these new historical-geographic complexes depended upon the deployment of transportation systems that were capable of cheaply and efficiently carrying massive quantities of bulky commodities across long distances. New technologies of production and transport integrated each zone into transnational commodity circuits. Each such system—including the railroad, the steamboat, and, in Brazil, the remarkable system of mule transport—adapted to specific local geographies, the material attributes of the crop, and the requirements of large-scale commodity circulation and consumption. These extended commodity frontiers meant that the sites of production were located farther from the centers of processing and consumption. Goods had to be transported over longer distances, and carriers were under pressure to increase capacity and lower costs. Thus, longer lines of communication themselves encouraged further increases in the scale of production in order to guarantee full cargoes and maintain profits for carriers. At the same time, the interdependence of increasing scale and cheaper unit costs in production and transport stimulated consumption. These general conditions intersected with distinct local environments and geographies to create specific social and economic histories in each zone.[7]

Because these new frontier zones were sparsely settled, they lacked an adequate labor supply to meet the requirements of the new crops. In each of them, the scale of slave production was dramatically increased in order to satisfy growing world demand for cotton, sugar, and coffee. The forced migration of chattel slaves supplied the demand for labor in each zone and shaped its respective plantation system. Despite abolitionist and British pressure to end the international slave trade, more than 2,400,000 Africans were transported from Africa to the Americas between 1801 and 1866, perhaps the highest level of activity for any comparable period in the history of the Atlantic slave trade.[8] More than 1,500,000 captives arrived in Brazil during this period and over 640,000 in Cuba. Of these, the overwhelming majority were destined for the Brazilian coffee zone and the Cuban sugar zone. In the United States, more than 1,000,000 slaves were taken from the Upper South to the cotton frontiers of the Deep South,[9] while in Brazil over 200,000 slaves were transferred to the new coffee frontiers of the Paraíba Valley and São Paulo after 1850.[10] At the very moment when modern industry, free trade, and the increasing strength of political liberalism and abolitionism are generally thought to have led to the end of the slave trade and the abolition of chattel slavery, more slaves were being transported across the Atlantic world and were producing more commodities on more land than ever before in the 400-year history of slavery.

In these far-flung commodity frontiers, slavery itself was remade in ways that conformed to the requirements of industrial production, capitalist world markets, and a postcolonial Atlantic political order. The particular material conditions required for the cultivation and processing of each crop structured the organization of the plantation and slave labor. Accelerating world demand for cotton, sugar, and coffee not only increased the number and size of plantations and restructured the organization of productive space but also concentrated more slaves, reconfigured labor processes, and intensified their labor in these new commodity frontiers. This new "second slavery" was characterized by increased output per slave, the incorporation of new production and transport technologies, and new strategies of land and labor management based upon new conceptions of time and space, quantification, measurement, and calculation.[11]

These previously marginal geographic zones emerged as key poles of the new world division of labor as each achieved unprecedented levels of production and rates of expansion. The U.S. South, western Cuba, and the center-south of Brazil each became the world's leading producer of its respective crop and anchored new commodity circuits that reconfigured the international division of labor. In place of the classic triangle trade between Europe, Africa, and the Americas as the basic structure of Atlantic commerce, the United States became the world's primary producer of cotton, supplying between 70 and 80 percent of the raw material for Britain's Industrial Revolution, and at the same time it emerged as the major consumer of Cuban sugar and Brazilian coffee. After 1815 the Atlantic slave trade reached perhaps its highest level, but Cuba and Brazil were virtually its exclusive destinations (see map PI.1). As production expanded in each zone and the volume of commodities in circulation reached unprecedented levels, each zone became more closely integrated into broader global networks of exchange, distribution, and consumption. The growing availability of cotton, sugar, and coffee shaped new patterns of consumption that contributed to a distinctively modern way of life.

The interaction of these various forces and relations reshaped the land and created distinctive working plantation landscapes in each of these new commodity frontiers. Each zone represents a distinct local response to the same world-economic conditions. In each there was an enormous increase in the scale of production. Land and labor were organized to maximize production and productivity. Monocultural agriculture expanded extensively and intensively. Plantation slaves were subject to more exacting rationalization of their working activity and more rigid hierarchy, racialization, and regimentation of their social lives. Production was more effectively integrated into the world market. Land and labor were subject to increasing rates of exploitation. Spatial ordering facilitated production and social control. However, in each zone the particular characteristics of each crop, the environment, topography, hydrology, the soil fertility, the available sources of power and means of transportation, and strategies of crop and labor management shaped particular configurations of landscape and formed singular spatial economies.[12] At the same time, the landscape and built environment embodied social and racial inequalities and expressed a symbolic order that sought to construct social meanings and legitimate authority. Thus, each landscape physically objectified these diverse material and physical conditions, social relations and processes, and expressed culturally formed symbolic meanings through which they were interpreted.[13] Nature, labor, power, and culture wove through plantation spaces and endowed them with specific identities and forms, even as the institution of the plantation unified the history of the Americas.

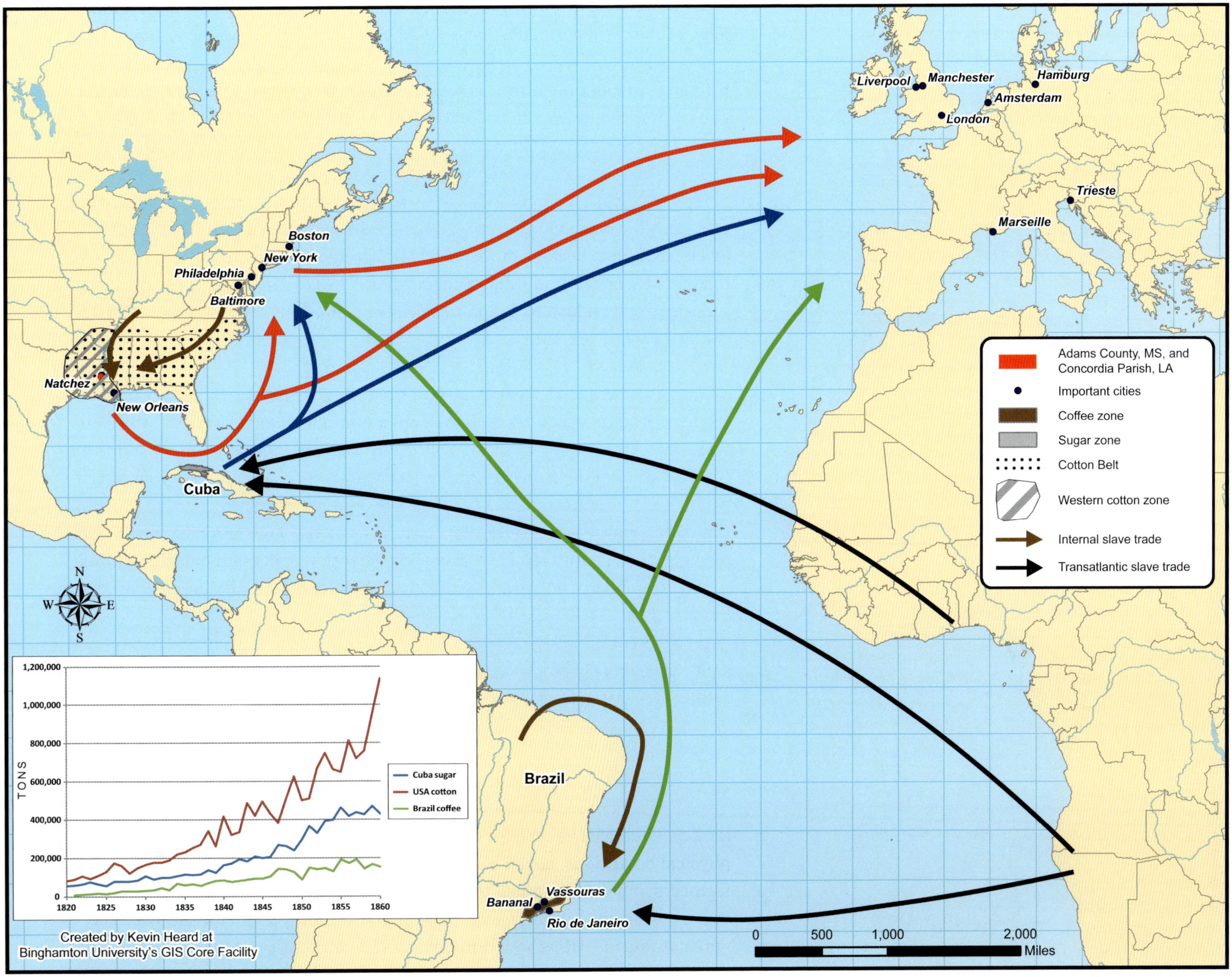

Map PI.1. *New Atlantic commodity frontiers, 1815–1868. Created by Kevin Heard, Binghamton University, GIS Core Facility.*

1
The Lower Mississippi Valley Cotton Frontier

The mechanization of the textile industry in Britain created growing world demand for cotton. The world cotton market expanded dramatically and continuously throughout the first part of the nineteenth century as this industrial raw material became the leading product in international trade.[1] The U.S. South soon emerged as the world's primary supplier of raw cotton. With the invention of the cotton gin, cotton spread rapidly across the South and revitalized slavery. At its height, the Cotton Belt stretched from the Carolinas to Texas. From the end of the War of 1812 to the beginning of the Civil War in 1860, U.S. cotton production climbed from fewer than 150,000 bales to over 4,500,000 bales. Even as world production increased sharply during the period between 1840 and 1860, the United States annually produced over 60 percent of the world supply and accounted for over 50 percent of U.S. exports by value. Between 85 percent and 90 percent of the U.S. crop was exported to Britain and accounted for nearly 80 percent of British cotton imports during the period before the Civil War. The slave plantations of the cotton South were tightly bound to the textile mills of Manchester.[2]

The growing world demand for cotton reshaped the physical geography of the South, subordinating it to the material conditions of cotton production and the socioeconomic characteristics of slave labor. Cotton requires no complex processing and can be adapted to different kinds of agriculture. It can be grown as a supplementary crop for small subsistence farmers, on small farms specializing in cotton, or on large-scale plantations as a monocultural crop. Each of these kinds of agricultural organization was found in the South as the lure of the cotton market and the promise of wealth attracted a variety of cultivators to the crop. Nonetheless, the cotton crop was dominated by the largest plantations with the most slaves. These plantations were concentrated in fertile river valleys, which offered both rich soils and access to world markets.[3] This combination of fertile soils and cheap water transportation had been key to development of southern tidewater plantation agriculture since colonial times. The Cotton Belt continued this pattern. From Georgia to Louisiana and Texas, access to cheap river transportation to the Gulf of Mexico made possible the development of extensive zones of cultivation dominated by large plantations. The acquisition of West Florida from Spain was a crucial development of the Cotton South because it provided a river outlet to the Gulf for the huge quantities of cotton produced in Georgia, Florida, and Alabama. The Apalachicola, Mobile, and (above all) Mississippi Rivers were vital arteries for the Cotton South, and the ports of Apalachicola, Mobile, and New Orleans became centers of the cotton trade. Without these transportation linkages, the development of the Cotton Belt would not have been possible.

The Natchez District along the Mississippi River quickly emerged as perhaps the most productive center of cotton cultivation in the South during the first half of the nineteenth century. The district included Wilkinson, Adams, Jefferson, Claiborne, and Warren Counties in Mississippi and Concordia, Tensas, and Madison Parishes in Louisiana. Its humid, subtropical climate with warm temperatures, abundant rainfall, long summers, and short, mild winters offered exceptional conditions for cotton cultivation. However, the lower Mississippi valley cotton frontier reached far beyond the Natchez District. The city of Natchez, in Adams County, Mississippi, was the hub of a cotton-producing hinterland extending from Mississippi and Louisiana to Arkansas and Texas. Natchez's strategic position on the Mississippi River, abundance of fertile land, and proximity to New Orleans allowed it to respond quickly to the growing demand for cotton beginning in the 1790s. By the 1830s, it became the region's major commercial and financial center and the seat of an enormously rich and powerful planter elite whose reach extended across the entire lower Mississippi valley and beyond.

The Mississippi River was the dominant environmental feature of the Natchez District and created the conditions that made it arguably the premier cotton-producing region in the antebellum South. The river's alluvial deposits were responsible for the region's exceptionally rich soils. In addition, the river and its tributaries provided an unrivaled transportation network that brought people, livestock, and supplies from the Upper South and the Midwest to the Natchez District and carried the region's cotton to New Orleans for shipment to world markets. It was a major route for the U.S. domestic slave trade, with Kentucky serving as the primary embarkation point for slaves taken from across the Upper South.

The *Map of the Alluvial Region of the Mississippi*, drafted by Charles Mahon and presented to the War Department by the U.S. Army Corps of Topological Engineers in 1861 (figure 1.01), was part of the federal government's efforts to gather scientific information about the interior of the continent in order to promote settlement and development through control of nature. The Corps of Topological Engineers produced the first scientific mapping of the West and played a role in providing infrastructure for transportation and settlement. The map employed the most advanced survey and cartographic techniques of the time to

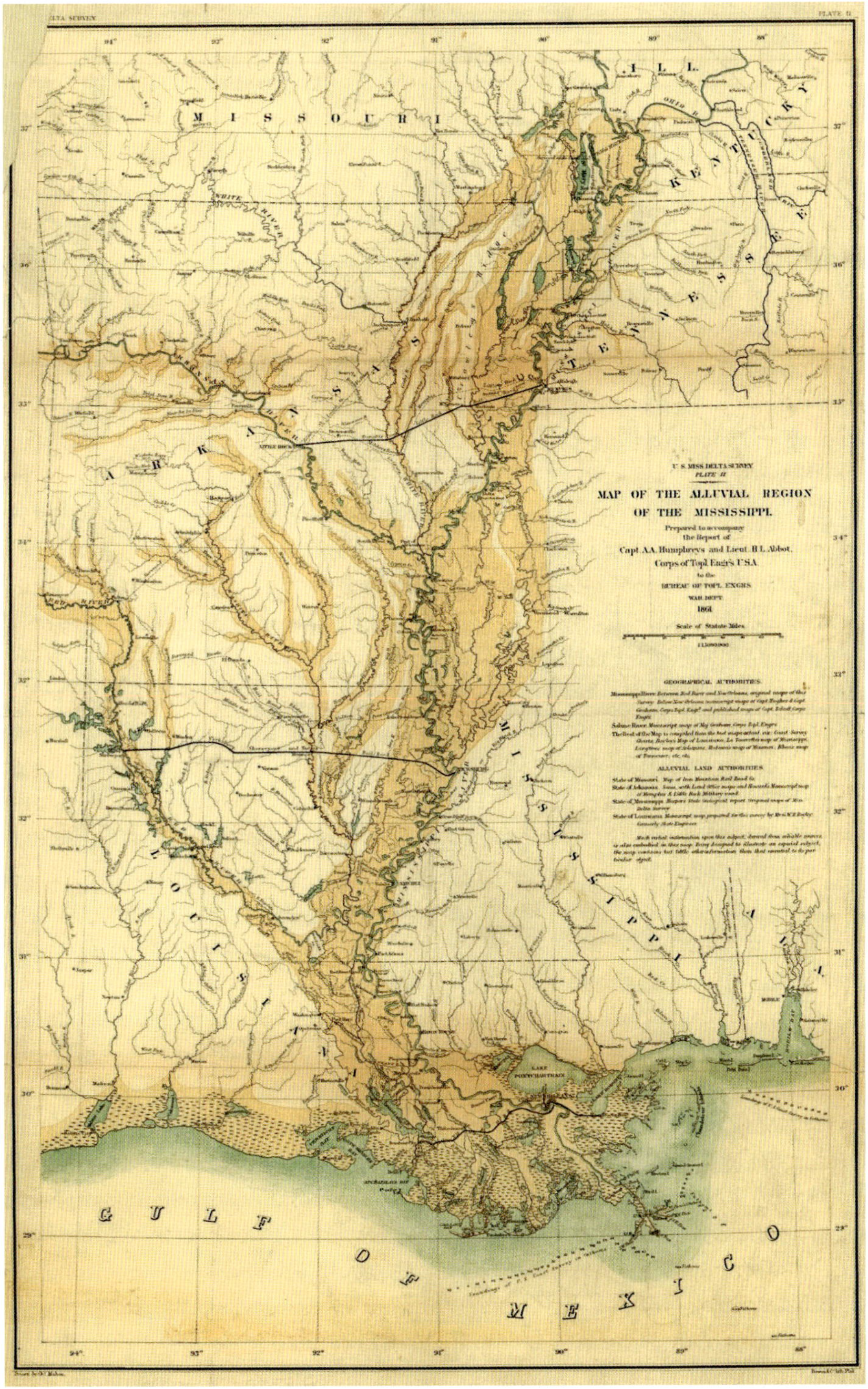

Figure 1.01. Map of the Alluvial Region of the Mississippi. *Charles Mahon, 1861. Library of Congress.*

precisely chart the geophysical features of this strategic region. It documents both the course of the Mississippi River and its tributaries and the soil region formed by its broad floodplain.

Although the Mississippi River made possible the development of the Natchez cotton frontier, it presented serious difficulties both for navigation and for the establishment of plantation agriculture. The river followed an irregular course that was subject to sudden and dramatic changes. Over millennia, it left deposits of rich alluvial soils over a broad expanse of territory that was regularly renewed by annual flooding. The resultant floodplain was low-lying, poorly drained, and densely forested. Because of the enormous volume of water, the river channel had no fixed course but could change drastically depending upon the volume and velocity of the water. The course of the river continually shifted, cutting new channels, creating sharp bends and new sandbars, and changing its course entirely. Such shifts formed cutoffs that transferred large spits of land from one side of the river to the other, changing physical boundaries, destroying and creating property lines, and altering navigation. The river also uprooted trees, which, as they became waterlogged, presented a danger that threatened boats. Their trunks sunk beneath the surface and became lodged in the bed of the river just beneath the surface of the water. Fallen trees formed another obstacle to navigation. As they became entangled with one another, they accumulated other material and began to form logjams even in the middle of the river. These logjams could create islands or "rafts," such as the notorious Red River Raft, which formed over 600 years and blocked navigation of the 150-mile-long stretch of river between Natchitoches and Shreveport. It took 50 years to clear the raft and open the river to navigation.[4]

Nonetheless, the lower Mississippi valley offered some of the most productive agricultural land on the North American continent. This land was highly prized for cotton and sugar cultivation; however, much of it remained uncleared and undrained. Cotton and sugarcane grew well where drainage permitted. The flooding left the heaviest deposits of silt closest to the riverbank. The best-drained lands were along these natural levees, and early settlement followed rivers.[5] The map indicates the contrast between the distribution of alluvial soils in the Natchez District to the south of Vicksburg and the extensive alluvial floodplain of the Mississippi delta, between the Mississippi and Yazoo Rivers north of Vicksburg. The delta was low-lying, swampy, heavily wooded, and subject to severe flooding. It required extensive drainage, levee construction, and forest clearance. It remained relatively unimproved and was fully exploited only after the Civil War, when it became the most productive cotton-producing region in the United States. Antebellum cotton cultivation began not on the alluvial lowlands but on the loess hills around Natchez on the east bank of the Mississippi River. There the topography offered some relief from flooding. The wind-deposited brown loam silt was extremely fertile but highly susceptible to erosion. With the U.S. purchase of Louisiana, Natchez planters expanded their operations across the river to the deep alluvial clay soils in Louisiana. There, cotton yielded as much as two bales per acre. As cotton production grew, it extended along the Mississippi River and later the Red River in Louisiana and the Arkansas River. Because of climate, sugar was the predominant crop south of Baton Rouge. Mahon's map also indicates the projected lines of the Vicksburg, Shreveport and Texas Railroad and the Memphis and Little Rock Railroad. These railroads were only partially completed in 1861. They supplemented river transport and brought more westerly cotton lands along the Red River and the Arkansas River into more rapid and direct contact with the Mississippi River.

Norman's Chart of the Lower Mississippi River indicates the dense settlement and exploitation of the land along the river (figure 1.02). It was drafted by Marie Adrien Persac and published by B. M. Norman of New Orleans in 1858. Persac, an engineer, architect, painter, and photographer, was educated in France. He gathered the material for the map by compiling information from parish records and by sailing down the river in a skiff, stopping every mile to survey relevant features and record every name for plantations on both banks of the river.[6] The map depicts the plantations along the Mississippi River from Natchez to New Orleans and gives the name of each. It has the effect of a promenade along the river, displaying the bounty of nature transformed into capitalist wealth.

This corridor was the nation's leading producer of cotton and sugar and had the densest slave population in the country. It was reputed to be home to more millionaires than anywhere else in the United States. Not only did the alluvial lowlands along the river allow easy access to transportation, but the annual silt deposits renewed the soil and formed a natural levee on the land closest to the riverbank. This natural levee was the highest and best-drained land along the river and was the preferred site for both building and cultivation. However, before cultivation was possible, the landscape had to be transformed in order to prepare the way for cotton and sugar monoculture. The complex ecologies of the lowlands were destroyed as African slaves were compelled to engage in the exhausting and dangerous task of clearing the dense growth of cypress, tupelo, and other water-tolerant trees, digging drainage ditches, and building levees to make the land suitable for plantation agriculture.[7] Before the Civil War, levee construction was left to individual initiative and was notoriously ineffective. Planting could begin only after the annual floodwaters receded.

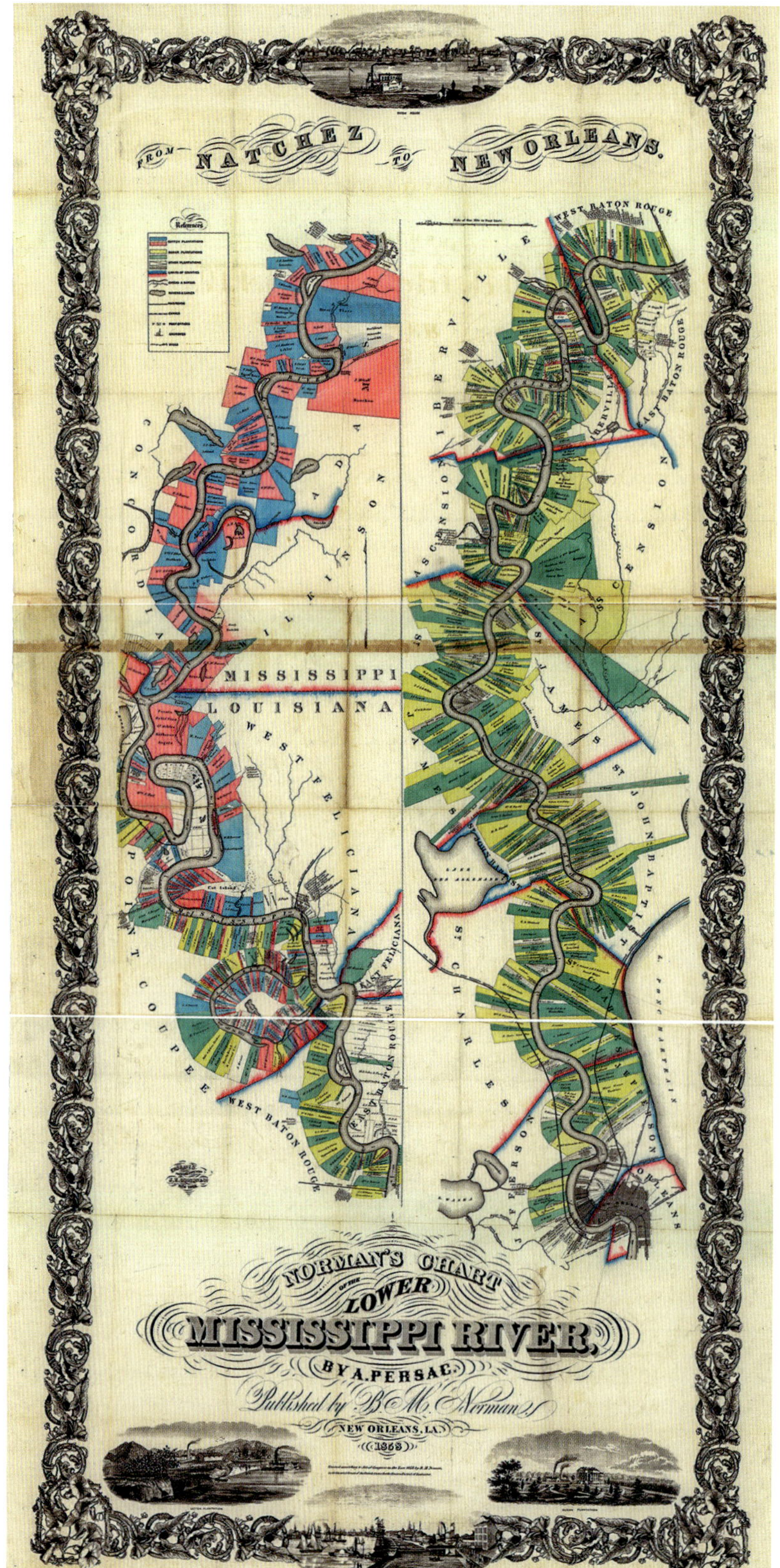

Figure 1.02. Norman's Chart of the Lower Mississippi River. *Marie Adrien Persac, 1858. Library of Congress.*

Persac's map also indicates the legacy of the region's diverse cultural history. Landholdings along the river were organized by the French long-lot system. The establishment of these properties preceded the cotton and sugar booms. All the properties fronted the river and had deep parcels that were perpendicular to the river. Each property had access to water and river transportation, while the long, narrow strips of land evenly distributed variations of soil, drainage, and topography across properties and allowed the inhabitants to live in close proximity to one another. This configuration could facilitate planting and harvesting, though the length of the holding could make transportation within the property more difficult. The twists and bends of the river created distorted pie-shaped sections in many places, and inheritance or sale could divide properties into narrow slivers. Finally, the map indicates the influence of climate on agricultural practices. The chart's coloring distinguishes the cotton zone (red and blue) from the sugar zone (yellow and green). The frost line is just north of Baton Rouge. Cotton was grown to the north of it, while to the south, sugarcane, which could not withstand frost, was cultivated.

The city of Natchez was the economic and social focal point of the district that bears its name. Natchez changed little after the Civil War, and Charles Babbit's 1891 survey map of Natchez and its suburbs delineates the distinguishing features of the city and its immediate environs (figure 1.03). The city of Natchez is located atop a bluff on the east bank of the Mississippi River, near the site of the former French Fort Rosalie. Its elevated position protected it from floods and made it defensible. The strip of land below the bluff provided access to the river and its traffic. Encircling the city proper was a band of suburban parkland containing the residences of one of the wealthiest and most distinctive planter elites in the South, the Natchez "nabobs." European presence in Natchez began in 1714–16 when the French established a fur trading post and constructed Fort Rosalie. Natchez was alternately a possession of France, Britain, Spain, and then France again. The first English settlers began to arrive in the late 1760s after the British victory in the Seven Years' War, and by 1783 the population reached about 500. With U.S. independence, it was at the far southwest corner of the new republic, bounded by French Louisiana and Spanish West Florida. During the 1780s, early settlers briefly produced tobacco that the Spanish allowed to be exported through New Orleans. When Spain changed its policy and denied the American farmers access to New Orleans, tobacco production collapsed and the planters soon turned their attention to cotton.

In 1835, James Tooley of Natchez, Mississippi's first native-born artist, rendered a panorama of the city of Natchez in the early period of the cotton boom (figure 1.04). The busy river port was the commercial and financial hub of the

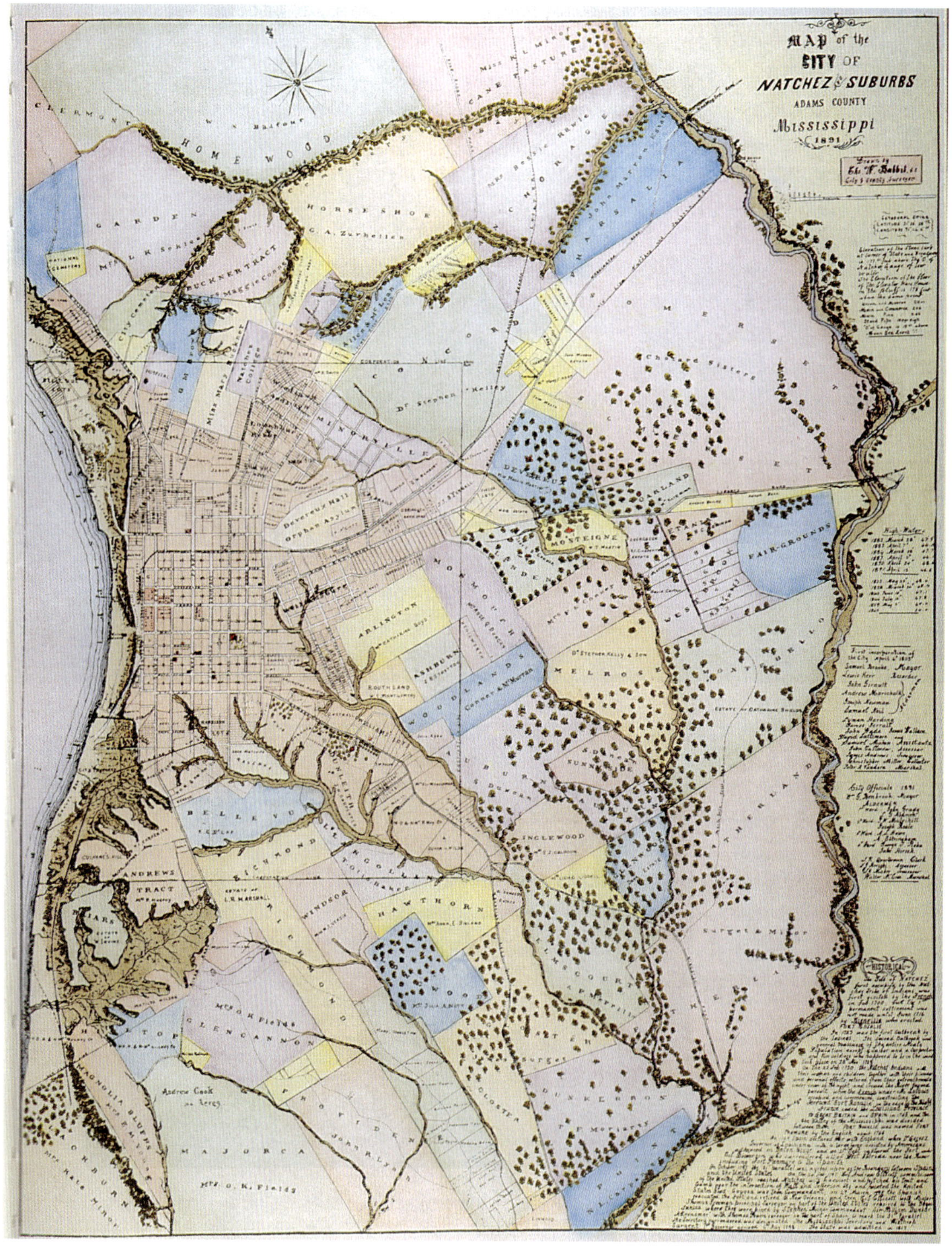

Figure 1.03. Map of the City of Natchez and Suburbs. *Charles W. Babbit, 1891. Courtesy of Historic Natchez Foundation, Miss.*

surrounding cotton hinterland. However, the city's economic importance to the region was not matched by urban development. By 1860, the total population of Natchez was only 6,600. Main Street ran east from the river for about half a mile and divided the gridded town in half. It was lined by a variety of stores that sold dry goods and fancy goods to the townsfolk and customers from the surrounding countryside. The center of town was also the site of the courthouse and nearby law offices as well as Presbyterian, Episcopalian, Methodist, and Catholic churches. Natchez also boasted three banks, including a branch of the Second Bank of the United States, which controlled the flow of credit to planters throughout the district and beyond. On the residential streets of the city, the mansions of wealthy cotton and land merchants were interspersed with the tasteful homes of the city's professionals. Finally, Natchez was a primary destination of the U.S. internal slave trade. The enslaved were transported down the Mississippi River or marched overland across the Natchez Trace, which terminated in Natchez. Slave auctions were held at the landing known as Under-the-Hill, in front of the courthouse, and by various slave dealers located along Franklin Street, while the biggest slave market in Natchez was at Forks of the Road, east of town. Only the New Orleans slave market was larger than that of Natchez.

Figure 1.04. Natchez on the Hill, from the Old Fort. *James Tooley, 1835. Courtesy of Historic Natchez Foundation, Miss.*

Figure 1.05. Natchez-Under-the-Hill. *A. R. Waud, woodcut,* Harper's Weekly, *July 14, 1866. Florida Center for Instructional Technology, Tampa.*

A. R. Waud's woodcut of Natchez-Under-the-Hill shows the city's river landing (figure 1.05). This narrow strip of land at the base of the bluffs was the city's physical link to the vast commercial network provided by the river. Steamboats connected Natchez with New Orleans, a two- or three-day journey. They carried cotton downstream and a variety of other merchandise upstream, while steamships and flatboats carried passengers (including slaves being brought for sale) and produce from the upper Mississippi and Ohio River valleys. Cotton warehouses and the offices of commission merchants were located on this landing, while stevedores, porters, boatmen, and travelers mixed with the denizens of the gambling houses, brothels, and barrooms that lined the foot of the bluff. New England traveler Joseph Holt Ingraham described Under-the-Hill as "the nucleus of vice for the Mississippi" in 1835, although he added that construction of mercantile houses, a hotel, and more diligent policing were bringing respectability to it.[8]

The presence of the planter elite was perhaps the distinguishing feature of Natchez. The "nabobs," as they were called (rather pejoratively by local townspeople), were a group of some forty close-knit families who accumulated exceptional wealth and status. The favorable conditions in the Natchez region attracted migrants from Massachusetts, New York, Pennsylvania, and Ohio as well as from the Upper South who came to make their fortunes in cotton. Closely bound together by blood, marriage, and interests, the Duncan, Farrar, Butler, Conner, Routh, Surget, Minor, Marshall, and other families were active cotton planters and succeeded in acquiring vast holdings of land and slaves. In addition, many of them also had sugar plantations in Louisiana. Stephen Duncan, reputed to be America's largest cotton producer and slave owner, had six cotton plantations and two sugar estates on which 1,041 slaves worked. Haller Nutt owned 800 slaves and 43,947 acres on twenty-one estates extending from Adams County to the Louisiana Gulf Coast. Levin Marshall owned five cotton plantations covering 14,400 acres in Adams County and in Louisiana that were worked by 817 slaves. Duncan and Marshall were said to each produce more than 4,000 bales of cotton a year, while the output of the properties of Samuel Davis and Francis Surget fluctuated between 3,000 and 5,000 bales. In addition to agriculture, many of the nabobs were active in banking, commerce, and finance and invested extensively in land, railroads, and stocks and bonds. Their ranks also included rich merchants and lawyers who acquired plantations through marriage or debt.[9] They were some of the wealthiest men in the South, if not the country.

By the 1830s, the extreme wealth of the nabobs set them apart from lesser planters and the Natchez townspeople. They began to coalesce as a closed, self-conscious group, establishing their social rank through the creation of status distinctions and remaining aloof from the town. Marriage "within their station" connected nabob clans through dense ties of kinship and property. Their horizons were national and international more than local. They confined themselves to their suburban villas and cultivated a cosmopolitan lifestyle. They were often well-read and well-informed. Some of them had impressive libraries or were inclined toward scientific pursuits. They summered in Saratoga Springs and Newport; were at home in Philadelphia and New York, where they maintained important business connections; and vacationed in Europe.

The mansion known as Auburn (figure 1.06) was built in 1812 for the wealthy attorney and planter Lyman Harding by the Philadelphia architect and builder Levi Weeks. Upon Harding's death in 1827, Auburn was purchased by Stephen Duncan, who added two recessed wings to the house. It was the first building to introduce formal architectural principles to Natchez. The classical front portico supported by two-story columns was one of the first of its kind. It became the model for plantation houses and mansions throughout the South.[10]

Haller Nutt's Longwood (figure 1.07) was under construction at the time of the Civil War but never completed after craftsmen brought from the North re-

Figure 1.06. *Auburn mansion, Natchez, Mississippi. Photograph by Grupo Bocaina.*

Figure 1.07. *Longwood mansion, Natchez, Mississippi. Photograph by Grupo Bocaina.*

turned home. Nonetheless, it is the most extravagant of the elegant mansions that remain the most distinctive feature of the Natchez landscape even today. These stately homes are commonly regarded as prototypical antebellum plantation houses. However, they were the residences of Natchez's remarkable planter elite. Located in suburban parklands around the city of Natchez—setting the elite apart from the town—these homes were often designed by architects or according to design books and were built on high ground to escape disease and flood. From these mansions, the privileged planters administered their far-flung plantations and looked after their business interests, and in them they held the visits, dinners, and balls marked by lavish display that confirmed their elite status.

Purchase of the Louisiana Territory in 1803 coincided with rising world demand for cotton. Together with the Battle of New Orleans in 1815, the Louisiana Purchase politically unified the entire region and presented new opportunities for the expansion of the cotton frontier. The extensive fertile soils of Louisiana became available for cotton cultivation, and control over the entire waterway, including the city of New Orleans and the mouth of the Mississippi River, provided unimpeded navigation all the way to the Gulf of Mexico for the entire Mississippi River basin.

Following the Louisiana Purchase, Natchez planters quickly acquired land and established plantations on the flat, fertile alluvial bottomlands across the river. Figure 1.08, showing part of John La Tourrette's map of Louisiana published in 1853, documents the cotton plantations in Concordia and Tensas Parishes, located directly across the river from Natchez, and provides the name of the owner of each property, including such members of the Natchez elite as Francis Surget, William Bisland, Steven Minor, Henry Chotard, Chancellor Quitman, and John Routh. The properties of the Natchez planters were most densely concentrated in Concordia and Tensas Parishes; however, the cotton frontier expanded on both sides of the Mississippi River. Plantations were also established in Wilkinson, Adams, Jefferson, Claiborne, and Warren Counties in Mississippi as well as in Madison Parish in Louisiana. The wealthiest of the Natchez planter elite also owned cotton plantations in the Mississippi–Yazoo delta, along the Red River in Louisiana, in Arkansas, and in East Texas, as well as sugar plantations in southern Louisiana. Acquisition of Louisiana also gave Natchez unrestricted access to New Orleans. The Mississippi River and, as the cotton zone expanded westward, the Red River in Louisiana formed the prime axes of cotton cultivation in the Natchez District.

Cotton plantations were most numerous along the Mississippi River. The census of 1860 enumerated 717 properties with more than fifty slaves belonging to about 640 individuals in the Natchez District. (Additionally, there were 686 slaveholdings of between nineteen and forty-nine slaves.) Some 79 percent of landowners had properties of 200 acres or more, and of these, 48 percent owned more than 1,000 acres. In Concordia Parish, which was entirely alluvial bottomland, 94 of 250 slaveholders owned 50 or more slaves; and 22 landowners (12 percent) owned between 500 and 999 acres, while 88 (48 percent) owned over 1,000 acres.[11] The district produced 400,000 bales of cotton in that year, one-tenth of the output of the entire South. Concordia, Tensas, and Madison Parishes produced 30 percent of Louisiana's cotton.[12]

La Tourrette's map of Louisiana records some 8,000 plantations in the state, as well as townships, sections, or mile squares; Spanish grants; settlement rights; railroads; canals; and other features. La Tourrette gathered information from the township maps in the Louisiana Surveyor General's Office and invited planters to provide the exact boundaries of their properties together with the name of the owner or "some fancy name if preferred" for inclusion on the map in return for a fee of twenty dollars, payable upon delivery of the map.[13] Such in-

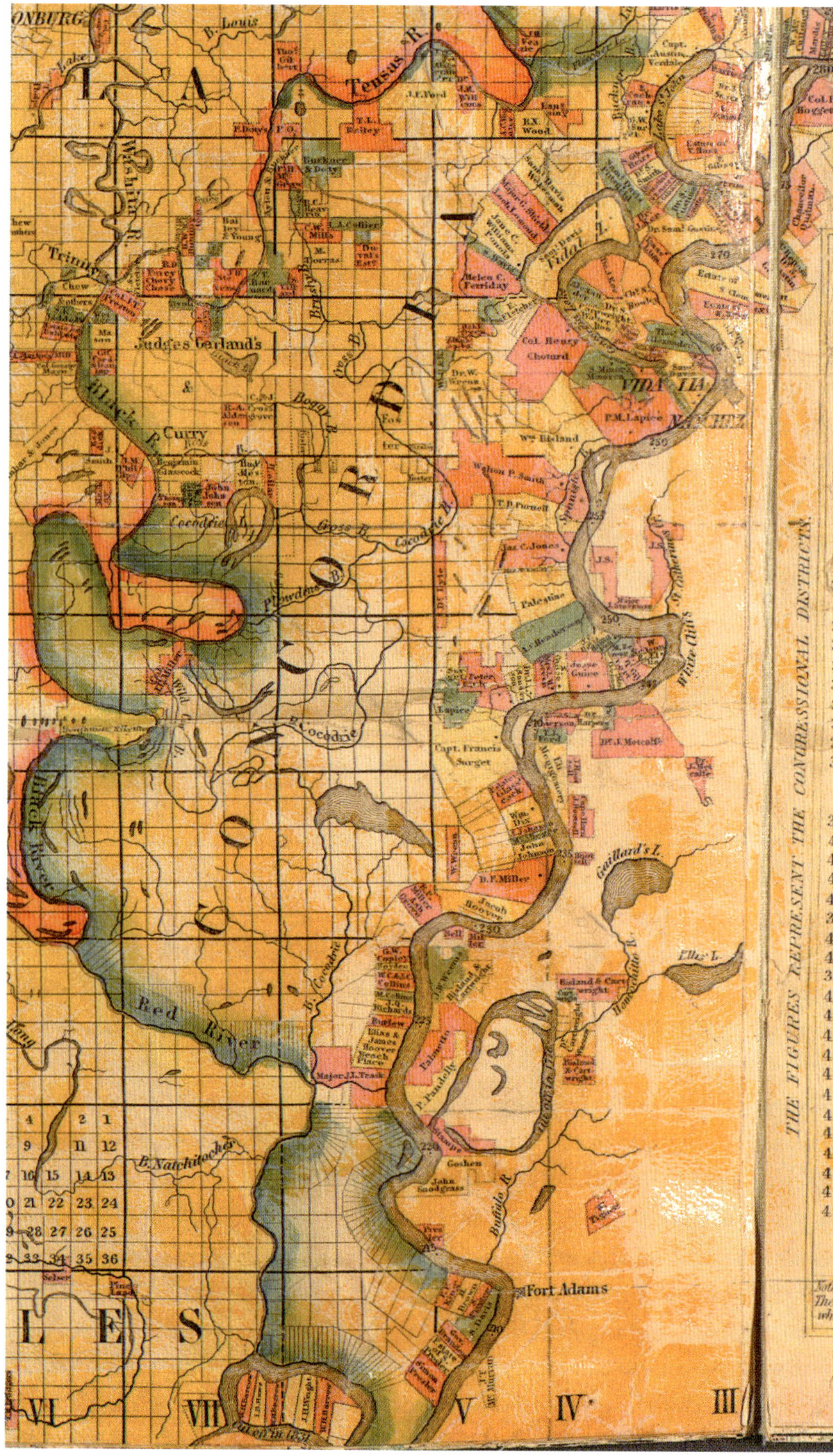

Figure 1.08. *Concordia Parish. Detail of John La Tourrette's reference map of the state of Louisiana, 1853. Library of Congress.*

scriptions not only recorded property boundaries but also provided a means to symbolically construct the collective identity of the planter class.

The map is testimony to the impact of the region's complex political and cultural history on the landscape. It indicates the intermingling of two different conceptions of property and organizing space—the French long-lot system and the American survey grid. The French system originated in the seigneurial system in France and was used in French Canada. It made no attempt to comprehensively organize rural space. Instead, it adapted to natural features and gave access to the river and the natural levee. As can be seen on the map, long lots predominated along the bank of the river, the legacy of early French settlement.

In contrast, the American survey grid offered abstract, universal geometric calculation of landed property. The American Public Land Survey System divided the land into a uniform rectangular grid. Using longitude lines as referents, the grid was universal and homogeneous. Beginning west of the Appalachians, it extended uniformly across the continent. In principle, this system could be extended across the globe. The survey grid organized space and established potential property boundaries even before settlement took place. It divided the country into uniform thirty-six-square-mile townships that could be combined to form larger units such as counties or subdivided into uniform sections, half sections, and quarter sections, which formed the basic units of property. Various natural and geographic features were noted within the grid, but they generally did not alter the distribution of the grid itself. (Hence, rural property was drawn up independent of access to water, forests, or other natural features.) In principle, roads were to follow the township lines, and towns were to form at their intersection.

Cheap water transportation made possible the development of the lower Mississippi valley cotton frontier. Early New Orleans photographer Jay Dearborn Edwards documented the city's rapidly changing economic landscape. His 1858 daguerreotype *Steamboats and Bales of Cotton near the Foot of Canal Street* (figure 1.09) dramatically emphasizes the mass industrial character of the cotton trade and suggests the great number of steamboats and the volume of cotton involved in the trade. The steamboat united the Midwest and the South. The first steamboat from Ohio arrived in New Orleans in 1812. By 1830, a thousand boats were active on the Mississippi, and the capacity of each boat had increased dramatically. The produce of the entire Mississippi River basin—flour, corn, salt beef, pork, and lard—together with cattle, horses, and mules from the Upper Midwest, slaves departing from Kentucky and Virginia on the "Second Middle Passage," and above all cotton from the lower Mississippi valley found their outlet in New Orleans. By 1860, over 3,500 steamboats arrived in New

Figure 1.09. Steamboats and Bales of Cotton near the Foot of Canal Street. *Jay Dearborn Edwards, ca. 1858. Historic New Orleans Collection (1985.238), La.*

Orleans carrying 2 million tons of freight worth nearly $2 billion. Further, the steamboat made possible traffic upstream. The voyage from New Orleans to Pittsburgh took fifteen to twenty days and made New Orleans into an entrepôt for consumer goods in the Natchez District, whether they arrived by river from the Midwest or the Upper South or by sea.[14]

The steamboat and the slave plantation system mutually reinforced one another to develop cotton monoculture and transform the riverine ecology of the lower Mississippi valley. Abundant and cheap steam transportation enhanced the value of land along the river, accelerated the migration of slave labor, and stimulated the growth of cotton production. The enormous quantities of cotton produced in the Natchez District required relatively cheap yet effective transport to carry it to market in New Orleans. The development of the system of steam transportation resulted in more cotton being carried less expensively compared with other modes of river transport. Additionally, it reduced the time of shipment to New Orleans and lowered freight rates. By the 1830s, the voyage from Natchez to New Orleans took from one to three days, and freight rates fell by three-fifths or four-fifths.[15] As the price of cotton dropped, planters needed to produce more cotton in order to cover fixed costs and required more steamboats to carry their produce. As the cost of transportation fell, shippers needed more cotton in order to guarantee full cargoes and maintain their revenues. More cotton required more steamboats, and more steamboats required more cotton.[16] Further, the steamboats' prodigious need for fuel contributed to the transformation of the riverine landscape. Plantation slaves and "woodhawks" with small woodyards alike felled trees to provide the steamships with firewood.[17] This spiral of expansion reached its geographic and environmental limits in the 1840s, when steamboat service covered all of the navigable waters of the cotton frontier.[18]

Steamboats serving the lower Mississippi valley were essentially custom-built for the cotton trade. Design was based on practical experience rather than on scientific engineering principles, and the boats were usually built in the shipyards of the Ohio valley. Construction boomed in the 1830s and 1840s, and the boats were often fragile as builders sought quick speculative profits.[19] Flexible keels and a shallow draft allowed the boats to pass over obstacles and navigate tributary rivers and streams. They were thus able to stop at landings along the river to take on cargo or fuel. (Upstream from the farthest points that the steamboats could go, keelboats and flat-bottomed boats extended the chain of river transport and carried cotton to intermediate transshipment points.) The long hulls of these boats were stabilized by "hog chains"—metal rods like those supporting suspension bridges—which allowed the flexible hulls to be lengthened and stabilized and prevented them from bending out of shape because of the weight of the cargo and engine. The decks were built in layers to maximize the horizontal cargo surface. The main deck was just above the waterline, and most of the ship's structure was above deck. The steam engine was located at the center of the main deck. Above the main deck was the "boiler deck," which contained often luxurious passenger staterooms and the long central parlor; above that was the "hurricane deck," which housed the crew; and above that was the pilot house, from which the boat was steered.

This design was suitable for cotton, which was light in relation to its volume. The bales of cotton were stacked on the open main deck, often reaching to below the pilot house. Cargo platforms hung from the hull, increased carrying capacity. Steamboats commonly carried over 1,000 bales of cotton, while exceptionally large boats like the *Sultana* could normally carry 3,500 bales.[20] The logic of steam transportation on the Mississippi was to carry cargo with speed over distance. High-pressure steam engines quickly predominated on the Mississippi, in contrast to eastern waters, where low-pressure engines were more common. The high-pressure engines were cheaper, lighter, simpler, and more powerful, but they were also more dangerous, and their use could lead to spectacular accidents resulting in loss of life and cargo.[21]

The growth of the lower Mississippi valley cotton frontier stimulated the social and economic transformation of New Orleans. By 1840, over 923,000 bales of cotton arrived at the New Orleans riverfront, and the city was the fourth largest port in the world measured by the value of its exports.[22] In contrast to Edwards's unadorned portrayal of the industrial character of the docks, Marie Adrien Persac's 1858 painting *Port and City of New Orleans* (figure 1.10) celebrates the commercial and financial success of New Orleans.

Originally drawn as a prototype for a decorative inset of the city for *Norman's Chart of the Lower Mississippi River*, it calls attention to the material elements of the city's prosperity: the Mississippi River, the confluence of riverboats and oceangoing merchant ships, and the flow of cotton from its upland source to the world market. Persac used a photographic technique that allowed him to accurately reproduce architectural and technical details in this painting. This view looks upstream from Marigny Street. It depicts the transfer of bales of cotton from the riverboats to oceangoing freighters. Moored to the docks in the foreground are tall-masted sailing ships coming up the river to take on cargo. The dark-colored side-wheel steamship in the middle of the river is likely a towboat used to convey the ocean vessels over the bar and upriver to the port, a journey of 100 miles that took three days. Upriver from the sailing ships moored in the foreground is the commercial district above Canal Street with the com-

Figure 1.10. Port and City of New Orleans. *Marie Adrien Persac, 1858. Historic New Orleans Collection (1988.9), La.*

mercial houses and residences of the American merchants. A cluster of riverboats is gathered there, unloading their cargo for transshipment to the ocean-going vessels. The earth levee served as an open-air loading zone for cotton and other goods. The image depicts carters and stevedores moving cotton bales along Market Street and loading them on ships. In the foreground, cotton bales are arranged along the levee in preparation for loading, while samples of cotton are displayed for inspection in the structure in the right foreground. Narrow wooden wharves and finger piers facilitated loading and unloading. Shortly after Persac completed this painting, the piers were filled in to form a continuous wharf that extended along the waterfront for miles.[23]

New Orleans's position on the Mississippi River made it the strategic node connecting cotton producers in the Natchez District with ocean routes and world markets. Persac's image calls attention to the complex material, commercial, and financial linkages that were required in order to transform cotton from the lower Mississippi valley into a global commodity. The painting suggests the variety of complex tasks that had to be integrated with one another in order to transship the cotton crop. Stevedores and carters had to unload the steamships and load the cotton bales onto carts to be taken to be weighed, sampled, and sold. The bales were then marked with the initials of their owner and his agent and carted back to the levee, where factors and shipping agents made up cargoes and oversaw the loading of the oceangoing vessels. While the riverboats were well suited to carry cotton, it was a different matter for the oceangoing ships. The high volume and low weight of the cargo made the ships unstable at sea, and they had to be carefully ballasted. Powerful steam presses, generating much more force those on than the plantations, reduced the bales to half their volume in order to prepare them for transoceanic shipping.[24]

This concentration of trade made New Orleans the key link in a chain of banking and finance that extended to New York, Philadelphia, and London. New Orleans merchants and brokers organized the flow of cotton to world markets, while the city's merchant houses and banks provided the credit that enabled planters throughout the valley to acquire more land and slaves and to continue producing cotton. New Orleans cotton merchants, who were frequently agents of New York or London banks, provided advances to the planters against the sale of the crop in exchange for the right to sell the crop on a consignment basis. Cotton was generally shipped on consignment by the firm that would eventually arrange its sale. Although some planters shipped their crop directly to Britain, the majority of the ships sailed to New York, where the cargo was unpacked, inspected, and consigned to a buyer in Liverpool before being reloaded on a transatlantic vessel. The long-term credit offered to cotton buyers by powerful New York financial institutions together with the federal subsidy given to the New York–to–Liverpool packet made New York freight rates much lower than elsewhere. Packet ships had to sail on a regular schedule and offered lower freight rates to make sure that they sailed with full cargoes. As a result of this advantage, New York became the major port supplying cotton to Britain's Industrial Revolution. The annual cycle of cotton production was underwritten by the continuous circulation of credit and debt.[25]

2
The Cuban Sugar Frontier

The extensive plains and favorable climate of the Spanish colony of Cuba offered ideal conditions for sugar cultivation. However, Cuba was a marginal sugar producer until the nineteenth century. Before then, Havana was the base for the Spanish merchant and naval fleets, its magnificent harbor the rendezvous point of the Spanish treasure flotillas carrying American silver back to Europe. By the mid-seventeenth century the hardwoods of Cuba's abundant and rich forests were the source of timber for the Spanish naval and commercial fleets, and Havana emerged as a major center of shipbuilding and repair. The forests were royal property and, being of strategic value for the Spanish Empire, placed under the jurisdiction of the Department of the Navy. Havana's position as a center of maritime activity for the Spanish Empire stimulated commerce, agriculture, including some sugar production, and stock raising in the area of the city.[1] But agriculture was, in general, strictly regulated throughout the island. Farming was restricted to lands close to settlements, and the major activity of the rural population was stock raising.[2]

Before the formation of the sugar zone, the majority of rural property in Cuba was distributed by grants from municipal governments. However, there was no uniform organization of rural property. Figure 2.01, the 1784 map of the Havana region, shows the distribution of the circular concessions that prevailed in the countryside. These vast haciendas were out of proportion to the small rural population. The larger holdings (*hatos*) ideally measured 22,512 hectares, while the smaller ones (*corrales*) measured 5,626 hectares. They were devoted to raising semi-wild cattle and pigs, respectively. Because of the peculiar circular shape and absence of boundaries of these vast parcels, they frequently overlapped with one another and were subject to legal battles over property rights. The holders of the concessions did not have absolute property rights. Rather, they had the right to use the land and its natural products together with the obligation to supply meat to settlements within their jurisdiction. Woodlands, streams, and pastures were considered communal property following Castilian custom. The navy had control of the forest, particularly species of tropical hardwoods of strategic value. The dark quadrilateral figures on the map represent royal livestock farms and timber haulage centers (*potreros del Rey*), from which neighboring estates were logged.[3] While farms producing local provisions existed either on the haciendas or in the spaces between them (*realengos*),

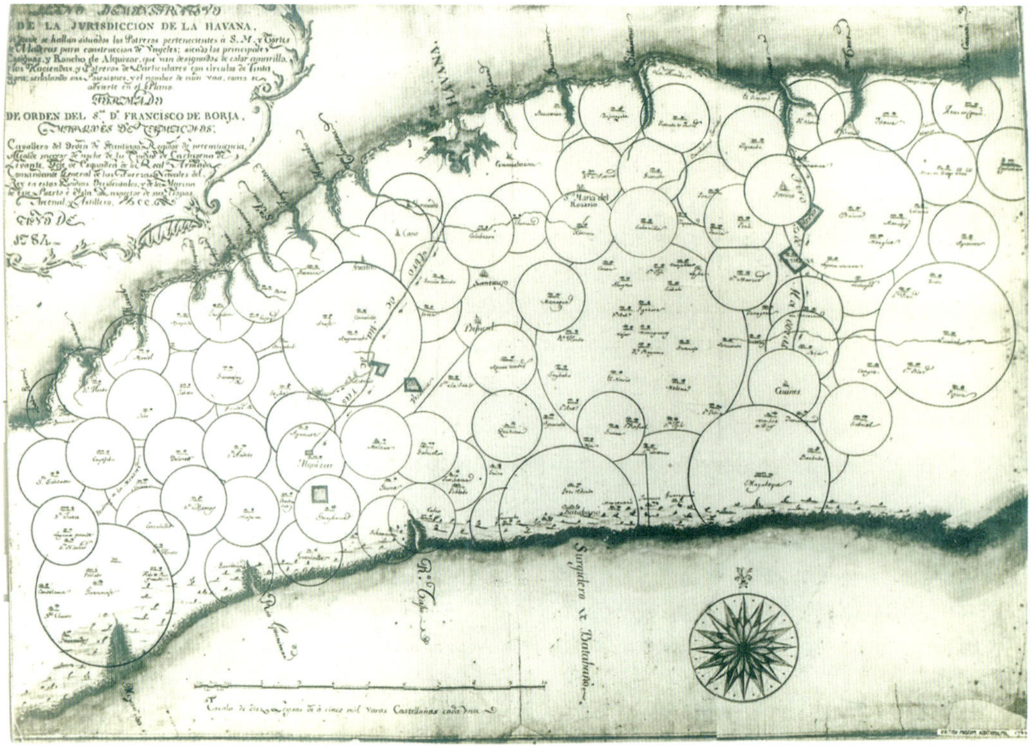

Figure 2.01. *Map of the Havana region, 1784. Biblioteca Nacional de Cuba José Martí, Havana.*

royal protection of the forest made it impossible to clear the land to engage in extensive agriculture. Nonetheless, the forest was a fundamental component of the type of livestock husbandry practiced in Cuba.[4] Until the end of the eighteenth century, the production of timber, leather, and meat defined Cuba's place in the Iberian Atlantic economy.

The Haitian Revolution destroyed the French colonial sugar industry, the world's largest producer, and provided Havana's planters with their opportunity to enter the international sugar market. In his *Discurso sobre la agricultura de la Habana y medios de fomentarla,*[5] Francisco Arango y Parreño, spokesman for the Havana elite, outlined the conditions that would lead to the growth of the sugar economy in Cuba: free trade in sugar, unlimited importation of slaves, and the systematic application of science to sugar production.[6] Sugar production began to slowly increase as new plantations were built on the fertile Artemisa plain between Güines and Quivicán to the south and southeast of Havana, where smallholders growing tobacco had previously settled. In 1792, 245 sugar mills were already in operation around Havana and Matanzas. By 1800, the number had climbed to 350 in the same region, with another 50 under construction.[7] This initial expansion of the sugar industry into the region outside Havana brought the sugar planters into conflict with the Department of the Navy over the proper use of the forest.[8]

However, the importance of transportation for the formation of the Cuban sugar frontier made itself felt even at this early stage of expansion. Without a cheap and efficient means of conveying large quantities of such a bulky product to the transoceanic shipping point, the enormous potential that the virgin soils of Cuba's interior offered for sugar cultivation could not be realized. Unlike on the smaller island centers of eighteenth-century sugar production like Barbados, Jamaica, Martinique, and Guadeloupe, overland transportation and the development of Cuba's extensive inland sugar frontier went hand in hand. The difficulty and high cost of overland transportation already emerged as a problem for the expansion of sugar production at the end of the eighteenth century. In response, the Havana planters appropriated a project to build a canal in order to transport timber from Güines to Havana shipyards. Such a canal would facilitate the extension of sugar cultivation into what was then the most fertile and most populous part of the interior of the island. The project of the Havana-Güines canal was discussed into the 1830s, but it was never built. However, the first railroad in Cuba was built between Havana and Güines in 1837.

Félix and Francisco Lemaur's 1801 map (figure 2.02) was created for the Güines-Havana canal project. Trained as military engineers, the Lemaurs offered a detailed visual inventory of economic resources of the rural hinterland of Havana and documented the early expansion of agriculture into the Cuban countryside. This pictographic representation of Cuban geography has its historical origins in landscape painting. By placing the vantage point above the image and eliminating the horizon, the cartographers projected the image on a flat surface and created a vertical or linear perspective view of the countryside.[9] There was not yet an established convention for the orientation of the map; the south coast is on the left side of the representation, while Havana is on the right. The map abstracts from a multiplicity of features to depict those resources and topography that were of interest to the sugar planters who sponsored the project—hills, the coastal plain forest, marshland, types of vegetation, roads, rivers, settlements, and farms, including seventeen sugar mills. These features are represented pictorially and symbolically and delineated by color and texture, for the map is meant to be seen, not read.[10] Inserted at the upper corners of the map are topographical views of sugar plantations. These interject a horizontal dimension of lived perspective that serves as a counterpoint to the verticality of the map and are emblematic of the transformation of the countryside by Havana sugar planters. These images are supplemented by text that provides the key to the towns, farms, roads, and important natural features depicted

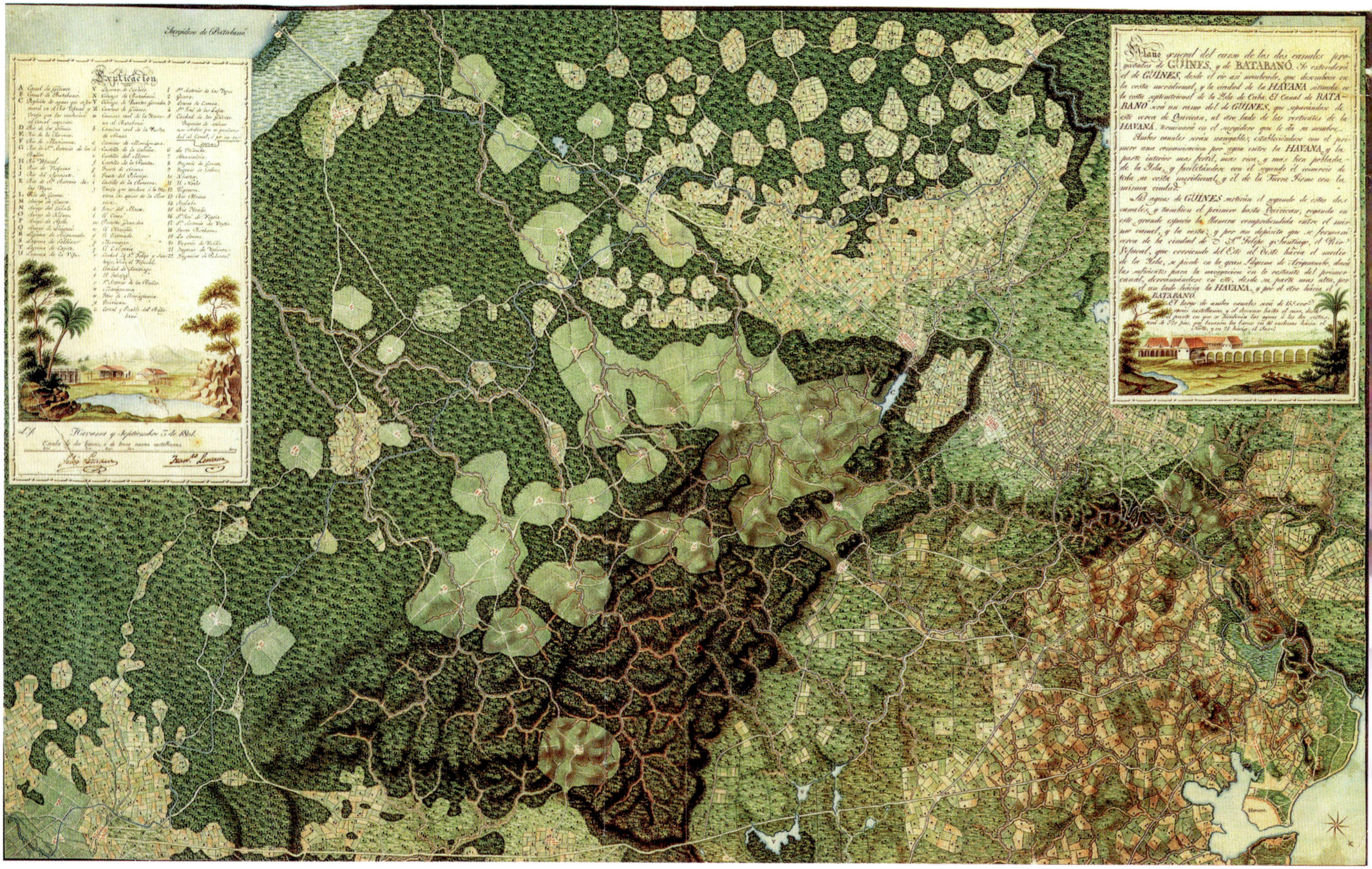

Figure 2.02. Plano general del curso de los dos canales proyectados de Güines y de Batabanó. *Félix and Francisco Lemaur, 1801. Ministerio de Defensa, Archivo del Museo Naval, Madrid, Spain. Clasificación 19 E-1–600 A.*

on the map (on the left) as well as a detailed description of the proposed canal in relation to the hydrography and geography of the region (on the right). By disclosing objects and spatial relations that could not otherwise be perceived, the map enabled the sugar interests to visually control the landscape and project the expansion of sugar production into a new area.

The expansion of large-scale commercial sugar production between 1792 and 1815 required the reorganization of rural property and the transformation of the natural environment. However, the navy's control of the forest inhibited the formation of new sugar plantations and aggravated the conflict between the sugar planters and the Department of the Navy over the disposition of the forest. By 1815 the decline of Spanish naval power in the Napoleonic wars and the growth of the Cuban sugar industry shifted the balance of forces in favor of the sugar interests, and a royal decree published in Havana in 1816 and finalized in 1819 effectively gave sugar planters absolute private property rights in land, including the right in perpetuity to cut down trees on their land. This decree cleared the way for massive deforestation and the subordination of the countryside to sugar monoculture.[11] The sugar frontier expanded rapidly onto the broad plains to the east and south of Havana.

The survey map or *agrimensor* map of the haciendas Banagüises, Jigües, and Rio Piedras in the heart of the Colón sugar zone registers the subdivision of three haciendas belonging to the Peñalver family, important members of the Havana elite, into regular parcels to be sold for the establishment of sugar mills in 1842 (figure 2.03). The property was first acquired at the end of the eighteenth century by Ignácio Rafael Peñalver Angulo y Cárdenas, the first marquis of Arco. Upon his death, the properties colored green were inherited by his son, the second marquis of Arcos, and those in yellow by his daughter, who had married her uncle, Nicolás de Peñalver y Cárdenas, who became the first Count of Peñalver shortly thereafter. Following the decrees of 1815 and 1816 that privatized land, this elaborate and precise survey map ordered the transformation of the landscape in anticipation of the sale of the properties. It organized the division of the land in advance of the extension of the rail line to the region, the conversion of the land to sugar mills, and the consequent rise in land values. The immense *hatos* and *corrales* were too large to be cultivated efficiently and were subdivided into smaller properties suitable for sugar plantations. The map delineates precise boundaries that established more or less uniform rectangular or rectilinear parcels. However, the preceding organization of property left its mark on the landscape as the properties bordering other *hatos* and *corrales* or particularly in the empty spaces between them (*realengos*) could have highly distorted shapes. The survey map marked precise and calculable boundaries for the new estates and established individual property rights over them, permitting owners to plan the location of fields, buildings, and pastures. The size and configuration of the sugar mills were determined by the technical conditions of sugar production that were current at the time. The flat topography of the region allowed for the purchase of contiguous properties. Because there was not a dense rural population, the alienation of land and the conversion of sugar was relatively free of conflict. The owners of such haciendas profited from the sale of their land, and some, like the Peñalver family, who constructed Ingenio El Narciso and the neighboring Ingenio El Progresso in the 1840s, kept some of the land to build their own sugar mills.

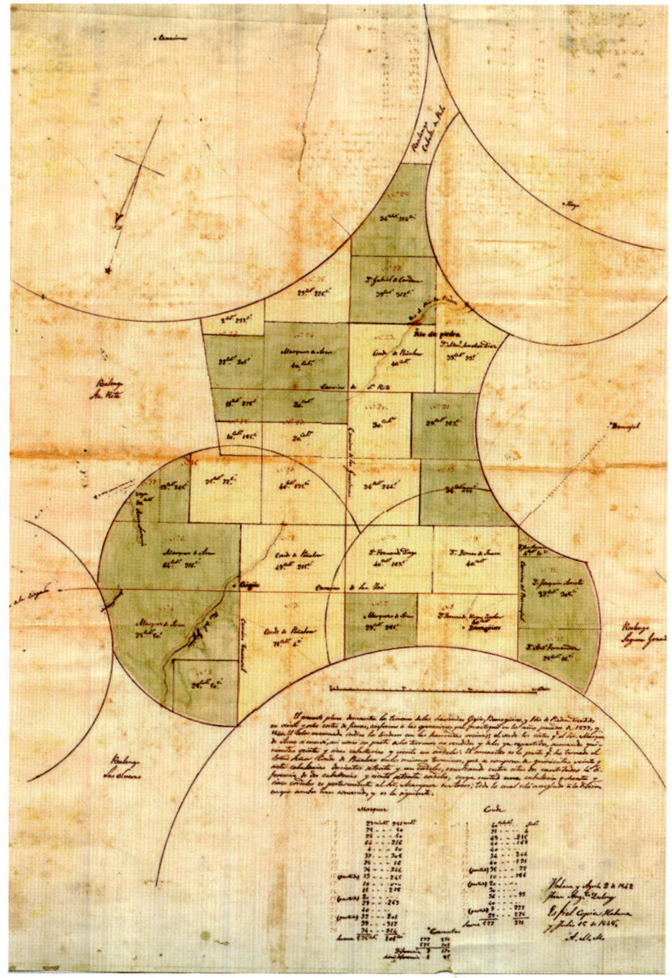

Figure 2.03. *Grants and titles of the Arcos family in the Banagüises and Jigües corrales and realengo Rio de Piedra and Santa Rita. Jéronimo de Villar, 1842. Fondo de agrimensores Serafín Sánchez Govín, Fundación Antonio Núñez Jiménez, Havana, Cuba.*

By the late 1820s, Cuba emerged as the largest sugar producer in the world and was rapidly expanding its output. The 1827 census registered 669 sugar mills in the western part of the island. Because of transportation problems, these were concentrated in the regions between the ports of Havana and Matanzas. In 1837, the construction of the first railroad in Latin America broke the transportation bottleneck and opened the extensive interior prairie to sugar cultivation.[12] The railroad was built by and for the sugar industry. Manuel J. de Carrera y Heredia's 1846 map of the railroad network between Havana and Júcaro (figure 2.04) documents the close relation between the railroad and the expansion of the plantation system. (The orientation of the map has north at the bottom and south at the top.) This survey map abstracts from the landscape to present only those features of interest to the railroad: sketched contours to indicate changes in topography; precise graphic representation of rivers, coastline, and hydrological features; symbols designating the location of plantations, towns, and cities; and lines indicating existing rail lines, those under construction, and the projected routes of new ones. It is an analytical representation that emphasizes scale, geometry, and precise calculable relations between selected features. In contrast to the Lemaurs' 1798 map for the project to build the Havana-Güines canal (figure 2.02), it is meant to be read, not seen.[13]

The map allowed the railroad to plan the location of its lines in close prox-

Figure 2.04. Plano general de los Ferro-Carriles construidos, en construcción y proyectados desde la Habana hasta el Júcaro. *Manuel J. de Carrera y Heredia, 1846. Biblioteca Nacional de Cuba José Martí, Havana.*

imity to the plantations in order to maximize the quantity of freight and minimize the distance to transshipment points in Havana, Matanzas, Cardenas, and Júcaro within the specific geography of the region. Conversely, the location of the rail line was a crucial element in determining where new mills would be constructed. The relation between the quantity of sugar produced, distance, and value determined the expansion of sugar into the interior. The abstract graphic representation of the map was instrumental in calculating and planning the integration of the railroad and sugar production. The interdependence of the railroad and the sugar mill generated pressure to expand sugar cultivation farther into the interior and to produce ever greater quantities of sugar. Up until 1837, the increase in Cuban production was due to the multiplication of sugar mills. After 1837, not only were there more mills, but sugar production was continuously restructured. During the 1830s and 1840s, sugar manufacturing was mechanized. New milling and refining technologies dramatically increased output. Each new innovation or improvement required more land and more labor in order to be efficient and profitable. The railroad created an open sugar frontier that allowed Cuban planters to build bigger plantations and incorporate new technologies as the Atlantic slave trade continued to supply necessary labor. At the same time, the farther the railroad network reached into the interior, the greater the amount of sugar that had to be produced in order to pay the costs of the construction and maintenance of the extended transportation infrastructure.[14] Thus, the railroad was the fundamental element for the extraordinary expansion of the Cuban sugar industry. It allowed planters to realize the unprecedented increases in both total output and productivity that enabled them to dominate the world sugar market. On the other hand, the extension of the railroad into the interior of the island accelerated the destruction of Cuba's biologically diverse forest environments. Not only were trees cleared to make way for cane fields, but wood was used for the construction of sugar mills and the railroad itself, and steam-powered locomotives and sugar mills consumed enormous amounts of it as fuel. The new landscape was dominated by monocultural production and transformed into a virtual sea of sugarcane.

The "Second Spanish Empire" was increasingly dependent on the wealth generated by the Cuban sugar industry during the first half of the nineteenth century.[15] The map of the Júcaro Railroad (figure 2.05) shows the heart of the Cuban sugar frontier at the height of its development. It documents the transformation of *hatos* and *corrales* into sugar mills and their relation to the rail line. The sugar mills depicted here include some of the largest and most productive mills on the island. Among the owners were some of the wealthiest planters in Cuba.

Figure 2.05. *Detail of* Plano del ferrocarril de Júcaro y sus inmediaciones. *G & W Endicott Lithography, 1844, New York. Fondo de agrimensores Serafín Sánchez Govín, Fundación Antonio Núñez Jiménez, Havana, Cuba.*

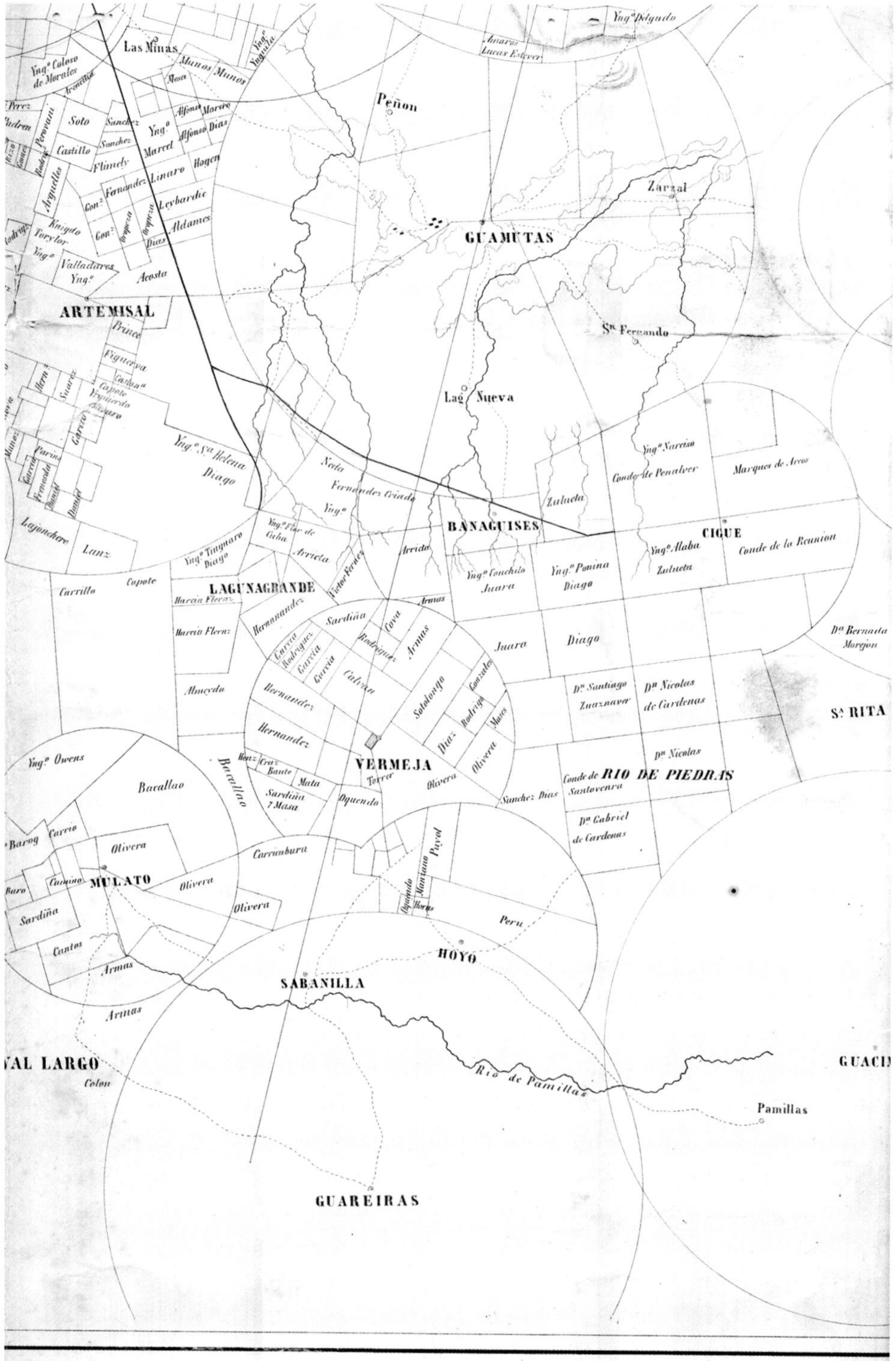

The map of Soledad Corral in Colón inventories property for purposes of taxation by the Spanish state (figure 2.06). It shows a *Corral* after its conversion to sugar, disclosing the close integration of the sugar mills and the railroad and indicating the importance of proximity to rail lines for the successful operation of a sugar mill. Eight large sugar mills dominate the territory shown on the map. With the exception of Ingenio Soledad (as distinct from Soledad Corral), which appears to have been founded in 1804, they were established in the 1830s and 1840s. Two of them, Ingenio Gratitud and Ingenio Soledad, have railroad stations on their property. The town of Bemba (today Jovellanos), built at the intersection of the rail lines, was the site of the largest iron foundry on the island, built to serve the needs of the sugar mills of the region. The presence of the foundry made Bemba the junction for the Cardénas, Cardénas and Júcaro, and Bahía Railroads, which reached farther into the sugar zone. The map also shows a considerable number of small properties, or *sítios de labor*, that specialized in the production of provisions for the plantations, as well as for the town of Bemba. The list of *censatarios* on the right of the map suggests that those holding those parcels had usufruct rights to the land in exchange for annually paying to the owner of the hacienda 5 percent of the value of the parcel stipulated by contract. In effect this amounted to a long-term lease.[16] The majority of the population in Soledad Corral were slaves who resided on sugar plantations. The majority of the population in the town of Bemba were white. In the Spanish conception of spatial order, this nucleus of white population served as a demographic and military counter to the enslaved majority on the plantations.[17] By accurately representing the productive units and means of transport of Soledad Corral, the map not only expressed the profound transformations of the Cuban countryside but also served as an effective instrument of Spanish control over the island.

The ever-increasing quantity of sugar arriving in Havana from the expanding sugar zone overwhelmed the facilities of the old city. The difficulties experienced in transporting and storing sugar and loading it on ships in the port of Havana led a group of investors to build large modern warehouses southwest of the town of Regla, across the harbor from Havana. These structures were made to handle the enormous quantity of sugar that passed through Havana on its way to North American and European ports. They were favorably located in relation to prevailing winds in the harbor and were built close to the water to facilitate the fast and efficient loading of ships. Construction began in 1843. The first warehouse measured 80 × 135 varas (1 vara = 7.74 feet). It was supported by internal pillars and had no interior walls. More and larger warehouses were subsequently built. The amount of sugar stored in the warehouses climbed from

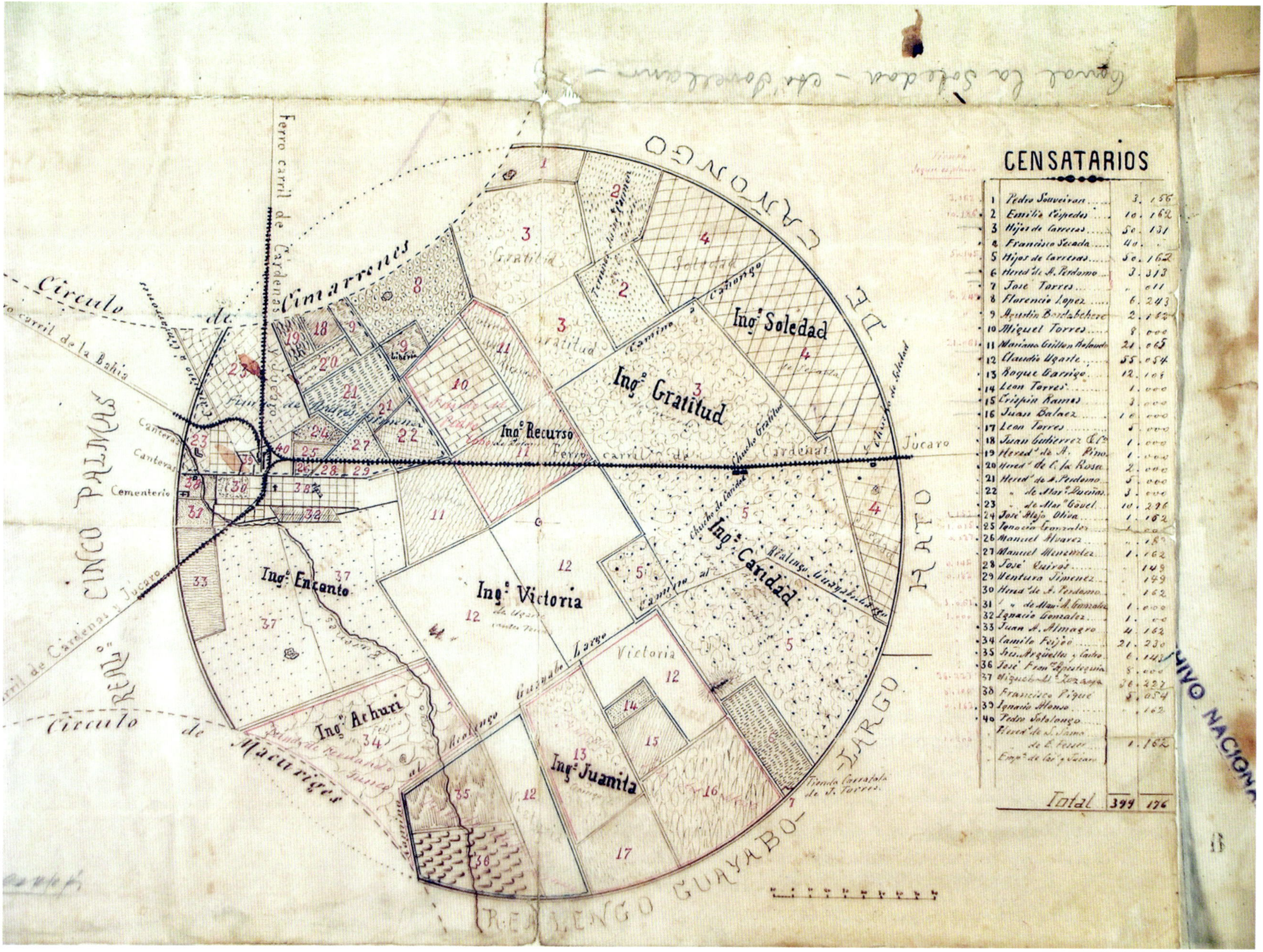

Figure 2.06. Soledad Corral.
Archivo Nacional de Cuba, Havana.

Figure 2.07. *Construction of the Santa Catalina warehouse, Regla, Cuba, 1858–60. The Getty Foundation, Los Angeles, Calif. Open access under the Getty's Open Content Program, Object Number: 84.XC.873.7777.*

46,848 boxes (*cajas*) in 1845 to 698,276 boxes in 1853. The warehouses were connected directly with the rail lines coming from the interior sugar zone. Inside the warehouses, designated spaces were set aside for the produce of individual sugar mills along the rail lines. Large overhead cranes moved the sugar from the trains to the warehouses and from the warehouses to the ships.[18] In order to take full advantage of these cranes, the majority of Cuban sugar was packed in large boxes instead of barrels. However, there was no effort to standardize the size of boxes until the mid-nineteenth century.[19]

George N. Bernard's stereograph view (figure 2.07) depicts the construction of the Santa Catalina warehouse at Regla. The immense two-story structure was designed by American engineer James Bogardus, the world's foremost expert in the use of structural iron. Construction began in 1858 and was completed in 1860. The iron frame was cast in New York and shipped to Havana. It employed the most advanced engineering technology of the time and held 200,000 boxes of sugar weighing between 400 and 500 pounds each. The Santa Catalina Bank and Warehouse Company, led by Eduardo Fesser, revolutionized the sugar trade by organizing the first company for the contract purchase and storage of sugar on a large scale.[20]

The 1857 map of railroads, steamship routes, and telegraph stations by José Maria de la Torre, professor of geography at the University of Havana, demonstrates the close interdependence between sugar production, the railroad, and the ports (figure 2.08). The railroad network and steamship routes coincide with the sugar zone, while the projected rail lines mark the future extension of the sugar frontier. The sugar mills were constructed in proximity to the rail lines. The railroad and steamship lines integrated the sugar plantations of the interior with the improved warehouses and port facilities of Havana and Matanzas and through them with the world market. They increased the volume of sugar that could be transported and the speed with which it could be carried. The telegraph allowed planters even in the farthest reaches of the sugar frontier to follow the movement of sugar prices and enabled merchants to follow the progress of the crop. Thus, the market for sugar began to form even before the crop was harvested. However, the remarkable feature of the map is that it presents not only the distance but also the time between stations. It represents the island as an abstract grid of homogeneous time and space. It thus made possible continuous calculation of time, distance, and price through which the Cuban countryside was integrated into world markets. This new conception of space and time was the premise of the development of the Cuban sugar industry and expressed the conditions of production in the new commodity frontiers.

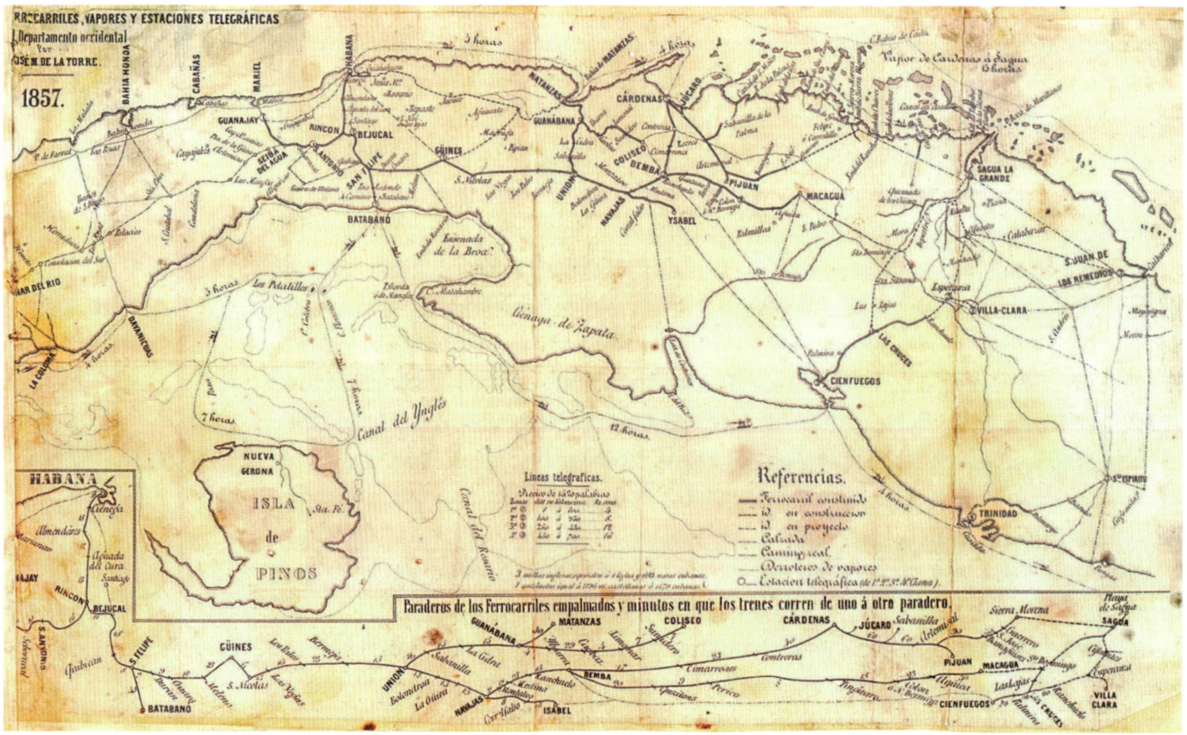

Figure 2.08. *Map of the Western Department of Cuba, with railroads, steamboats, and telegraph stations. José Maria de la Torre, 1857. Fondo de agrimensores Serafín Sánchez Govín, Fundación Antonio Núñez Jiménez, Havana, Cuba.*

3
The Brazilian Coffee Frontier

The emergence of the Paraíba Valley coffee frontier transformed world coffee production and created a mass market for coffee. After 1815, the conditions of world coffee production and consumption changed dramatically. The Haitian Revolution and the dramatic withdrawal of Saint Domingue from the European economy completely altered the configuration of the world coffee and sugar markets. New producing regions emerged, and world production increased. Coffee adapted readily to new conditions of urban life and industrial work rhythms. It found ready consumers in the growing middle and working classes. Initially the zones that most benefited from the vacuum created by Saint Domingue were those that had produced coffee before 1790, especially in the British West Indies. However, by the mid-1820s a clear differentiation between old and new producing regions emerged. Encouraged by Spain's Bourbon Reforms that liberalized trade, Cuban planters were well prepared to take advantage of the new conditions of the world market. Cuba became a major coffee producer. Many coffee planters were refugees from Saint Domingue who settled in the mountainous region of eastern Cuba because of its geographic proximity and favorable environmental conditions. These new immigrants played a decisive role in transferring technology and knowledge of coffee cultivation to Cuba. This knowledge was quickly passed along to planters who were building coffee plantations in other parts of Cuba, and by the 1830s Cuban coffee planters employed around 50,000 slaves and were producing almost 30,000 metric tons of coffee annually.[1] However, in the west of the island, where the majority of plantations were located, coffee and sugar competed for the same natural resources and for slave labor. With the rise of the sugar industry during the same years, coffee production declined in the west and was concentrated in the eastern part of the island.

Brazil also entered the world coffee market during the period after the Haitian Revolution and the Napoleonic wars. Coffee had been cultivated in the state of Grão-Pará e Maranhão as early as the 1720s as part of the same movement that introduced the crop to Martinique and Surinam. During the 1770s the plant was adapted to Brazil's center-south region and cultivated at country houses and on small farms around Rio de Janeiro. But the decisive moment for Brazil becoming the world's dominant coffee producer was the emergence of the Paraíba Valley as the new coffee frontier during the 1820s and 1830s. With almost limitless land at their disposal, Brazilian planters adopted a strategy of extensive cultivation and large-scale production at the expense of quality. Their profits derived from low costs per unit and high volume. The great quantity of low-cost Brazilian coffee created a mass market, particularly in the United States, over the first half of the nineteenth century.

The exploitation of the Paraíba Valley built upon key elements of the infrastructure that were already present in Brazil because of the gold economy. During the eighteenth century the mining district of Minas Gerais, located in the interior of the country, was the largest producer of gold in the Americas. The Paraíba Valley lies between Minas Gerais and Rio de Janeiro. In order to prevent contraband, the Portuguese crown outlawed settlement between the mining zone and the coast. The consequence of this prohibition was that a vast area of virgin land was made available for coffee cultivation. East-west and north-south roads crossed the valley to connect Rio de Janeiro to the gold fields of Minas Gerais and to São Paulo. Further, this region possessed a very efficient transport system based on mule trains that was well-suited to the rugged terrain of south-central Brazil. Finally, and perhaps most crucially, a large-scale bilateral slave trade between ports of Central Africa and Rio de Janeiro controlled by merchants in Rio de Janeiro ensured an adequate supply of labor as the coffee frontier expanded.

Nonetheless, the cycle of coffee production did not follow straightaway on the decline of the mining industry. The immediate response to the Haitian Revolution in Brazil was the recuperation and expansion of sugar production in the northeast littoral. Sugar also began to be cultivated in other parts of the country, and the production of provisions and cattle raising for the internal market became important activities.[2] The impetus for coffee production may have come from the flight of the Portuguese court to Rio de Janeiro because of the threat of Napoleon's armies in 1804. The population mushroomed in the new seat of the Portuguese Empire, and Rio de Janeiro became one of the largest cities in the Americas. In order to meet the need for food in this rapidly growing city, the crown constructed roads to directly link the zone producing provisions south of Minas Gerais to the new court. These new roads would become the central axes for the development of coffee cultivation in the central Paraíba Valley. Their opening generated immense land hunger, and two of the most important coffee municipalities in the world, Vassouras and Valença, were soon to be established on their margins. The exiled monarchy also needed to expand trade in order to increase its revenue. For this reason, the Portuguese state encouraged coffee production. Coffee was to become Brazil's major export crop in the nineteenth century and supported the power of the country's dominant landowning elite.[3]

The formation of coffee plantation agriculture in Brazil depended upon political actions that were coordinated at the level of the Portuguese imperial government in order to create the institutional conditions necessary to set activity in motion and to regulate the world coffee market. In conjunction with the demographic growth of the court, the opening of the ports to free trade after 1808 had an immediate impact on the demand for slaves. During the first decade of the nineteenth century, an annual average of 10,000 slaves disembarked in Brazil. During the following decade (1811–20), under the new commercial regime, this figure practically doubled.[4] A portion of these slaves were destined for the growing coffee plantations whose proprietors had at their disposition a complete commercial system (warehouses, merchant houses, and the like) that had been built there previously for the exportation of sugar, leather, cotton, and other products.[5] The period of the formation of the great coffee fazendas of the Paraíba Valley coincided with the period of the illegality of the transatlantic slave trade (1835–50) and the acquisition of slave gangs that, according to the terms of the imperial law of November 7, 1831, were formally free. Without an internal structure that gave political and juridical security to masters who possessed illegally enslaved Africans, Brazil certainly would not have supplied endless sacks of coffee to the ports and warehouses of the Northern Hemisphere.[6]

Slave owners invested decisively in coffee during the decade beginning in 1810 in response to rising world market prices. Before the opening of the ports, annual exports averaged about 400 metric tons for the period from 1797 to 1811. In the five-year period of 1812–16, the annual average rose to 1,500 metric tons in response to direct access to the world market and rapidly rising prices. In the following five-year period (1817–21), production increased fourfold, climbing to 6,100 tons annually. Production more than doubled during the years of independence (1822–23), reaching 13,500 tons, and then nearly quintupled over the next ten years, with production reaching 67,000 tons in 1833. This latter figure was the equivalent of total world production in 1790. By 1828, the value of Brazilian coffee exports surpassed that of sugar, and Brazil emerged as the world's leading coffee producer, well ahead of the rest of its competitors (Cuba, Java, Jamaica, Haiti). Thus, it was no accident that the period from 1822 to 1833 marked the clear differentiation of the world coffee market between old and new producing regions.[7] This process of differentiation had been set in motion some three decades earlier. Beyond Brazil's complete domination of the world coffee market throughout the nineteenth century, the unheard-of volume of its production was central for the transformation of the nature of the market itself, which passed from restrictions linked to luxury consumption to a qualitatively distinct scale of mass consumption.[8]

Almost all of Brazilian production came from a single region. The valley of the Paraíba do Sul River, or simply the Paraíba Valley, encompassing lands in the provinces of São Paulo, Rio de Janeiro, and Minas Gerais, underwent a complete transformation in the course of two generations. Relatively unoccupied in 1800, the valley acquired all the characteristics of a slave plantation region over the next fifty years.[9] The Paraíba Valley is located on a high plateau between the Serra de Mantiqueira and the slopes of the Serra do Mar. It runs in a southwest-to-northeast direction parallel to the coast. The climate is moderate year-round. Winter months are dry with relatively cold nights. The temperature is higher in the summer, and there are torrential downpours; the average rainfall is between forty to sixty inches annually. Knob-like hills known locally as "half oranges" (*meia laranjas*) running parallel to the Paraíba River form the topography of the valley, which has been described as "a sea of hills." The area is well-watered and drained by streams that flow between the ridges. The mountainous terrain was covered by the dense Mata Atlantica rainforest. The clay loam and sandy loam soils were shallow and moderately fertile, and they were further enriched by the biomass of the virgin forest, but they retained little vegetable mold from the forest.[10] Removal of the forest cover and its replacement by coffee monoculture deprived the soil of vital nutrients.

Conrado Jacob de Niemeyer was one of the principal cartographers of nineteenth-century Brazil and the author of *Carta geral do império do Brasil*, published in 1845 and awarded a prize by Emperor D. Pedro II the following year. In 1857, at the height of the coffee boom in the Paraíba Valley, the Assembly of Rio de Janeiro commissioned him together with Pedro D'Alcantara Bellegarde to make a detailed map of the province, which took four years to produce. Published in 1861, the map offers a striking presentation of the new spatial complex forming the slave-coffee frontier (figure 3.01). Around the border of the full map (not pictured here) are detail maps of the principal towns that arose in the Paraíba Valley to facilitate the export of coffee and of the primary coastal entrepôts from which the coffee destined for the port of Rio de Janeiro was shipped in the years before the railroad. Niemeyer also inscribed on the map all the great coffee plantations and, in the case of the most important ones, the names of the plantations or their proprietors.

We may divide the Paraíba Valley into three subregions. The upper Paraíba, with emerging land occupation up to the zone of Queluz and Rezende at the present division between São Paulo and Rio de Janeiro, was already occupied at the beginning of the seventeenth century by Paulistas seeking to enslave Indians. The lower Paraíba, extending from São Fidélis up to the falls of the Paraíba River, roughly corresponding to Campos de Goitacases, had been occupied since the second half of the seventeenth century, first for cattle raising and later for sugar production. In contrast, the central Paraíba Valley (figure 3.01), from Barra Mansa to the region of São Fidélis, was open to coffee cultivation on an unprecedented scale. Occupation had been blocked, as mentioned above, by the official Portuguese policy of "forbidden zones" that was adopted in the 1730s. This ordinance sought to prevent contraband trade in gold by prohibiting construction of new roads and trails in the mountain areas where there were no checkpoints and the forest patrols (*patrulhas do mato*) were not active. Clandestine prospectors and small-scale squatters were certainly present on lands to the east and west of the Caminho Novo or Estrada Real before revision of the ordinance in the 1780s, as well as a small band of Coroado Indians on the north bank of the Paraíba River near the present-day town of Valença. However, systematic settlement was effectively blocked.[11] As a result, there was an enormous quantity of virgin land in the central Paraíba Valley at the end of the seventeenth and beginning of the eighteenth centuries. These lands presented no effective obstacles to settlement and offered excellent conditions for coffee cultivation. They were no more than 150 kilometers distant from the myriad of natural anchorages located along the coast to the south of the port of Rio de Janeiro, and they possessed an adequate transportation infrastructure because of the mining economy.[12]

Coffee production in the Paraíba Valley was premised on the virtually unlimited availability of land. Vast lands of the Paraíba Valley offered exceptional conditions for large-scale coffee cultivation. Their high elevation and distinctive topography provided cool temperatures, adequate soil and rainfall, and good drainage for coffee production. In their pursuit of high profits, Brazilian coffee planters adapted traditional slash-and-burn agriculture on a giant scale. Planters believed that coffee had to be grown on soil overlain by primary forest. They employed traditional techniques to burn off the forest cover and reduce the trees to ash, which would add nutrients to the soil. Partially incinerated trunks were simply left to rot. Once the forest was cleared, the rich humus soil that had been deposited for centuries was initially highly productive but subsequently deteriorated.

The map of four of the plantations belonging to Antonio Clemente Pinto, baron of Novo Friburgo (figure 3.02) and one of Brazil's richest planters, owning fifteen plantations and about 2,000 slaves, shows the patchwork of coffee groves, second-growth scrub, and primary forest that was created by the pattern of hillside cultivation in the Paraíba Valley.[13] There are no elevations on the map. The lines made by the "()" symbol mark the ridgelines of the hills. Together with the direction of the streams, they give some indication of the topography

Figure 3.01. *Detail of Pedro d'Alcantra Bellegarde and Conrado Jacob de Niemeyer's map of the province of Rio de Janeiro, 1861.* Carta chorographica da província do Rio de Janeiro mandada organisar por Decreto da Assemblea Provincial de 30 de Outubro de 1857. Encarregada aos engenheiros Pedro d'Alcantra Bellegarde e Conrado Jacob de Niemeyer (1858–1861). *Biblioteca Nacional do Brasil, Rio de Janeiro.*

Figure 3.02.
Brazilian coffee fazendas: Aldeia, Gavião, Cafés, and S. Martinho, Municipality of Cantagalo, Rio de Janeiro, n.d. Arquivo Nacional, Rio de Janeiro, Brazil.

of the area. The coffee plantings were extensive, and for each plantation there is a symbol indicating its seat, where the resident population lived and the coffee was processed. The plantings were often distant from the plantation nucleus. Coffee bushes were initially planted in vertical rows on the slopes facing the sun. As yields there declined, planting shifted to less favorable sites on the plantation, creating a chaotic pattern of new coffee groves, declining coffee groves, second-growth vegetation, and uncleared rainforest. Coffee bushes planted this way produced much higher initial yields, even if they required constant weeding, but they had an oscillating yield from harvest to harvest.[14] Further, in contrast to the more common shade-grown coffee, all of the berries ripened at the same time and could be picked simultaneously. However, removal of the forest canopy exposed the plants directly to the sun, resulting in lower quality fruit. Thus, the Paraíba Valley mass-produced cheap, low-quality coffee. Paradoxically, these practices put coffee in the reach of new consumers and broadened the market. The coffee trees bore fruit for as many as thirty years. However, clearance of the forest cover and the practice of planting the coffee bushes in vertical rows on the hillsides resulted in the loss of soil fertility and massive erosion during the rainy season. The available records indicate that the yield of coffee plants in the Paraíba Valley were extremely high in the early decades but declined over the course of the nineteenth century.[15] When yields began to decline, planters moved on to new lands rather than replant old groves. The coffee frontier migrated farther into the interior of the valley, where more extensive tracts were available, and the same pattern was repeated. The key to the expansion of Brazilian coffee production and its domination of the world market was the presence of virtually unlimited tracts of virgin soil and the mobility of its slave labor force. Coffee production in Brazil was an "itinerant culture,"[16] and the coffee fazenda was not a seigneurial estate fixed in space.

The transportation geography of the Paraíba coffee frontier differed from that in the southern United States and in Cuba. In the southern United States, major rivers linked fertile inland valleys to the sea, while in Cuba the flat terrain facilitated the construction of an extensive railroad network. In Brazil, though, the Paraíba River runs parallel to the coast, is itself not navigable, and does not offer an outlet to the sea. In order to market the growing output of the 1820s, it was necessary to overcome the obstacles presented by the mountainous terrain of the Paraíba Valley and the distance to the ports on the coast. The transportation network was the major contribution of the mining economy to coffee cultivation during the nineteenth century. In response to the requirements of the mining industry in the second half of the eighteenth century, a complex system of raising and commercializing mules linked the southern part of Portuguese

America to the *capitanias* of São Paulo, Rio de Janeiro, and Minas Gerais, furnishing the primary means of transport to the entire center-south of the colony. With the stimulus of the world market, this system was immediately mobilized to transport the coffee production of the Paraíba Valley (figure 3.03).[17] Given that the new plantations were no more than a seven-day journey from the ports of the coast (taking as a reference the customary journey of three leagues a day) and given the relatively low cost of acquiring and maintaining mule trains until the mid-nineteenth century, the cost of transporting coffee (involving the cost of freight, the volume of coffee, and the distance to the ports) was viable with the system of mule trains.[18] As coffee production expanded farther into the valley, there was more pressure on the transportation system. During the 1840s, railroad technology capable of operating on the steep slopes of the Serra do Mar was developed in Scotland, the United States, and the Alps, but it became available in Brazil only in the 1850s. In 1855 construction began on the Dom Pedro II Railroad. The railroad ran the length of the valley and brought the more distant fazendas closer to the port at Rio de Janeiro. Still, mule trains remained the primary means of transport for the coffee economy well into the 1860s. Despite the beginnings of industrialization and the increasing quantity of coffee taken to market, mule trains remained an efficient means of transport in the mountainous terrain of the Paraíba Valley.

Figure 3.03. *Mule train carrying coffee. Marc Ferrez, ca. 1885. Museu Afro Brasil, São Paulo.*

Victor Frond's engraving (figure 3.04) provides a panorama of Rio de Janeiro's busy harbor at the height of the coffee trade. Capital of the Brazilian Empire, Rio de Janeiro was the commercial hub of the Paraíba Valley coffee zone. Its harbor gave the valley access to the trade of the world. Among the buildings along the shoreline is the warehouse belonging to Maxwell, Wright and Company of Baltimore, the largest exporter of Brazilian coffee in the nineteenth century, an indication of the new commodity circuits of the second slavery.[19]

The new commodity frontiers of the U.S. South, Cuba, and Brazil were formed at the intersection of multiple material, social, economic, and political processes of varying scope and extent. The interaction and combination of these forces and relations configured these distinctive geographic-historical complexes. Each frontier comprised new combinations of natural resources, material processes of production, and slave relations. In each region, the natural environment was dramatically restructured in response to the pressures and opportunities of the world market. In each, diverse ecologies were transformed as vast tracts of land were dedicated to the commercial production of a single nonindigenous crop. In each, slaves were imported on a scale not seen before in order meet the enormous demand for labor. In each, transportation infrastructures and commer-

Figure 3.04. Panorama of Rio de Janeiro. *Victor Frond, engraving, 1859. Charles Ribeyrolles,* Brazil pittoresco *(Rio de Janeiro, 1859).*

cial and financial institutions integrated the zone and bound it together with world markets and transnational consumers. Thus, these commodity frontiers anchored new commodity circuits that integrated their production into a new world-economic division of labor that was as much geographic as it was economic. Within each zone, this same combination of forces reconfigured the productive units themselves. The number of plantations producing cotton, sugar, and coffee multiplied, and land, slave labor, and technology were combined in new ways in order to maximize the production of each crop.

Part II
Spatial Economies and Plantation Landscapes

The slave plantation integrated the new commodity frontiers of the lower Mississippi valley, Cuba, and Brazil into the world-economic division of labor. In each of these zones, more and larger plantations than had existed previously in any region of the Atlantic economy produced ever greater quantities of cotton, sugar, and coffee to satisfy growing world demand. While the plantations of these new productive zones shared general traits with the plantation regimes that preceded them, the plantation as a form of socioeconomic organization was far from being fixed, static, or rigid. The form of plantation organization was dramatically reconstituted in the new productive spaces as part of the expansion of the nineteenth-century world economy. Each of the new slave commodity frontiers was relatively uninhabited and offered few obstacles to the creation of new plantations. In each zone, the availability of extensive new lands, of a geographically mobile slave labor force, and of new production and transportation technologies restructured and reordered the plantation itself. These new spatial and organizational structures made possible the mass production of tropical and semitropical staples that anchored the commodity circuits forming the new industrial division of labor.

However, nature was not a blank slate upon which the world market simply inscribed the optimal conditions of production. Rather, the natural environment shaped the social and material relations of plantation production. Specialization in a given crop required appropriate environmental conditions, and particular environments offered some possibilities for the purposes of plantation agriculture, but not others. Thus, whatever general features they may have had in common, the Mississippi cotton plantation, the Cuban sugar ingenio, and the Brazilian coffee fazenda represent distinct responses to the natural environment. In each instance, the social and productive organization of the slave plantation had to be accommodated to the material and physical characteristics of the place in which it was produced and of the particular crop that it cultivated.[1] Each production process had to be adapted to distinct environments and spatial contexts: topology, soils, drainage, the availability of water and fuel, the varieties of vegetation, kinds of animal and insect species, physical location, and access to transportation all had to be taken into consideration when organizing the plantation and its activities. At the same time, the introduction of a new primary crop entailed the selection and manipulation of certain aspects of the pre-plantation natural environment. Complex ecologies were simplified and subordinated to monocultural production of the principal crop. Forests were cut down, fields were cleared, swamps were drained, irrigation and drainage ditches were dug, and roads and buildings were constructed.

The adaption to and transformation of nature for the purposes of establishing plantation monoculture was inextricably linked to the material characteristics of each crop. Cotton, sugar, and coffee each had its own "botanical economy." The characteristics of each plant varied, including whether it was grown from seed, from a cutting, or, in the case of coffee, from a tree; the plant's pollen-producing capacity; the length of the growing season; the length of time before the plant bore fruit; the timing and length of the planting and harvest seasons; the length of time that the plant continued to bear fruit from the same planting; the number of plants that could grow in a given area; the ratio of seed to yield and yield per plant or per area of land; the size, shape, and form of the fruit—fiber, stalk, or bean; and the processing required to transform it into a marketable product.[2] These various physical characteristics of the crop determined the operations required to cultivate and process each crop, the way that the land was ordered, the size of the slave labor force, the division of tasks, and the routines and rhythms of work.

Under market pressure to increase output and productivity, the planters of the new commodity frontiers utilized various strategies to maximize the surplus product within this material and social framework. They increased the extent of land under cultivation and, where possible, deployed new technologies. But because the labor force was secured through the physical appropriation of the person of the worker, slavery was not labor-saving. Technological innovation could increase output but did not result in the reduction of the size of the labor force or the costs of reproducing it. However, slave labor was geographically mobile and could be reconstituted on an extended scale and within new divisions of labor. In the zones of the second slavery, more slaves were deployed, divisions of labor were restructured, new technologies were incorporated, and work routines were modified and intensified. By these means, planters could establish greater economies of scale and increase output per slave.

The restructuring of the production process had to be synchronized with the possibilities and limits presented by the environment and the physical characteristics of the crop. In each commodity frontier, the transformation and reordering of the physical landscape created distinct spatial economies.[3] With more extensive areas under cultivation, greater masses of material had to be carried over increased distances for processing, preparation for shipment, and storage. The interplay of the physical environment, the material characteristics of the crop, and the capacities of the slave labor force established the optimal scale of production in given circumstances. It formed a material-spatial economy determined by the quantity of material that could be processed in a determinate space *in a given time*.[4] The institutional form of the plantation was recast in order to secure and regulate the spatial, material, and social integration of these restructured productive spaces. The plantations in the new commodity frontiers required careful management of both land and labor and their coordination with one another. Ideally, the location, size, and shape of fields and the placement of buildings for production and storage of the crop, for the residence of the supervisory and technical staff, and for the slave quarters were laid out so as to take optimal advantage of the resources offered by the physical environment, to establish the integration of the production processes required for each crop, to facilitate the physical movement of the produce through the plantation space, and to secure control over the activities of the slave labor force.

The transformed and reordered landscape structured productive activities and social life within the plantation unit. Since its inception in the sixteenth century, the plantation had been a type of industrial agriculture whose operations required calculation and measurement. However, with the increases in scale and severe pressure to maximize output and efficiency, quantification, measurement, and calculation became central to the organization and operation of the plantations of the new commodity frontiers. The larger the scale of production and the greater the mass of material to be manipulated, the more necessary were coordination and timing to integrate production processes. Quantification and measurement of the crop promoted standardization of process and product. Production techniques and planting knowledge became increasingly uniform and reproducible. They could be codified and transmitted by means of standardized planting and management manuals. The division of fields into regular plots and planting the crop in standardized rows created a more or less uniform and homogeneous landscape that facilitated measurement and calculation as a means of manipulating the relation of space, volume, distance, and time within the plantation. The size of plots, the mass of material produced, and its movement through the different phases of processing and production within the estate were subject to quantification and measurement throughout the entire crop cycle. The volume of material and the length of time it took to process at each stage became regular, predictable, and quantifiable. The entire process, from planting to final product, could be envisioned, calculated, and planned. Calculable space was transposed into calculable time and subjected to mathematical planning and control. The simplified and ordered productive landscape was translatable into abstract and schematic instruments such as maps, diagrams, and tables that allowed activities to be controlled and coordinated over the entire landscape in order to maximize the surplus product.[5]

The physical organization of the landscape had to be coordinated with the activities of the slave labor force. The reconstructed landscape and built environment served as a means to discipline and control the slave laborers. The reduction of the productive landscape to uniform, homogeneous, calculable space allowed the quantification and measurement of labor. Quantification and calculation served as a means of regulating the relation between nature and labor and between space and time in ways that conformed to the characteristics of each crop. Tasks and work routines could be standardized and measured against the size of the field and mass of material to be treated. Time discipline and greater intensity of work could be imposed on the slave labor force. A given quantity of work had to be performed in a given period of time. Slaves were reduced to abstract, calculable units of labor, and a new conception of management regulated labor and shaped a culture of control.[6] Calculation of the quantitative relation between land and labor enabled planters to compel the slaves to produce larger crops and greater surpluses on the more extensive plantations. The interaction and mutual formation of the physical space of the plantation and the material processes of production together with strategies for managing the landscape and for controlling the labor force structured the relation of space and time and formed the spatial economy of the plantation. From this perspective, it is more useful to regard the plantation as the product of a flexible and dynamic grammar of space and power than as a template that was serially replicated in each zone.

4
The Lower Mississippi Valley Cotton Plantation

The Natchez District was a center of agricultural innovation. Perhaps its most important contribution to the rise of the southern cotton kingdom was the development of a new strain of cotton that was ideally suited to the material and commercial needs of southern planters, Petit Gulf. A botanical painting of Petit Gulf cotton (figure 4.01) was included in Benjamin L. C. Wailes's *Report on the Agriculture and Geology of Mississippi*, a compendium of the state's geological and agricultural resources and practices, commissioned by the Mississippi state legislature in conjunction with the establishment of the University of Mississippi. The painting of the Petit Gulf cotton plant calls attention to the importance of reproducible scientific images drawn from life as a means of organizing, standardizing, and disseminating botanical knowledge and influencing agricultural practices.

Cotton was first introduced into the United States in the 1780s. The size of the cotton plant depends on climate and soil. In average soil, the plant grows to about five feet in height. In fertile soil, it grows to twice that height.[1] The branches are long and jointed and occasionally bifurcated. A boll containing the fiber and seeds grows at each joint. It is accompanied by a broad indented leaf growing from the same joint and rests on a footstalk three or four inches long. The woody fiber of the plant is white, spongy, and brittle but covered with a tough, pliant skin. The cotton plant is tuberous. Its roots penetrate deeply into the ground. Consequently, it is less affected by drought than other plants. The cotton fiber grows out of the seed as the plant matures and fruits. The fruit of the cotton plant is a compartmentalized boll filled with fiber-covered seeds that is enclosed by a protective calyx or pod. The bolls are egg-shaped, rather smaller than the egg of the domestic fowl, and pointed at the extremity. The plant begins to flower at the beginning of June, and the growing season lasts until about the first of November, when the plant is killed by the frost. When fully mature, the boll expands widely. The open calyx becomes tough, brown, and somewhat horny in texture. The fiber or lint remains attached to the boll and has to be plucked from it.[2] The seeds adhere to the lint and must be separated from it in order for the cotton to be spun into cloth. The bolls on the same plant ripen at different times. Pickers must return to the same plants throughout the harvest season. For this reason, cotton plantations were more compact than sugar or coffee plantations.

Figure 4.01. *Petit Gulf cotton. 1854. Wailes,* Report on the Agriculture and Geology of Mississippi, *Plate III, 138–39.*

Petit Gulf cotton offered significant advantages over the other major commercial varieties cultivated in the United States. Historian Joyce Chaplin, in her work on agricultural innovation, contrasts Petit Gulf cotton with Sea Island cotton, which is a high quality long-stapled hybrid variety of cotton. Its seeds easily are removed and its long spiral-shaped fibers can be spun into finer and stronger thread suitable for laces and luxury cloth. However, it cannot be grown any further than thirty miles from the coast. Cultivation of Sea Island cotton was confined to the Sea Islands of Georgia. [3]

Georgia upland cotton, another variety, was distinguished by its short, course lint and its small, fuzzy green seeds. It was difficult to separate the lint from the seeds, a process done by hand before the invention of the cotton gin. The cotton gin made possible the widespread cultivation of upland cotton throughout the interior regions of the South. Yet it was far from satisfactory. It was a poor-quality, low-price variety that was highly susceptible to rot and other diseases and pests.[4]

Mexican cotton and varieties based on it predominated in Mississippi. Mexican cotton was apparently introduced into Mississippi by Walter Burling of Natchez from Spanish Louisiana in 1806. This variety had long fibers and large seeds covered with felt-like down. It was known for its "vigorous growth," large boll, and ease of picking. It ripened earlier than other varieties of cotton then in use. When ripe, the boll opened widely, and the expansion of the lint made it easier to pick. Further, many bolls on the same plant ripened simultaneously. Three to four times more Mexican cotton could be harvested in a given amount of time than other varieties. In addition, the plant was not susceptible to rot or a range of other diseases and pests that plagued upland varieties. However, the fiber was coarse and the lint was exposed to wind, rain, and dirt and could fall out of the boll if not picked rapidly.[5]

New varieties of cotton were continually being produced in the Natchez District either by chance or by intentional cross-breeding following the introduction of Mexican cotton to the lower Mississippi valley.[6] Petit Gulf was a hybrid developed from Siamese, Georgia upland, and Mexican cotton by Rush Nutt and other planters in Rodney, Mississippi, north of Natchez, and patented in 1820.[7] It improved on the best qualities of Mexican cotton and its hybrids and possessed all the physical, ecological, and commercial characteristics desired by the planters. Unlike the hybrid of Georgia upland and Mexican cotton, it did not revert to the inferior qualities of Georgia upland. It grew prolifically and was disease-resistant and immune to cotton rot. It bloomed two weeks earlier than other varieties, which prolonged the picking season. Its long, fine fibers were suitable for high-quality cloth, and the seeds were relatively easy to remove.

Most importantly, its physical characteristics facilitated picking. Petit Gulf and its descendants bloomed in large, wide-open bolls. But unlike Mexican cotton, the lint was more firmly attached to the plant and did not fall to the ground if not picked quickly. If 50 pounds had been an average day's work for an adult picker with other varieties of cotton, the quota might go up to 200 pounds a day for Petit Gulf. By the mid-1830s, not only were Petit Gulf and its hybrids the mainstay of the lower Mississippi valley, but this variety spread to all cotton-growing states in the South, and the production of cotton seed provided a lucrative source of income for Natchez District planters.[8]

The features represented on the survey map of Cedar Grove plantation in figure 4.02 are characteristic of an antebellum cotton plantation in Adams County, Mississippi. Founded in 1830 by Absalom Sharp, a cotton merchant from Pennsylvania, Cedar Grove had 925 acres of land and ninety-one slaves in 1860. Typical of the physical landscape of Adams County, the terrain is hilly, and cultivated fields are broken by woodland and gullies. The map indicates the gullies that formed around the stream running through the property. The friable soil of Adams County was very fertile but highly susceptible to erosion and silting. In contrast to Cuban sugar mills and Brazilian coffee fazendas, the spatial plan of Mississippi valley cotton plantations was not normally structured around a centralized nucleus of buildings. The map of Cedar Grove shows the dispersed pattern of organization that was common in the region. The master's house and its dependencies are located in the small rectangular grove of trees on the southwest side of the property. The slave cabins are located in the middle of the fields at some distance from the master's house and are arranged in a line facing the overseer's cabin. The cotton gin is the larger building set at a distance behind the slave quarters. It is centrally located in relation to the fields, but because of fear of fire, it is far from other buildings. The location and structure of the buildings defined a strict social and racial hierarchy among masters, overseers and supervisory personnel, and slaves and facilitated surveillance and supervision of the plantation's working activities. The map shows that Cedar Grove was contiguous with other plantations. The proximity of plantations facilitated control of the enslaved populations. At the same time, inevitable interactions between plantations allowed slaves to extend their communities to nearby properties and form distinct neighborhoods.[9]

The material characteristics of cotton shaped the spatial organization of the plantation, its work routines, and conditions of everyday life. Because the same cotton plant kept yielding new fruit throughout the harvest season, the slaves kept returning to pick from the same fields. Consequently, in comparison to sugar and coffee, the fields were compact rather than extensive. Corn was

Figure 4.02. Map of Cedar Grove. *Charles W. Babbit, 1877. Courtesy of Historic Natchez Foundation, Miss.*

commonly grown alongside cotton, and fields were rotated every few years. Corn was grown as a row crop and used to feed both slaves and livestock. The size of the slave labor force had to be coordinated with the extent of the fields and the amount of cotton that could be grown. Cotton needed no elaborate processing but did require more labor to harvest than to plant and cultivate. Consequently, the peak demand for labor at harvesttime determined the optimal size of the plantation and its labor force. However, the size of the labor force required for the harvest had to be measured against the need to keep the enslaved workers occupied throughout the agricultural year. A balance had to be struck between the extent of the fields that were planted, the cotton yielded per acre, and the size and work capacity of the slave labor force. There had to be enough slaves available to harvest the crop during the picking season. During the remainder of the year, the slave population was occupied with a round of tasks including preparing the fields, planting the cotton, caring for the standing crop, cultivating corn, clearing land, building and maintaining roads, digging and clearing ditches, repairing damage from erosion, gathering wood, and various domestic activities that were performed during the time between planting and harvest. Having too many "idle hands" both was unproductive and presented a discipline problem for planters and overseers.

The crude ratio between the number of "hands," the extent of the fields, and the size of the yield determined the scale of production. In his travels through the southern cotton kingdom, Frederick Law Olmsted reported that wealthy planters around Natchez grew a bale and a half of cotton per acre on fresh land and that a slave picked between four and eight bales over the course of the harvest. Their plantations commonly had from 50 to 100 slaves. There was, of course, a certain amount of variation, but planters in the Natchez District commonly regarded 100 slaves as the optimal number of hands. That number expressed a rough equilibrium between the yield of the land, the capacity of the labor force, and the capital invested. It maximized the amount of labor available at harvesttime but kept the slaves fully occupied thought the rest of the year. When the planters reached that number, they would divide the slaves and stock a new plantation. At times they would have three or four adjoining plantations, each with its own overseer but belonging to the same man. More frequently they struck out for new land and built a new plantation elsewhere.[10] Thus, in contrast to more extensive Cuban sugar ingenios and Brazilian coffee fazendas, the lower Mississippi valley presented a pattern of dispersed smaller plantations.

The planter's residence at Cedar Grove (figure 4.03) is representative of the homes of the Natchez gentry. These prosperous planters were resident on their estates, which were working cotton plantations. The tasteful construction of the "big house" reflected the prosperity of the plantation, and its architectural features and location distinguished the owners from smaller and poorer cotton planters, whose crude cabins were hardly different from the slave quarters.[11] Nonetheless, the architecture of this particular residence, like that of other cotton plantations in the region, stands in sharp contrast to the elaborate villas of the Natchez "nabobs." The substantial houses of the gentry imparted a sense of stability and order to their properties. Their homes were also emblems of the respectability of the owners and their families, and they marked the social cohesion among this group. The "big house," whether the residence of the owner or of the estate manager, was the administrative and symbolic center of the planta-

Figure 4.03. *A planter's cottage, Cedar Grove, Natchez, Mississippi. Photograph by Grupo Bocaina. Courtesy of Lyda Jordan.*

tion. It embodied the authority and prestige of the owner and was the apex of the social and racial hierarchies that defined the plantation community.[12]

English-born A. R. Waud gained fame during the Civil War as a battlefield illustrator for the *New York Illustrated News* and then *Harper's Weekly*. Woodcuts like those made from Waud's drawings were an important way of transmitting visual images in mass-circulation newspapers and reviews before the invention of lithography and photography. His sketches in *Scenes on a Cotton Plantation* (figure 4.04) present a striking portrayal of plantation slavery. The sketches—made at Buena Vista plantation in Clarke County, Alabama, and published in *Harper's Weekly* in 1867—are noteworthy both for the visual information they provide and for their interpretation of plantation slavery. They are assembled in a way that creates an idealized portrait of the cotton plantation as at once a unit of production and a human community. Waud's carefully constructed composite image carefully documents the processes of cotton production on the working landscape as it provides a sentimental portrayal of the slave community. His drawings imply an integrated and harmonious though hierarchical plantation community unified by the patriarchal authority of the slave owner. The exploitation of nature and labor depicted at the center of the image is enveloped in the web of paternalist relations that are portrayed around its outer edge. Waud's artwork naturalizes and racializes the slave community by making it a permanent part of the plantation landscape.

These illustrations draw attention to the contradictory demands of the plantation as a human community and as a productive enterprise. Because the plantation was formed by means of the physical appropriation of human beings as chattel property, the activities and conditions of life of the enslaved population were subordinated to the requirements of production and to the necessity of social control both inside and outside of work. Management of slave labor and strict regulation of the resident plantation population were dependent on one another. Despite the evident limitations of Waud's interpretation, the visual juxtaposition of these two dimensions of slave life draws attention to the deep and multiple tensions and conflicts generated within the slave plantation and to the complex ways that they may be related to one another. It thus helps account for the distinctive spatial and architectural features of the plantation.

The sketches in the outer panels depict the social life of the plantation and envelop the productive process presented in the inner set of images. The power and authority necessary to control both dimensions of slave life came from a single source, the slave master. The dominant figures are those of the master and the overseer at the right of the illustration. It was the master who organized production and managed the dependent slave labor force. But Waud's sketches

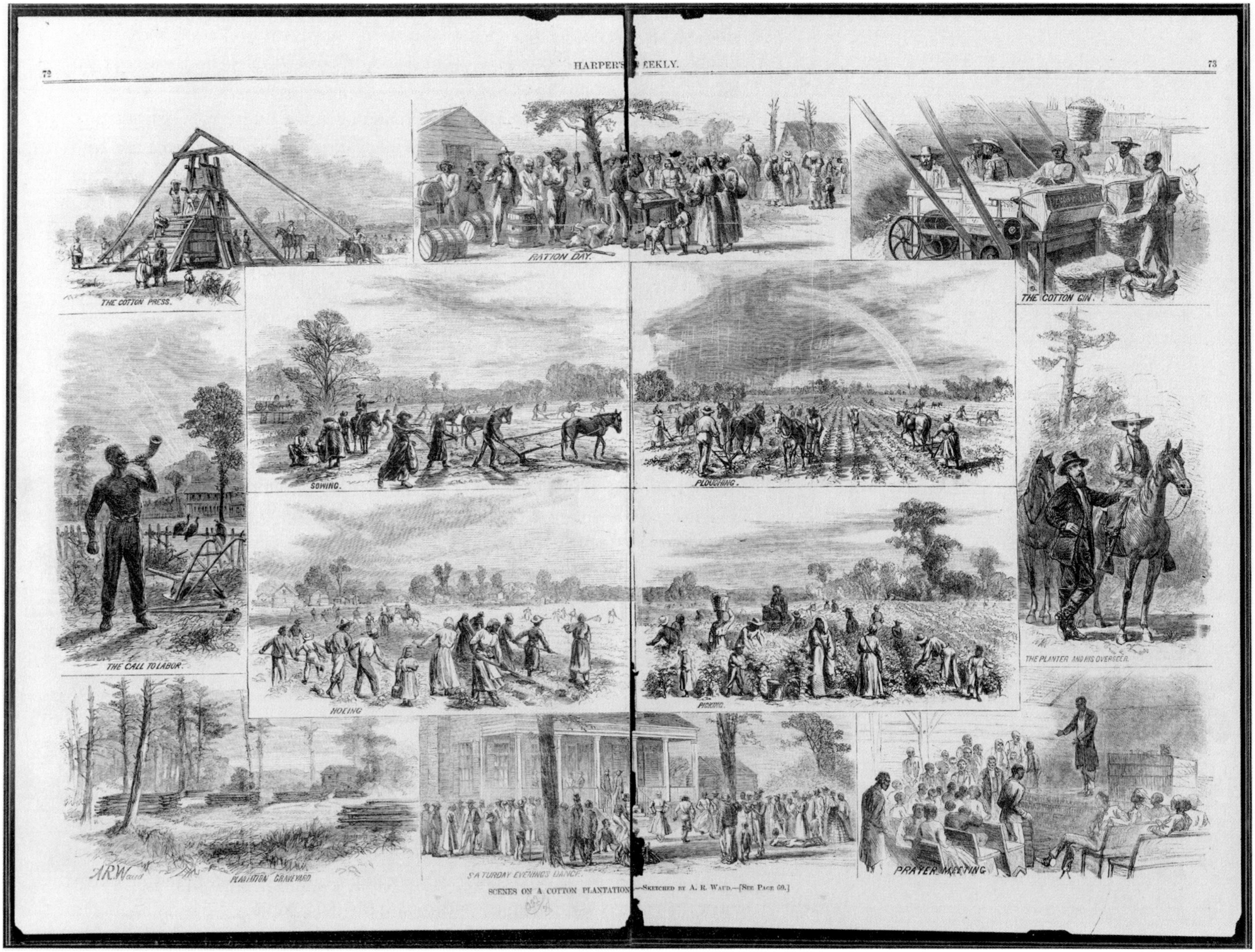

Figure 4.04. Scenes on a Cotton Plantation. *A. R. Waud,* Harper's Weekly, *February 2, 1867. Library of Congress.*

also emphasize the authority of the planter over the plantation community. The slave owner exercised his domination over the enslaved population of the plantation as his personal command over a given group of people. The prestige of authority, class, and race, and not simply wealth and property, set the slave plantation owner above everyone else and defined his distinctive role.[13] In Waud's depiction, the planter's dress and his association with the horse distinguish him from all others and endow him with authority and status. Alongside him is the mounted figure of the overseer, who carried out the master's will and was responsible for direct physical control over the slave population. The remaining outer panels present idealized and paternalist vignettes of the plantation community. Here, the images of the slaves receiving rations, the slave prayer meeting, the Saturday evening dance, and the slave graveyard are presented as expressions of the master's paternal benevolence. Such a presentation obscures the ways in which slave diet and cuisine, religious beliefs and practices, music and dance, and kinship and burial were created by the enslaved themselves out of the harsh conditions of plantation life and expressed their own conception of community. Such a view might easily be inverted to emphasize conflict between master and slave. Plantation life and labor entailed the continual interplay of resistance and accommodation, reward and punishment. What may appear at first as a simple distinction between master and slave, black and white, was in practice traversed by multiple deep tensions and conflicts. A complex web of intertwined social, racial, occupational, age, and gender distinctions and hierarchies at once formed the plantation community and profoundly divided it.

The lives of enslaved workers, whether they were engaged in cotton, sugar, or coffee production, were dominated by long hours of agricultural labor throughout the crop cycle. The yearly round of labor coalesced into set routines, which might be subject to contestation, negotiation, or resistance if norms of conduct were violated. But force and violence were always present to compel the fulfillment of the required tasks.

The four interior panels of Waud's illustration are remarkable for their detailed depiction of collective slave labor throughout the annual cycle of cotton production. Here Waud portrays the major tasks entailed in cotton cultivation: plowing, or "bearing off" to prepare the field; sowing the seed; hoeing to "scrape" or thin out the cotton plants and to weed the fields; and finally picking the mature crop.

Cotton cultivation required a tremendous amount of labor throughout the year. Preparation for planting began in January, when the cotton stalks left standing from the previous year were cleared from the fields. During this period, slaves were also engaged in repairing roads, fencing, cleaning ditches and repairing damage from erosion, hauling manure to the fields, and preparing plows and hoes.[14]

Planting generally began in April. Early in the century, planting was done with hoes, but by the 1830s plows were in common use. First, a team of mules or oxen plowed "water furrows" six to eight feet apart, which created ridges to facilitate drainage. A lighter plow was run in the center of these ridges to make the "drill" in which the seed was deposited. A girl carrying seed in her apron followed the plow and sowed the seed in the drill. On some farms the seeds were covered with a hoe, but on more progressive farms a horse-drawn harrow was used. By the 1830s, such planting gangs were able to plant ten to fifteen acres per day.[15]

The seeds were sown thickly. When the shoots began to appear in about six to ten days, the cotton was "scraped" in order to give the more robust plants room to grown. A light plow was run along the drill, throwing earth away from the plant. Then laborers with hoes chopped or cut away the excess shoots and intruding weeds, leaving single cotton plants growing from a mound of dirt about two feet apart. This operation demanded a high degree of skill on the part of the laborers. The use of the plow lightened the load of the hoe gang and allowed planters to increase the acreage that they could successfully cultivate. Scraping ordinarily took place in early May and took about two weeks. About two weeks later, another hoeing took place to clear weeds and grasses. Another plowing threw dirt from the furrow onto the root of the growing plant. Two weeks later, another hoeing took place to clear weeds and grasses. The cotton plants were then able to mature without being threatened by encroaching grass and weeds. In July, furrows were plowed between the rows for drainage in case there were heavy rains. The crop could then be "laid by" until the cotton began to ripen.[16] During this period, masters directed the slaves' efforts toward the cultivation of corn and peas. There was no relaxed period while the cotton crop was maturing.[17]

The harvest season began in late July or early August. Picking was the bottleneck of cotton production. More hands were required to pick the cotton than to plant it. The greater part of the available labor force was employed in picking until the harvest season ended around Christmas, though it could extend into January or February of the following year.[18]

The images in the upper right and left corners of Waud's montage show the final stages of the crop cycle of cotton production with representations of the two important machines required to prepare the cotton for market. The cotton gin separated the fibers from the seeds, and the cotton press compressed the cotton into bales. If the weather was good, the cotton was taken directly to the gin, but generally it was spread on scaffolds where it was left to dry and cleaned of any trash that was mixed in with the cotton. Picking, trashing, ginning, and pressing cotton were carried out continuously from August to December.[19]

Separation of the seed from the fiber was essential for large-scale commercial production of cotton. Eli Whitney's wire-toothed cotton gin, patented in 1794, opened a new era of agricultural development. However, Whitney did not reap the full benefits of his invention. He was neither able to meet the demand of planters for the new machinery nor enforce his patent. Further, Whitney's gin was effective at removing the seed but damaged the lint and did not produce the quality that textile producers wanted. Consequently, his invention was followed by both legal challenges and experimentation and efforts at gin construction throughout the cotton South.[20]

The Mississippi cotton frontier was beyond the reach of the legal disputes surrounding Whitney's invention. In 1795, Daniel Clark in Fort Adams in Washington County, Mississippi, south of Natchez, commissioned a cotton gin after seeing a sketch of the Whitney gin. James Bols, Barclay, a slave mechanic, and a blacksmith named Hughes built a prototype gin at Clark's Sligo plantation in violation of Whitney's patent.[21] Their prototype substituted round iron saws cut by hand from hoe blades for the wire teeth of Whitney's apparatus. It cleaned 8 pounds of seed cotton in fourteen minutes and promised to do 1,000 pounds per day.[22] Local planters responded enthusiastically to Clark's experiments, and the Natchez District became a center of testing and innovation. Local millwrights, mechanics, and blacksmiths, several migrating to the area to take advantage of the growing demand, began to specialize in the construction of gins. A variety of locally produced saw gins were in use in Natchez between 1795 and 1800. These differed in size and source of motive power. However, there were no forges or foundries in the Natchez District, nor were there sawmills for woodwork. Parts were made of bar iron or wrought iron sheet by local blacksmiths.

In 1817, local gin maker Eleazer Carver returned to Bridgewater, Massachusetts, where there were skilled workmen and an industrial infrastructure, and began to produce saw gins for the southern market. While southern gin makers remained active, new industrial techniques made their presence felt, and there was rapid improvement in the ginning equipment. New and efficient running gear replaced crude, handmade machinery. Saw blades were cut from cast sheet steel with steam-powered precision machine tools. The new blades were cheaper and more durable than the old handmade blades. They damaged the fibers less than the old saws did and produced higher quality cotton. The lower cost of mass-produced gins made them available to more planters, and they became more widely used. After 1837 the size and efficiency of gins improved significantly. Gins were larger and faster, with more saw blades. Gin stands were about six feet in width and enclosed a horizontal cylinder and brush running on iron axles. Improvements were also made in the design and manufacture of the blades. Forty to eighty high-quality cast-steel saws were mounted on the cylinder with greater precision to ensure accuracy and uniformity. These together with other improvements more than quadrupled the efficiency of the gin.[23]

The value of cotton depended upon the technical quality of the gin and the care taken in ginning. Planters were concerned to process the large quantities of cotton that they produced within the time constraints imposed by world market conditions. Consequently, they favored speed and quantity over quality. The development of large, multicylinder saw gins met the planters' demand to process greater quantities of cotton more quickly, but these gins broke the fibers and produced lower-quality cotton. Gradually the quality of cotton came to be defined by fiber cleanliness rather than by length. The larger gins were powered by horses or mules. Operated with care, a gin stand with four mules could turn out four bales of 450 pounds each per day, but it could be pushed to as many as five or six. By the 1830s, steam engines were beginning to replace draft animals on larger plantations. Steam power raised ginning capacity considerably, and steam engines often drove several gins and the cotton press at once. Wailes records a gin house in Washington County, Mississippi, where a steam engine powered four eighty-saw stands and the press. Those planters who had large, powerful gins often ginned their neighbors' crop, and some Natchez merchants erected public gins in Natchez, Washington, and other strategic points. The gins produced an enormous amount of seed, only a small portion of which was need for the next year's crop. The remainder was fed to the cattle, used for manure, burned, or simply left to rot. It was not until the 1830s that cottonseed oil was marketed.[24]

Improvements in the gin design changed the industrial architecture of the plantation. Early gin houses were mounted on the ground in a simple shed. However, by the 1830s, with the introduction of animal and steam power, they became more elaborate two-story structures, such as the gin house at Killarney plantation in Concordia Parish, Louisiana, across the Mississippi River from the city of Natchez (figure 4.05). Made of wood, they typically measured 40 feet × 60 feet. The gin stand was on the upper floor, resting on high blocks or pillars to accommodate the running gear on the ground floor. Directly beneath was the "horse path," where from one to four horses or mules turned a shaft that transmitted the motive force to the gin (figure 4.06). The current of air generated by the gin blew the lint into a room located directly behind the gin stand that was designed for receiving and storing it. In some arrangements, especially those with steam power, a large press for baling cotton was located on the ground floor

Figure 4.05. *Cotton gin house, Killarney plantation, Concordia Parish, Louisiana. Lemuel Parker Conner Family Papers, Mss 1403, Louisiana and Lower Mississippi Valley Collections, Louisiana State University Libraries, Baton Rouge.*

below the receiving room. Ginned cotton was thrown from the packing room into a reservoir, where it was tramped down by slaves. When there was a sufficient quantity, the upper door was closed and a powerful screw mechanism compressed it into a solid bale. Fire was always a danger in the gin house, and for this reason it was located away from other buildings.[25]

A variety of presses of local manufacture were in use. The screw press pictured in Waud's *Scenes on a Cotton Plantation* and in figure 4.06 could be found on small and medium-sized plantations. Made of wood, the large screw mechanism was turned by a mule or horse. Its great disadvantage was that cotton lint had to be carried from the gin to the press. It took much more time and effort to bale the cotton, and work could be done only in fair weather.[26] More popular on the larger plantations of the Natchez District was a horizontal press with two heavy wooden screws. Both gins and presses were installed in the same building and could be driven from a common power source, whether draft animals or steam engines. The horizontal configuration of the screws allowed the press to fit easily under the floor of the gin stand.[27] Cotton was initially packed in long cylindrical bags that weighed about 300 pounds. This method was abandoned in the Natchez District when local mechanic and gin wright David Greenleaf invented a practical cotton press. The use of compressed bales facilitated transportation of the massive quantities of cotton that were produced and protected them from dirt, water, and fire. Whichever type of press was used, the cotton box was lined with Kentucky hemp bagging to cover the upper and lower side of the bale. The cotton lint was then packed into the box and compressed into a solid mass. Ropes were passed around the bales to secure the covering and tied, and the openings in the hemp bagging were sewn together with twine. The screw was released, and the cotton swelled within the ropes. The bales were weighed, numbered, and marked with the name of the planter and his plantation. They were then hauled by wagon or cart to the nearest shipment point and consigned to the planter's agent or a commission agent. The weight of the bales was not uniform. Bales pressed in Mississippi weighed between 400 and 500 pounds, in contrast to those in the south Atlantic states, which generally weighed between 300 and 325 pounds. Shipping charges were calculated by number of bales rather than by weight. The larger bales resulted in lower transportation costs.[28]

Development of the Natchez cotton frontier's extensive and fertile lands depended on securing an adequate supply of labor. This demand for labor was satisfied by the interstate slave trade. Between 1820 and 1859, over 300,000 slaves from Virginia, Maryland, and the Carolinas endured the "second middle passage" that carried them to Mississippi and Louisiana.[29] The flux of slaves transported to Natchez for sale followed closely upon the fortune of the cotton economy. It rose with the rapid expansion of cotton cultivation during the 1830s, subsided during the depression decade of the 1840s, and rose again with boom

Fig. 2. Old Plantation Gin House and Screw.

Figure 4.06. *Gin house and cotton press. 1899. Tompkins,* Cotton Mill, Commercial Features, *5.*

of the 1850s. This forced migration transformed the demography of the region and created an overwhelmingly black majority population. Initially, sales took place at various sites in Natchez, but they were soon moved to the slave market at Forks of the Road, located on the Natchez Trace, just outside of town. Natchez became the biggest slave market in the Lower South after New Orleans and supplied the entire district. The excerpt of a registry of slaves brought to Natchez for sale certifies to the good conduct of those being transported (figure 4.07). The registry provides a record of those who experienced the interstate slave trade. They were predominantly in their late teens and early twenties and fairly evenly divided between males and females. Thus, they were at the prime age for work and sexual reproduction. These young people were uprooted from their kin and communities in the Upper South and transported down the Mississippi River or marched overland to Natchez. They then had to form new communities in the harsh conditions of Mississippi and Louisiana cotton plantations.[30]

The unprecedented expansion of cotton production in the lower Mississippi valley between 1820 and 1860 rested upon the labor of enslaved African Americans. Improvements in the botanical characteristics of the cotton plant and more powerful and effective cotton gins meant that more acreage could be planted. Large bolls and easy detachment from the pod of Mexican and Petit Gulf cotton hybrids facilitated picking, but human hands were still required to pluck the cotton bolls from the plant. Large-scale cotton planters instituted changes in the organization, intensity, and pace of work and transformed the character of American slavery.[31] The system of gang labor was the nearly universal norm on lower Mississippi valley cotton plantations. Organizing the slaves into large gangs—composed of women and men alike—supervised by white overseers mobilized the productive force of collective labor and facilitated supervision and control. The lives of the enslaved populations resident on cotton plantations were systematically subordinated to labor. Slave gangs worked from dawn to 10:00 A.M. and then resumed work from 2:00 P.M. until dusk. Slaves' free time on half Saturdays and on Sunday, widespread before the introduction of cotton, gave way to the demands of the cotton crop.[32]

Planters and overseers were concerned with increasing the rate of production and drove slaves to perform more labor in less time while prolonging the working day. At harvesttime, each slave was assigned to a row of cotton and given a sack to hold the cotton. A basket was placed at the end of the row to receive the cotton once the picker finished the row. Picking was a tedious and repetitious task. The cotton lint had to be plucked from the plant. The stalks and stiff, sharp leaves tore at the pickers' hands. It required dexterity rather than strength, and skilled laborers picked with both hands.[33] The contents of the bag were then

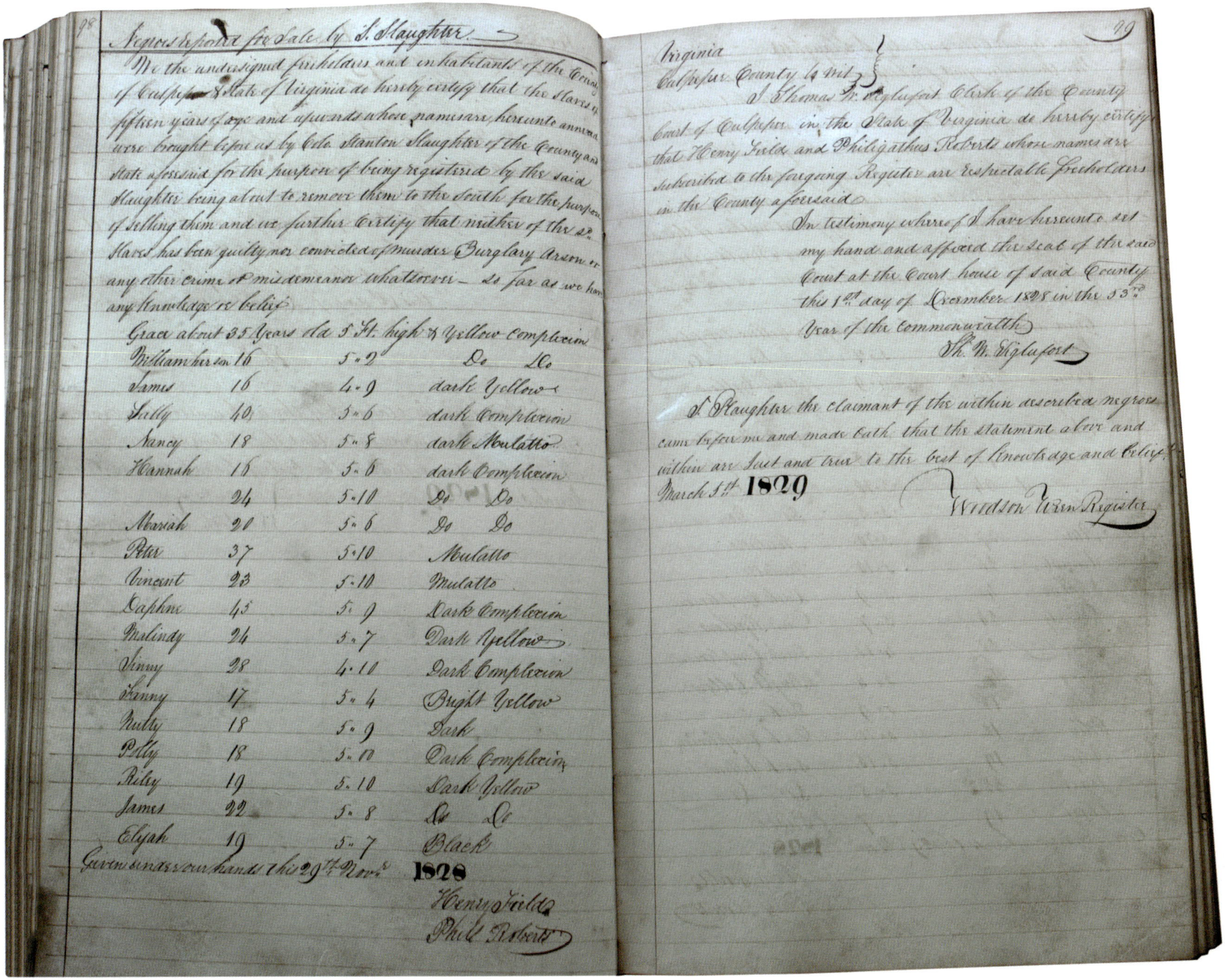

98 Negroes exported for sale by S. Slaughter

We the undersigned freeholders and inhabitants of the County of Culpeper & State of Virginia do hereby certify that the slaves of fifteen years of age and upwards whose names are hereunto annexed were brought before us by Colo. Stanton Slaughter of the County and State aforesaid for the purpose of being registered by the said Slaughter being about to remove them to the South for the purpose of selling them and we further certify that neither of the sd. slaves has been guilty nor convicted of murder Burglary Arson or any other crime or misdemeanor whatsoever — so far as we have any knowledge or belief

Name	Age	Height	Complexion
Grace about	35 Years old	5 Ft. high	& Yellow Complexion
William her son	16	5 " 2	Do Do
James	16	4 " 9	dark Yellow
Sally	40	5 " 6	dark Complexion
Nancy	18	5 " 8	dark Mulatto
Hannah	16	5 " 6	dark Complexion
	24	5 " 10	Do Do
Mariah	20	5 " 6	Do Do
Peter	37	5 " 10	Mulatto
Vincent	23	5 " 10	Mulatto
Daphne	45	5 " 9	Dark Complexion
Malindy	24	5 " 7	Dark Yellow
Jinny	28	4 " 10	Dark Complexion
Fanny	17	5 " 4	Bright Yellow
Nutty	18	5 " 9	Dark
Polly	18	5 " 10	Dark Complexion
Riley	19	5 " 10	Dark Yellow
James	22	5 " 8	Do Do
Elijah	19	5 " 7	Black

Given under our hands this 29th Novr 1828

Henry Field
Phil Roberts

99

Virginia
Culpeper County to wit

I Thomas W. Eglufort Clerk of the County Court of Culpeper in the State of Virginia do hereby certify that Henry Field and Philigathus Roberts whose names are subscribed to the foregoing Register are respectable freeholders in the County aforesaid

In testimony whereof I have hereunto set my hand and affixed the seal of the said Court at the Court house of said County this 1st day of December 1828 in the 53rd Year of the Commonwealth

Th. W. Eglufort

S. Slaughter the claimant of the within described negroes came before me and made oath that the statement above and within are Just and true to the best of knowledge and belief

March 5th 1829

Woodson Wren Register

Figure 4.07. *Excerpt from the registry of slaves transported for sale to Adams County, Mississippi. Courtesy of Historic Natchez Foundation, Miss.*

deposited in a basket for transport to the gin. The following excerpt from the memoir of former slave Solomon Northrup, a freedman from New York who was kidnapped and sold as a slave in Louisiana, describes cotton picking from the perspective of an enslaved worker:

> When a new hand, one unaccustomed to the business, is sent for the first time into the field, he is whipped up smartly, and made for that day to pick as fast as he can possibly. At night it is weighed, so that his capability in cotton picking is known. He must bring the same weight each night following. If it falls short, it is considered evidence that he has been a laggard, and a greater or lesser number of lashes is the penalty.
>
> An ordinary day's work is considered two hundred pounds. A slave who is accustomed to picking, is punished, if he or she brings in a less quantity than that. There is a great difference among them as regards this kind of labor. Some of them seem to have a natural knack, or quickness, which enables them to pick with great celerity, and with both hands, while others, with whatever practice or industry, are utterly unable to come up to the ordinary standard. Such hands are taken from the cotton field and employed in other business. Patsy . . . was known as the most remarkable cotton picker on Bayou Boeuf. She picked with both hands and with such surprising rapidity, that five hundred pounds a day was not unusual for her.
>
> Each one is tasked therefore, according to his picking abilities, none, however, to come short of two hundred weight. . . .
>
> The cotton grows from five to seven feet high, each stalk having a great many branches, shooting out in all directions, and lapping each other above the water furrow.
>
> Sometimes the slave picks down one side of a row, and back upon the other, but more usually, there is one on either side, gathering all that has blossomed, leaving the unopened bolls for a succeeding picking. When a sack is filled, it is emptied into the basket and trodden down. . . .
>
> The hands are required to be in the cotton fields as soon as it is light in the morning, and, with the exception of ten or fifteen minutes, which is given them at noon to swallow their allowance of cold bacon, they are not permitted to be a moment idle until it is too dark to see, and when the moon is full, they often times labor until the middle of the night. They dare not stop even at dinner time, nor return to the quarters, however late it be, until the order to halt is given by the driver.
>
> The day's work over in the field, the baskets are "toted," or in other words, carried to the gin-house, where the cotton is weighed. No matter how

fatigued and weary he may be—no matter how much he longs for sleep and rest—a slave never approaches the gin-house with his basket of cotton but with fear. If it falls short in weight—if he has not performed the full task appointed to him, he knows he must suffer. And if he has exceeded it by ten or twenty pounds, in all probability his master will measure the next day's task accordingly. So whether he has too little or too much, his approach to the gin-house is always with fear and trembling.[34]

Slaves had no protection from outbursts of extreme violence, but Northrup's testimony discloses the role of routine, day-to-day violence in managing the labor force and maximizing the output of the slave gang. The combination of row planting and gang labor enhanced calculability and productivity throughout the crop cycle. Enslaved workers were compelled to continuously perform mechanical tasks from dawn to dusk under the strict supervision and discipline of overseers and drivers and the constant threat of violence. Repetitive toil, with every movement subject to arbitrary control, animated the collective productive force of the slave gang. Such activity resulted in physical and mental fatigue that were key elements of social control and labor discipline.

The drive to increase the number of bales per acre per hand governed lower Mississippi valley cotton culture.[35] Picking averages increased dramatically. Near the end of the eighteenth century, an average hand in Natchez District could gather about 75 pounds of seed cotton a day. By 1837, average workers were picking in excess of 150 pounds of seed cotton daily, and skilled pickers brought in 300 pounds or more. On average, each hand picked from 250 to 300 pounds of seed cotton per day in the 1850s. Planters who in 1800 hoped to produce two bales 400 pounds of ginned cotton per hand per year were trying to produce six to eight bales per hand per year by 1837.[36] The natural environment and the bodies of the enslaved were the price of the high rates of cotton production.

Planters in the lower Mississippi valley were increasingly concerned with the level of output achieved by their slaves. Thomas Affleck of Washington, Mississippi, just outside of Natchez, formulated a standardized record book to facilitate plantation management by overseers (figure 4.08). First published in 1847, this best-selling handbook was issued annually in different sizes for different-sized plantations until the outbreak of the Civil War: one for 40 hands or fewer, one for 80 hands or fewer, one for 120 hands or fewer, and one for 160 hands or fewer.[37] Although cotton plantations were far from uniform, quantification and calculation made their presence felt in the management of slave cotton production and extended the reach of the world cotton market into the daily rhythm of the plantation. *Affleck's Cotton Plantation Record and Account Book* offered

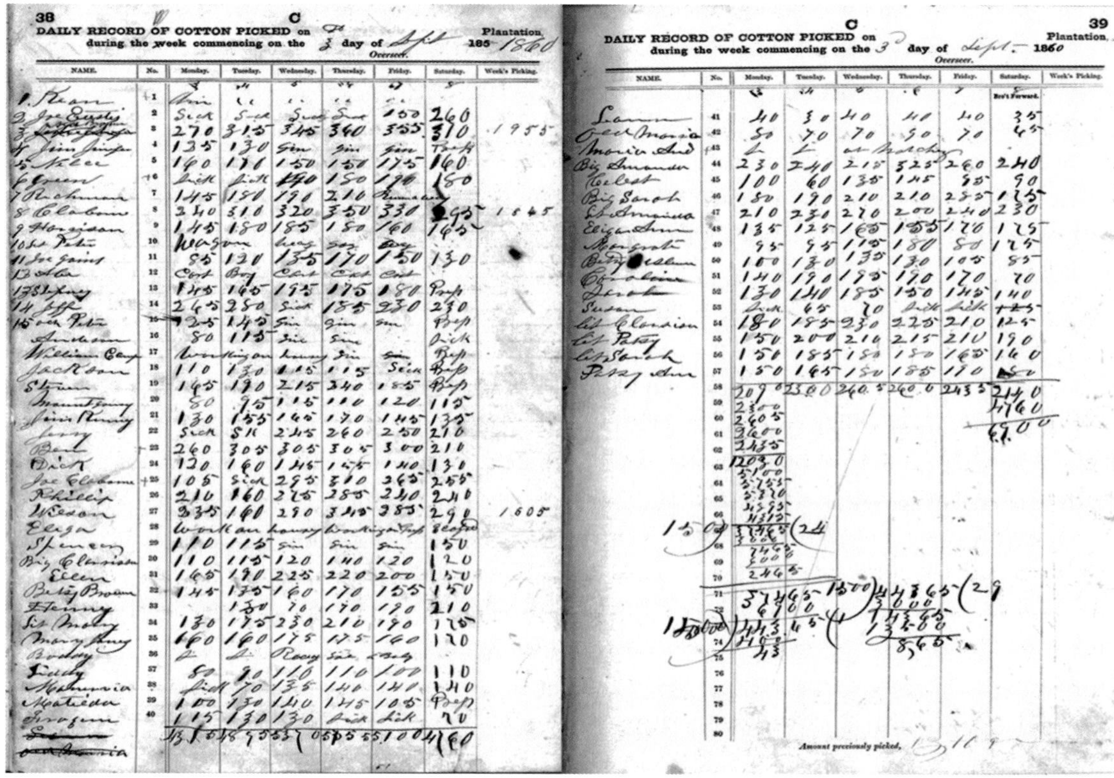

38
DAILY RECORD OF COTTON PICKED on Plantation during the week commencing on the 3 day of Sept 1860
Overseer.

NAME. | No. | Monday. | Tuesday. | Wednesday. | Thursday. | Friday. | Saturday. | Week's Picking.

39
DAILY RECORD OF COTTON PICKED on Plantation during the week commencing on the 3 day of Sept 1860
Overseer.

NAME. | No. | Monday. | Tuesday. | Wednesday. | Thursday. | Friday. | Saturday. | Week's Picking.

Amount previously picked,

Figure 4.08. *Excerpt from the standardized account book published by Thomas Affleck belonging to G. R. Clark (overseer), Eustatia plantation, Washington, Adams County, Mississippi, 1861. Ohio History Society, "The African-American Experience in Ohio," http://dbs.ohiohistory.org/africanam.*

preprinted forms that allowed the planter to quantify and track each aspect of the production process together with practical essays on aspects of plantation management. Its abstract logic provided an objective representation of the various practices of the slave cotton plantation that gave coherence to its structure. It allowed plantation owners and overseers to have a synoptic overview of the natural-material processes of cotton cultivation, slave labor management, and the financial determinants of marketing cotton.[38] This restricted and codified focus permitted systematic calculation and control of the plantation's natural and material resources and of the activities of the slave labor force. The overseer could evaluate past activities, direct present ones, and plan future ones, and the owner could assess the performance of the overseer without even having to see the fields.[39]

Affleck's Cotton Plantation Record and Account Book centralized record-keeping and required the overseer to fill out daily record sheets. The focal point of Affleck's plantation management guide was the exact measurement of the output of each slave each day of the week. Figure 4.08 is a page from Affleck's handbook showing the amount of cotton picked daily by each slave for the week of September 3, 1860, on the Eustatia plantation in Washington, Mississippi. Here, land and labor are reduced to the amount of cotton as their abstract, quantitative common denominator. The rows and columns schematically represent the geometrically ordered rows of cotton in the fields. Each slave is indicated by name but is represented as an abstract unit of labor, a "hand." As each slave is assigned to a standardized row of cotton, the rows of figures in the book measure the amount picked by each hand, and the sums at the bottom of each column enumerate the daily output of the whole gang each day. Affleck's accounting system permitted systematic measurement and calculation of the pounds of cotton produced by slave and by the acre and of the number and size the cotton bales. Bales were equated with the price of cotton. Total yield, total expenditure, and total profit could then be calculated. Thus, time was equated with money. Working days were converted to bales of cotton, and bales of cotton were converted into dollars.[40] In this way the entire production process was subordinated to the logic of the market.

The interplay of the growing world demand for cotton, the particular environment of the lower Mississippi valley, the physical requirements of cotton production, and the social relations of slave labor shaped the spatial economy and working landscape of the lower Mississippi valley cotton plantation. The interrelation of the requirements of cotton production, land, and labor set the parameters of the spatial economy of the cotton plantations of the Natchez District and determined the form of their architectural structure.

Winter Quarters plantation house, in Tensas Parish, Louisiana (figure 4.09), began as a simple hunting cabin built by Job Routh in 1805. In the 1850s, Haller

Figure 4.09. *Winter Quarters plantation house, Tensas Parish, Louisiana. Photograph by Grupo Bocaina.*

Figure 4.10. View of Winter Quarters. *Justin Sancan, October 1858. Photograph by Mark Coffey. Courtesy of Pilgrimage Garden Club, Natchez, Miss.*

Nutt renovated the house to make it a suitable residence for his family. And yet, Winter Quarters remained a simple house incorporating diverse architectural styles. Nutt was closely associated with the Natchez elite. He owned 43,000 acres of land and 800 slaves. On the eve of the Civil War, he was worth over $3,000,000. Winter Quarters covered a remarkable 2,000 acres and had 300 slaves and several cotton gins. (Interestingly, this is exactly three times what was regarded as the optimal size of a cotton plantation.) In the late 1850s Nutt contracted with Philadelphia architect Samuel Sloan to design Longwood, his ornate villa in Natchez. Construction began in 1860 but was never completed because of the Civil War.[41]

Justin Sancan's *View of Winter Quarters* (figure 4.10) depicts a scene of daily life on the plantation. In the foreground, slaves are drying cotton. The drying ground has a pasture to one side and a garden behind it. Caring for livestock and raising vegetables complemented cotton production. The garden appears to be organized under the supervision of the planter or overseer rather than under the control of the enslaved population. On the other side of the garden are the slave cabins as well as storage buildings nearest the bayou and the road that runs alongside of it. The cabins are arranged in parallel rows forming an alley that facilitates the control of the circulation of the slaves. Beside each of the cabins is a raised coop, presumably for chickens. The coops were undoubtedly elevated to protect their contents from the alligators that inhabited the bayou in front of the property. The planter's house is in the trees on the other side of the slave cabins. Behind the buildings on the side away from the river are cotton fields and alongside them the wooded areas that were common in the Natchez plantation district. In the background, other cotton plantations can be seen, including John Routh's Hollywood, suggesting the close links of family and property that bound the Natchez elite together. They are built along the bayou in accordance with the French long-lot system.

Figure 4.11 shows the 1849 deed map to Stephen Duncan's Saragossa plantation. Duncan established 940-acre Saragossa in the 1820s and sold it to William St. John Elliott, who owned the property from 1835 to 1853. It was one of six cotton plantations that Duncan owned and was literally a work camp. There was no planter residence there. Duncan lived five miles away at his Auburn villa. The property had about seventy slaves between 1823 and 1840. The map shows two rows of four cabins. Here too the cabins are built around a central alley that is commanded by the overseer's house.[42]

Figure 4.11. *Saragossa plantation map, Adams County, Mississippi. Courtesy of Historic Natchez Foundation, Miss.*

Figure 4.12, a photograph of one of the Saragossa slave cabins, is from the Historic American Building Survey. The rude slave housing stands in stark contrast to the homes of the wealthy plantation owners. The slave cabins of Sara-

Figure 4.12. *Saragossa plantation slave quarters, Adams County, Mississippi. Historic American Building Survey, Library of Congress.*

gossa plantation, just south of Natchez, were typical slave housing in the United States. Such cabins generally measured 16 feet × 18 feet and were often divided into two separate living units housing four persons each.[43] The buildings remained in use well into the twentieth century; the windows were undoubtedly put in after the Civil War.

The natural and social forces mobilized by the ever-growing world demand for cotton crystallized in the working landscapes of the slave plantations of the lower Mississippi valley. The built environment of the plantation, of course, expressed the power of the master and the subordination of the slaves. But more to the point, the spatial economy of the plantations synchronized nature and slave labor in ways that conformed to the material conditions of large-scale commercial cotton production. Simplification of the natural environment and the introduction of row agriculture, the botanical modification of the cotton plant, improvements in the cotton gin, the employment of gang labor, and new techniques of labor management shaped the characteristic features of the working landscape. The physical organization of the plantation secured social control of the enslaved population and facilitated greater rates of exploitation of its labor. By increasing output per slave as well as aggregate output, the Mississippi valley cotton plantations achieved unprecedented levels of production and lowered raw material prices. They fueled Manchester, England's mills and made cotton textiles the leading commodity in world trade.

5
The Cuban *Ingenio*

Sugarcane (figure 5.01) is a large grass of the family *Graminae*. The variety (*Saccharum officinarum*) primarily cultivated in the New World until the end of the eighteenth century, known as creole cane, was brought by Columbus on his second voyage in 1493. Sugarcane grows best in tropical climates, where it receives an abundance of heat and water, but it can also be grown in subtropical climates. Cold is prejudicial to the plant, although it can be grown in areas with marginal frost. Sugarcane successfully adapts to a variety of soils. The plant has a tall stalk, which commonly grows twelve to fifteen feet in height. Its cross-section is cylindrical and is between three-quarters of an inch to two inches in diameter. It is covered with a rind that is tough at the lower part of the stem and becomes softer toward the top. The fibrous pith contains the sucrose. The stem is divided into joints consisting of a node and a section of stem. The node is identifiable by a band that encircles the stem. Each node contains the primordia of a bud and a root. The plant is reproduced asexually by planting and covering a section of stem containing at least one node. The leaves are attached to the stalk and completely surround it. They are narrow and sharp and are up to five or six feet in length. Sugarcane is grown from cuttings and takes from twelve to eighteen months to mature, depending on the variety and the environment. Several crops (known as ratoon crops) can be grown from the same planting. The yield from each successive ratoon crop diminishes. Generally, after the third ratoon crop the yield is too low to be profitable and replanting is necessary, although there can be some variation in this depending on soil, climate, and other local conditions.[1] Cuba was in an advantageous position in this regard. There, as many as seven, ten, or more harvests could be obtained from the same planting.

Although the harvest may last for six months to a year because of the amount of cane planted, each individual stalk must be cut as soon as it is ripe and processed as soon as it is cut. If the cane is not harvested promptly, it will lose the juice or the proportion of sucrose in the juice will diminish. Once cut, the cane must be ground and the juice extracted and boiled into sugar within eighteen to thirty-six hours, or it will deteriorate and not crystallize. The sucrose content of the plant is the natural and technical limit of sugar production. Sugarcane contains 7 percent sucrose. The goal of improvements in milling technology was to grind greater quantities of cane and more effectively extract the juice containing the sucrose from the cane stalks. (By the nineteenth century the crushed cane stalks, or bagasse, were an important source of fuel for the boiling house.) Sucrose is indistinguishable in taste and chemical composition no matter its source, and it yields a qualitatively uniform product. The great variety of types and grades of sugar are all the same substance and differ only in chemical purity and the degree of crystallization. Once the juice is extracted from the cane, various chemicals are added to remove impurities from the cane juice. The resulting liquid is then slowly heated in order to evaporate the liquid and concentrate the sucrose. When the liquid becomes supersaturated, crystals begin to appear. When this magma is ready to "strike," it is rapidly cooled in order to complete the crystallization process. Various means are then used to separate the crystals from the remaining liquid, which are either distilled into rum or other eau-de-vie or consumed in the form of molasses by slaves and animals. Each of these operations is dependent on those before it, and the operations have to be performed sequentially in order to obtain crystallized sugar. Large-scale sugar production requires these processes to be carried out simultaneously, continuously, and as quickly as possible over extended periods of time.[2]

The physical characteristics of sugarcane imposed a distinctive spatial and

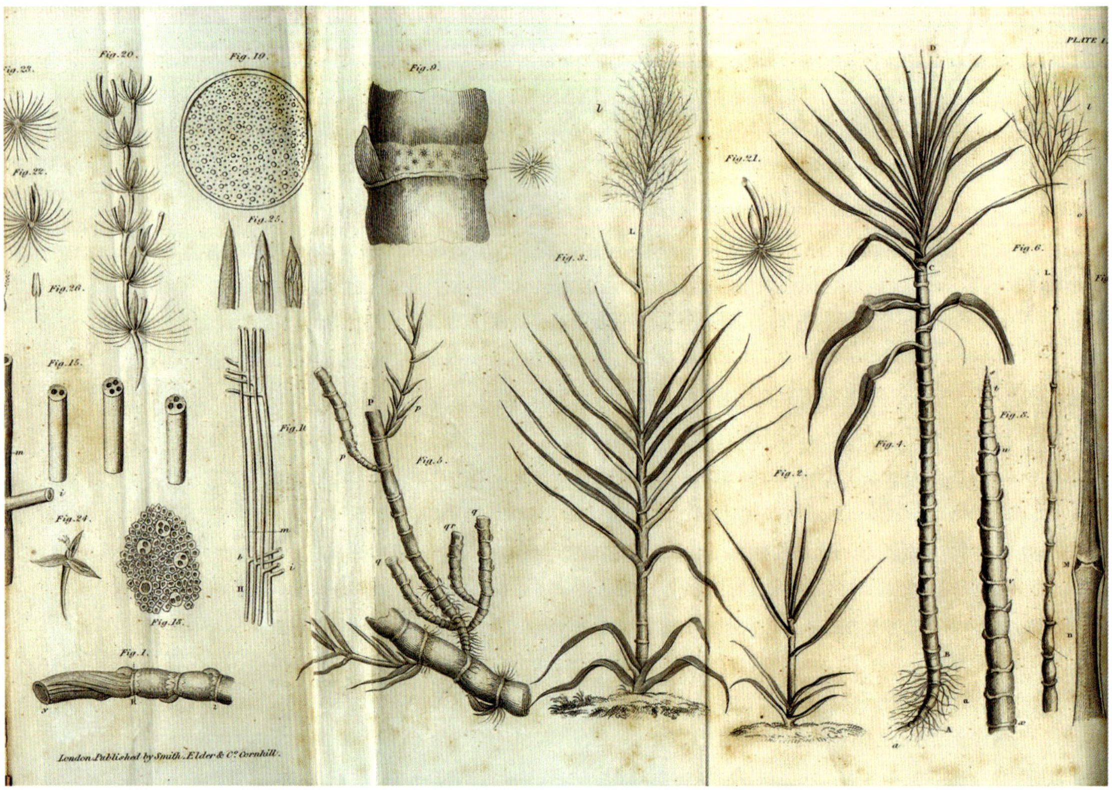

Figure 5.01. The Nature and Properties of the Sugar Cane. *London, 1843. Biblioteca Nacional de Cuba José Martí, Havana.*

temporal order on large-scale sugar production and made the sugar plantation a prototypical "factory in the field." The execution of all the sequential phases of the manufacturing process—cutting, hauling, grinding, clarification, evaporation, and crystallization—had to be coordinated with one another within a limited period of time in order to secure the material and social integration of the process. The interdependence of these agricultural, mechanical, and physical-chemical operations implies not only a *qualitative* relation but also a *quantitative* relation between these sectors. It established a proportional relation between sectors that determined the scale and spatial organization of the plantation and the size of the labor force and imposed an economy of time and space on producers. The entire process, from planting to final product, required speed, continuity, and coordination and entailed constant calculation of the quantity of material—whether in the form of cane, syrup, or crystallized sugar—the distance between sectors, and the time required to perform each operation. The area under cultivation had to be coordinated with the capacity of the mill and refinery. No more cane could be cut than could be ground; no more could be ground than could be boiled. The grinding mill and refinery had to be located in physical proximity to the fields and to one another. The need to carry out these operations simultaneously required the assignment of specialized groups of workers to each task and a division of labor formed by the distinct technical operations involved in sugar manufacture. The working activities of slaves were subject to strict industrial time discipline in order to ensure the integration of the overall process and maximum output. The material and social integration of these diverse processes imposed industrial organization and discipline not just on the sugar factory but on the agricultural operations as well. The scale and rhythm of activity dictated by the mill reverberated through the fields.[3]

The need to maintain the proportional relations between the distinct but interdependent operations entailed in sugar production set the parameters for technological innovation and the historical development of the sugar mill. The plan of the Paroy sugar plantation (figure 5.02) depicts the spatial organization of a sugar plantation in Limonade, Saint Domingue, in the 1780s. The estate covered 294 acres, of which 200 were planted in cane and had an enslaved population of 179. It had a water-powered vertical grinding mill and two Jamaica trains (see below) with five kettles each to refine the sugar. In 1784 it produced about 55 tons of semi-refined sugar (*sucre terré*) and 36 tons of muscovado sugar. The plan represents the structure of production that prevailed before the scientific and industrial transformation of the sugar mill during the nineteenth century. It embodies enlightenment principles of rational organization; emphasizes the measured, calculated, and geometrically uniform arrange-

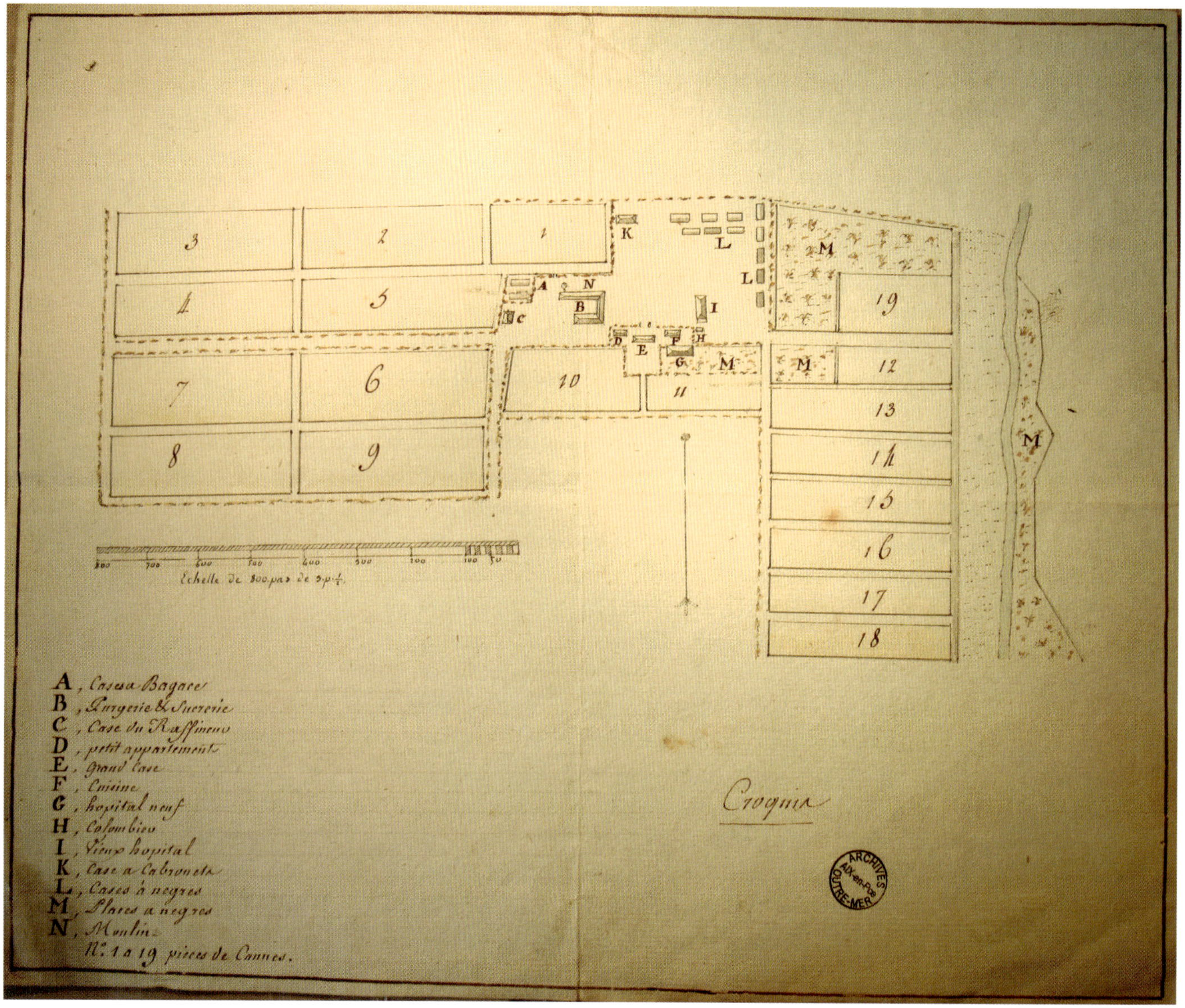

Figure 5.02.
Plan of the Paroy sugar plantation, Limonade, Saint Domingue, ca. 1780. Photograph by Rafael Marquese. Fonds Le Gentil de Paroy, AP 164, 1/7, Archives nationales d'outre-mer, Aix-en-Provence, France.

ment of space that maintains the spatial and temporal integration of agricultural and manufacturing operations; and maximizes output. Its spatial economy is organized to efficiently coordinate the activity in the fields with the mill and refinery. Fields were laid out in uniform geometric plots that were calculated to yield a determined amount of cane. The amount of cane planted in each was coordinated with the capacity of the mill. Because the cane was planted over several months, different cane pieces ripened at different times. Thus, the amount of cane cut could be synchronized with the capacity of the mill and boiling house over the duration of the entire harvest season. The lanes between fields allowed carts to carry cut cane to the mill. Distance and time were calculable. The mill, the boiling house, and the curing house (where crystallization of the sugar was completed) were in close proximity with one another to facilitate transportation from the fields to the mill and the integration of the entire process. Control of the slave labor force was integrated with control over the processes of sugar production. The master's house, the slave cabins, and auxiliary buildings were placed together in a central location near the mill and refinery. This cluster of buildings formed the productive and social nucleus of the plantation. Lands unsuitable for sugar were given over to pastures, fields for food crops grown as estate crops, and slave provision grounds. Locating such secondary activities in a distinct place not only made efficient use of the land but simplified management and control of the slave labor force. The plan enabled the planter to establish visual control over the landscape and to control and coordinate the activities required for sugar-making over the course of the crop cycle.[4]

William Clark's series *Ten Views of* [or *in*] *the Island of Antigua* (1823) depicts the labor processes and technology that characterized a plantation such as the Paroy plantation. *Holeing a Cane-Piece* (figure 5.03) shows a field being prepared for the planting of cane cuttings. Planting methods depended on the nature of the terrain and convention. Hole planting was prevalent into the nineteenth century, although innovative planters adopted plows where conditions permitted. (By the mid-nineteenth century, more extensive fields and shortage of slaves stimulated some planters in Cuba to use plows.)[5] All the agricultural operations were performed by gang labor under the direct supervision of drivers and overseers. Planting was very laborious work. Holes measuring two feet square and nine inches deep were dug with a hoe. Several cane cuttings were placed in each hole and covered with dirt. The plant began to sprout in about three weeks and required careful weeding as it grew. Each slave had to dig about twenty-eight holes an hour, depending on soil conditions. The holes were dug in parallel rows, and the fields were laid out in rectangular plots with wide lanes between them that served as firebreaks and allowed the passage of carts. The careful measurement of holes and the layout of the fields at the inception of the crop cycle allowed calculation of the quantity of cane that would be available over the course of the crop cycle into harvest season.[6]

Cutting the Sugar-Cane (figure 5.04) depicts the harvest. Cane cutting was the most demanding operation in the crop cycle and lasted six to seven months a year. The cane stalks were cut with a cutlass, cleaned of leaves, and loaded onto carts for transport to the mill. Sugar manufacture required many skilled tasks,

Figure 5.03. Holeing a Cane-Piece. *William Clark,* Sugar Production in the Island of Antigua, *1823 (published London: Infant School Society Depository, 1833). Courtesy of the John Carter Brown Library, Brown University, Providence, R.I. [Converted to gray scale by authors.]*

Figure 5.04. Cutting the Sugar-Cane. *William Clark,* Sugar Production in the Island of Antigua, *1823 (published London: Infant School Society Depository, 1833). Courtesy of the John Carter Brown Library, Brown University, Providence, R.I. [Converted to gray scale by authors.]*

Figure 5.05. A Mill Yard. *William Clark,* Sugar Production in the Island of Antigua, *1823 (published London: Infant School Society Depository, 1833). Courtesy of the John Carter Brown Library, Brown University, Providence, R.I. [Converted to gray scale by authors.]*

Figure 5.06. Interior of a Boiling House. *William Clark,* Sugar Production in the Island of Antigua, *1823 (published London: Infant School Society Depository, 1833). Courtesy of the John Carter Brown Library, Brown University, Providence, R.I. [Converted to gray scale by authors.]*

which were performed by male slaves. Females played a prominent role in field labor.

A Mill Yard (figure 5.05) shows oxcarts arriving at the mill with cut cane. The grinding mechanism depicted inside the millhouse has three vertical cylinders. It was inexpensive and could be powered by wind, water, animal traction, or, later, steam. Because of the vertical placement of the cylinders, cane stalks passed through only the bottom part of the rollers. Since it did not utilize the entire surface of the rollers, such a mill could produce only about 170 tons of sugar per year, whatever the source of power. Larger plantations had to build a second mill to produce more sugar.[7]

Interior of a Boiling House (figure 5.06) depicts the refining process. The syrup was first held in a cistern, where various substances were added to it in an attempt to precipitate impurities that inhibited crystallization of the sugar. The impurities were skimmed off and the resulting syrup passed to a series (train) of open kettles to be boiled down into sugar. As the liquid became more concentrated, it was ladled into progressively smaller and hotter kettles until it was ready to "strike," or be crystallized into sugar by rapid cooling. This process was imperfect. The kettles were made of copper or cast iron and varied in size and shape. It was difficult to control the heat in the open kettles, and the liquid was exposed to dirt and humidity. Skimming and ladling the syrup mixed impurities back into it and made it difficult to control the concentration of the liquid. The sugar that was produced was brown or "muscovado" sugar with high molasses content. After the sugar had cooled sufficiently, it was taken to the curing house and placed in clay or metal cones, where the molasses was drained off and the crystallization completed. The molasses was usually made into rum.

The "Jamaica train" (figure 5.07) was perhaps the most important technical innovation in sugar refining of the eighteenth century. It first appeared in Barbados around 1725 and spread quickly throughout the French, Spanish, and British Caribbean. In the French sugar colonies it was known as the "English train," in the Spanish colonies as the "French train," and in the English colonies as the "Jamaica train." By the 1820s it had been reintroduced in Cuba and was widely adopted under the name "Jamaica train."[8] Before the invention of the Jamaica train, each kettle had its own fire. The amount of fuel consumed in the boiling process was enormous. Sugar manufacture was typically destructive of the forest, leaving sugar mills chronically short of fuel. The Jamaica train arrangement not only saved fuel by having only one fire but also allowed crushed cane stalks to be used as fuel. The length of the train and the size of the kettles had to coordinate with the capacity of the boiler to generate and distribute heat throughout the length of the train. The number and size of the kettles determined the quantity of

Figure 5.07. *Jamaica train ruins. Ingenio San Ysidro, Trinidad, Cuba. Photograph by Grupo Bocaina.*

syrup that could be processed at one time. On the other hand, the proper amount of heat had to be distributed to each kettle. There was no standard arrangement of the boiling kettles. Each sugar master had his own scheme for how the kettles were to be configured. Between four and six kettles in a train were most common, and a widely practiced solution to the problem of increasing the volume of syrup that could be processed was to have a common furnace for more than one train. Sugar making was an "art." Each head boiler had his own techniques for reducing the syrup to sugar, but he had to know the particular characteristics of the furnace, of each kettle, and of each batch of cane, as these all affected the conduct of the process. Once the boiling started, it could not be easily stopped. Once the harvest began, work went on around the clock day after day, pausing only when it was necessary to clean the kettles. Field slaves were normally pressed into a night shift after a day in the fields in order to keep the process going.[9]

Thus, the sugar plantation already exhibited its agro-industrial character in the eighteenth century. Activities in the fields, boiling house, and mill were interdependent and had to be closely coordinated with one another. Planning, measurement, and calculation were necessary throughout the crop cycle and manufacturing process. Tasks involved in sugar making had to be executed quickly and in coordination with one another. The qualitative and quantitative integration of these processes created a series of potential bottlenecks and thresholds. Each step in the production process represented a potential constraint on the transformation of the production process. Improvements or increases in output could be introduced in any one of the sectors until it reached a threshold that put pressure on the other sectors. It then created a bottleneck and a new set of problems. Thus, each sector was a potential obstacle to transforming the production process. Changes in technique could not be introduced randomly, and no single innovation would necessarily transform the production process. It did no good to add a steam-powered grinding mill, for example, if the size of the fields and the labor force and the capacity of the boiling house were not increased commensurately. The three-cylinder vertical mill, by far the most common type of mill in the Caribbean, established the technical limit for sugar production before the technological transformations of the nineteenth century. Its output could not be increased, even if it were powered by a steam engine, because of the vertical orientation of its rollers. It thus fixed the scale of production and the quantitative and qualitative integration of fields, mill, and refinery. It was the primary bottleneck for the transformation of sugar production at the beginning of the nineteenth century. If planters desired to increase the amount of sugar that they produced, their only option was to build another mill and refinery and to bring more land under cultivation.[10]

The growth of the Cuban sugar industry coincided with the transformation of sugar manufacture from an artisanal process into a fully mechanized process. Beginning in the 1820s, improvements in the steam engine and the invention of new milling and refining technologies broke through the limits established by the three-cylinder vertical mill. In Cuba, more than anywhere else in the world, it was possible to effectively incorporate these innovations and transform the processes of sugar making. As each sector of sugar manufacture was mechanized, Cuban planters were able to extend the sugar frontier farther into the interior of the island and establish bigger plantations that allowed them to successfully incorporate the new machinery. However, technological changes did not by themselves drive the transformation of the sugar plantation. Innovation in any particular sector of sugar production represented only a partial transformation of the overall process. It created new conditions and new limits with different potential consequences. Technical innovation and mechanization were not linear processes. Change was discontinuous. There was no technical necessity of adopting any particular technique. Instead, there was considerable experimentation with different techniques. A variety of combinations coexisted with one another. The semi-mechanized mill and the mechanized mill represented independent paths of development, and the former could not be converted into the latter. Planters and manufacturers experimented and found diverse solutions to the problems of sugar manufacture as they responded to the pressures of the world sugar market. Nonetheless, the process of restructuring the plantation was cumulative. As new and larger sugar plantations were established, various innovations were adopted, and the quantity of material to be processed grew, the various sectors of production became more tightly integrated. Quantification, calculation, and more precise synchronization of the various sectors throughout the process became increasingly important. Both process and product became more and more standardized, and the conditions were created for the complete mechanization of sugar manufacturing.[11]

Between 1855 and 1857, a series of lithographs of Cuba's most advanced sugar mills was published in Havana as *Los ingenios: Colección de vistas de los principales ingenios de azúcar de la isla de Cuba*, executed by French engineer and lithographer Eduardo Laplante (Louis Eduard de Laplante Dorson) under the patronage of Cuban sugar planter Justo Germán Cantero. The images were produced at the high point of the development of lithography, before it was eclipsed by photography as the means for the mass production and circulation of images. In part because of the demands of the tobacco industry for cigar bands and box covers, Havana was one of the most important centers of lithography in the world. Cantero spared no expense in preparing the luxury edition of *Los ingenios*. The Havana lithography firm of Luis Marquier produced a folio-sized volume that is "beyond reproach from a technical point of view because of the meticulous attention to detail with which the machinery is reproduced" and regarded by many as the most beautiful book ever published in Cuba.[12]

Cantero was a wealthy sugar planter from the city of Trinidad. He owned five sugar mills that his wife had inherited on the death of her previous husband and was actively engaged in improving them by incorporating the newest technology available. Laplante was born in France and came to Cuba around 1848 as the representative of a construction firm that installed machinery on sugar mills. Because of his work, he traveled extensively throughout Cuba and came into contact with the more important planters of the period. He was therefore familiar with Cuban sugar mills and the technical details of the new machinery. He was also a distinguished painter and lithographer and, after 1849, devoted himself principally to lithography.[13] Cantero commissioned Laplante to create a series of images of the most productive sugar mills in Cuba. The mills that were chosen were "those that are most notable for the large scale of their production, those that have established some improvements or reforms of recognized utility, and those that because of their particular circumstances shed some light on the sphere of production and elaboration or give some useful idea for its history."[14] Cantero's purpose was to make known the improvements and advances made by these planters in order to promote technological innovation among Cuban planters.

Los ingenios consists of twenty-eight detailed, full-color lithographs by Laplante. They are drawn from life and are intended to accurately depict the sugar mills and their productive apparatuses. Combining illustrative elements with an unsentimental topological and documentary approach, they emphasize accurate observation and measurement. Laplante's images document the spatial articulation of the material processes of production, the new milling and refining machinery, and the architecture of the slave plantation on the Cuban sugar frontier. They are accompanied by descriptive inventories of the productive infrastructure of each mill by Cantero and by several engineering drawings that provide comprehensive visual information on key aspects of the new productive technology. At the same time, Laplante's representations capture the tensions within the social life of the plantation. At certain times of the year, especially during the harvest season, when rain and mud were not obstacles, the masters, normally resident in the towns, traveled to the countryside for leisure and recreation. The *casa grande* became a center of social life, with invited guests, formal dinners, music, dances, and holiday festivals. As they meticulously document the technical organization of the ingenios, Laplante's images also record the construction of an artificial landscape for the enjoyment of the master and his family, with formal gardens, statues, fountains, ornamental plants, dovecotes, and vegetable gardens that stand as a counterpoint to the productive landscape and underscore the privilege of the master.

Laplante's technical knowledge and artistic ability enabled him to create superb visual documentation of the changing technology of sugar making and the organization of the sugar mill. His interior views record the progressive mechanization of each step in the process of sugar manufacture—grinding, clarification, evaporation, crystallization, and separation of the sugar from molasses. He presents an industrial landscape that is justified by improvement and progress—the "rational subordination" of nature to a nonnative plant destined for the world market. His images allow us to accompany the industrialization of sugar making and the restructuring of the spatial economy of the plantation. Cantero's texts provide technical information that cannot readily be conveyed visually, and they permit comparative analysis of the technical features and political economy of each mill. *Los ingenios* is at once a product of the dramatic transformation of the Cuban sugar economy and one of the most complete graphic accounts of a process of manufacture in the nineteenth century.[15]

The grinding mill was the first sector of sugar manufacture to be mechanized. By the 1830s, powerful, high-compression steam engines, often of U.S. fabrication, became increasingly common in Cuba. These engines allowed the development of horizontal grinding mills, which were sometimes used in tandem. These mills utilized the entire surface of the cylinders. They could grind more cane and obtain more juice from a given quantity of cane. However, there were no improvements in refining technology through the 1830s. In order to process the greater quantity of syrup produced by the grinding mill, planters increased the number of Jamaica trains to create the semi-mechanized mill. Ingenio Progreso (figure 5.08) represented a different response to the imbalance between milling and refining that combined old and new technologies. Progreso had a forty-horsepower steam engine built at the West Point New York Foundry that drove two horizontal grinding mills and a smaller twelve-horsepower engine of English manufacture. The powerful grinding mills required a huge amount of cane in order to be used efficiently, and Progreso had 1,300 acres planted in sugarcane. The T-shaped factory contained both the mill and the refinery, rather than each being located in a separate building. As Laplante's lithograph indicates, the mill was located in the transverse section of the building, which facilitated the unloading of the enormous quantity of cane stalks that fed the mill and the removal of the cane trash. The refinery had a "mixed train." Five Jamaica trains and one half train were used to reduce the juice to syrup. How-

Figure 5.08. *Ingenio Progreso. Cantero and Laplante,* Los ingenios, *1857.*

ever, the final crystallization was done in a vacuum pan, visible at the far end of the refinery. The vacuum pan was the most important innovation in nineteenth-century sugar manufacture. By evaporating the liquid in a vacuum, crystallization could take place in a controlled environment at a low temperature. More sugar and sugar of much higher quality was produced from a given quantity of syrup. However, the vacuum pan represented a large capital investment and required a much greater volume of syrup than open-kettle boiling to be profitable. Progreso produced over 1,400 metric tons of sugar, nearly 70 percent of which was high-quality white sugar.[16]

Laplante's image of Ingenio San Martín (figure 5.09) shows the interior of a fully mechanized sugar mill. San Martín had 1,845 acres planted in cane.

Figure 5.09. *Ingenio San Martín. Cantero and Laplante,* Los ingenios, *1857.*

The volume of material to be processed, whether in the form of cane, syrup, or sugar, was much greater than in previous types of refinery. It had to be moved quickly and efficiently from field to factory and from one sector of the factory to another to ensure the overall integration of the process. The mechanization of the mill created an almost continuous flow process. A system of pumps and gravity feeds moved the syrup through the multilevel structure, and carts on iron rails transported the crystallized sugar within the mill. In addition, gaslights provided adequate lighting within the building and allowed production to continue into the night. The grinding mill and refining apparatus were housed in a single T-shaped building that was 402 feet long and 156 feet wide. The powerful horizontal 40-metric-horsepower steam grinding mill, built by the firm of

J. F. Cail in Paris and operated by M. Ducry, a representative of the Cail firm, was capable of processing 20,000 boxes of sugar a year. It was equipped with conveyer belts to feed cane into the mill and to remove the crushed stalks. After the juice was extracted, pumps carried it to the raised platform, where the clarifiers were located. There, lime was added in order to precipitate the chemical impurities contained in the cane juice. After heating the liquid short of boiling and leaving it to stand, a scum containing the impurities rose to the surface. Instead of trying to skim off the scum, as had been the practice with open-kettle boiling, a spigot was opened at the bottom of the clarifier to drain out the cane juice. Ideally the liquid contained only sucrose and water. San Martín had ten clarifiers that held 1,660 liters of liquid each. The large number of these devices suggest the great quantity of juice that was being processed. The juice then passed through the large cylindrical carbon filters at the bottom of the platform to remove any remaining particles. It was then pumped into one of two sets of triple-effect vacuum pans, pictured in the center of the image.[17]

The triple-effect vacuum pan revolutionized sugar manufacture. It amplified the scale of production and made possible the giant mechanized mill that was the dominant feature of the Cuban sugar frontier. The boiling process that took place in the triple-effect vacuum pans was completely mechanized and subject to precise measurement and control. Each set of vacuum pans operated in a series. The heat generated by the first boiler powered the second, and the second powered the third. The condensers pictured in front of the vacuum pans converted the steam from each boiler into water for the next. This arrangement greatly economized on fuel and water. After crystallization, the remaining molasses was separated in a battery of steam-powered centrifuges, pictured in the lower right-hand corner. The remaining molasses was drained from the crystallized sugar on the curing platform in the upper-right portion of the image. San Martín had six steam generators to supply energy to the refinery.[18] The triple-effect vacuum pans required another increase in the scale of the entire operation. Because of their cost and the enormous amount of cane that they required, only a limited number of ingenios could employ them.

Laplante also created images of various details of the interior of Cuba's mechanized and semi-mechanized mills that document other machines and techniques that were employed. By moving his perspective to the back of the mill, he documents the final steps in sugar manufacture in the images below.

The lithograph of Ingenio Santa Rosa (figure 5.10) calls attention to the multilevel structure of the factory building. Not only did new mill buildings have to be taller and span a greater area in order to accommodate the machinery, but they were built on multiple levels to bring the machines in closer proximity to one another, to utilize gravity to move the cane syrup from one process to another, and to facilitate the circulation of condensed steam throughout the plant. At the bottom in the foreground of the image are the furnaces for the six steam generators above them. The generators provided energy and heat for all the operations in the refinery. Steam power increased the fuel requirement. Dried cane trash could be used to heat the generators, but firewood and coal from the United States and Great Britain became significant imports to Cuba. At the upper right of the image are twelve clarifiers that received the cane juice from the mill behind it. Once the chemical impurities were removed from the juice in the clarifiers, a gravity feed conveyed it to the carbon filters below. The juice was then pumped into the triple-effect vacuum pan, located on a platform on the main floor, where it was converted into sugar. To the left of the vacuum pans, Laplante provides a detailed representation of the condenser, which converted the steam from the vacuum pans back into water so that it could be reused, and of the six centrifuges, which separated the molasses remaining in the sugar from the crystallized sugar by centrifugal force.[19]

Even after the sugar was processed in the centrifuges, it still contained molasses. Laplante's lithograph of Ingenio Ponina (figure 5.11) shows the extensive curing platform. The sugar was placed in inverted cones to drain the molasses from the sugar and complete crystallization. Laplante also portrays the internal iron railway and metal-wheeled carts used to transport the heavy sugar cones inside the factory. It is worth noting that Ponina had two single-effect vacuum pans built by Charles Derosne's firm in France and an English vacuum pan built on Derosne's model.[20]

The lithograph of Ingenio Victoria (figure 5.12) shows the final steps of the refining process. Large basins were placed beneath the curing platform to catch the molasses as it was drained from the cones. The molasses was then re-refined into low-grade sugar in the open pans pictured in the center of the image. The crystallized sugar was lowered to the main floor of the mill by a pulley system. There it was packed into large boxes that could weigh up to 500 pounds. Once the sugar was packed, it was shipped, usually by rail, to the port in Havana, Matanzas, or Cárdenas.[21]

The architectural plan of Ingenio Santa Rosa (figure 5.13) documents the integration of all the constituent processes of sugar manufacture in a single structure and the increasingly standardized arrangement of the factory. It is one of several such drawings that present a similar arrangement of the factory. As the sugar manufacturing process became mechanized, the layout of the machinery became more uniform. The location of the mill, clarifiers, carbon filters, vacuum pans, steam generators, condensers, clarifiers, and curing platform

Figure 5.10. *Ingenio Santa Rosa. Cantero and Laplante,* Los ingenios, *1857.*

Figure 5.11. *Ingenio Ponina. Cantero and Laplante,* Los ingenios, *1857.*

Figure 5.12. *Ingenio Victoria. Cantero and Laplante,* Los ingenios, *1857.*

were functionally determined. Their proximity facilitated the material and social integration of the manufacturing process. The factory building had to accommodate the size and placement of the machinery. Mechanization and the growing scale of production required architectural innovation. The T-shaped building was increasingly common for large mills. The grinding mill was perpendicular to the transverse refinery. The single integrated structure and multilevel construction facilitated the coordination of the various partial manufacturing processes and the continuity of production. The larger dimensions of the building encouraged the use of new materials like lightweight and durable zinc roofs instead of tile and, later, iron beams in place of wooden ones. Laplante's view of the Armonia mill (figure 5.14) corresponds closely to the plan of Ingenio Santa Rosa and confirms the increasingly standardized arrangement of the machinery within the mill. It also suggests the importance of the platform as a vantage point from which visual control of the entire manufacturing process could be established. Further, the correspondence of the plan to Laplante's depiction of Ingenio Santa Rosa (figure 5.10) testifies to the technical accuracy of his drawings.[22]

The mechanization of the Cuban ingenio required the transformation of the spatial economy of the sugar plantation. Laplante's lithographs reveal the changing relation between mechanization, the scale of production, and the architectural and spatial organization of the plantation. With the mechanization of sugar refining, more land had to be brought under cultivation and more slaves employed. A greater quantity of cane had to be converted into sugar, and the distance from field to mill increased. Field workers had to keep up with the capacity

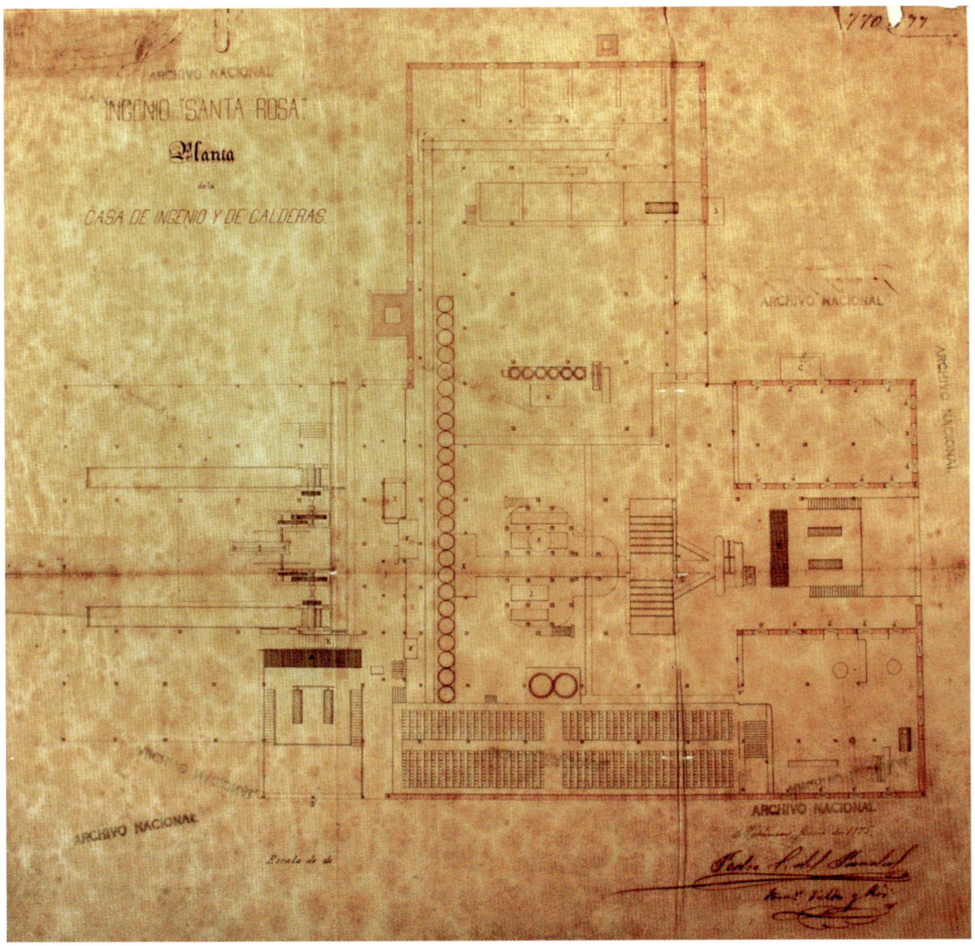

Figure 5.13. *Plan of Ingenio Santa Rosa, mill and refinery. Archivo Nacional de Cuba, Havana.*

Figure 5.14. *Ingenio Armonia. Cantero and Laplante,* Los ingenios*, 1857.*

of the new machinery to process the cane if the latter were to be effectively utilized. Speed and coordination of the movement of material through the different sectors of sugar production became more important as the capacity of the sugar mills increased. Calculation of the quantity of material—whether cane, syrup, or crystallized sugar—distance, and time played a more prominent role in integrating field, mill, and refinery. Laplante's representations of the industrial and residential nucleus of the plantation, or *batey*, provide a vantage point from which to understand these changes in the spatial economy of the Cuban ingenio. Technical innovation and mechanization followed a geographic pattern. The larger, more technologically advanced semi-mechanized and mechanized mills were concentrated in the expanding eastern part of the sugar frontier, while the older mills that were no longer competitive were to be found in the original part of the sugar frontier between Havana and Matanzas.

The first operation in sugar manufacture to be mechanized was the grinding mill. Ingenio San José a La Angosta (figure 5.15), belonging to the Conde de Fernandina, was an older plantation in the hilly terrain of the Mariel Valley, to the east of Havana and outside of the new sugar frontier of Matanzas and Cárdenas. San José a La Angosta is an example of an existing sugar plantation that early on substituted steam power for ox-power for the mill. Cantero records that an eighteen-horsepower low-pressure steam engine was installed at San José a La Angosta; however, he does not indicate the type of mill that was used. Some early applications of steam power continued to use vertical, three-cylinder mills. These mills were bigger and better constructed, with more resistant materials than earlier versions of the three-cylinder mill. They could handle continuous and more intense workloads and process more cane, but they were subject to the same limitations as the earlier vertical mills and did not qualitatively transform the grinding process. However, by the 1820s, the English firm of Fawcett and Preston began selling low-pressure steam engines in combination with all-

Figure 5.15. *Ingenio San José a La Angosta. Cantero and Laplante,* Los ingenios, *1857.*

iron horizontal mills. Because the orientation of the rollers was horizontal, they could grind across the entire surface, and the all-iron construction meant that they were much sturdier and more pressure could be applied to the cane stalks. The integrated steam engine and horizontal iron mill revolutionized the process of crushing the cane stalks and extracting the juice. However, the structure of plantations such as San José a La Angosta remained unchanged. While the mill could produce more juice, the new problem was boiling down the greater volume of juice into sugar. Solutions had to be sought within the existing technological possibilities. The response to the improved grinding technology was to increase the number of Jamaica trains.[23]

Laplante's lithograph indicates the adaptation of San José a La Angosta's preexisting spatial economy to the new technical conditions in the factory and to the greater quantity of cane that had to be processed. The tall chimney at the center of the image indicates the location of the steam engine and the mill. The boiling house is a separate building behind the mill. Two of the chimneys each provided heat for two Jamaica trains. The third chimney indicates the distillery. The building with the fenced-in yard in the right foreground is the overseer's house with a large storage building and carpenter's shop attached to it. To the right of the mill and boiling house are workshops and storage buildings. To the left are three sheds for drying cane trash for use as fuel for the mill and refinery. Together these buildings formed a compound that enclosed all the manufacturing processes, which were in close proximity to one another. The slave cabins are arranged irregularly outside of this compound. The spacious big house of the owner, with an extensive English garden, is on the hill above the factory. A reservoir that supplies water for all of the needs of the plantation is below the owner's house and garden and forms the fourth side of the compound. The scale of production was considerably larger than the Paroy plantation in Saint Domingue but less than the more improved plantations in the sugar frontier proper.

Ingenio Monserrate (figure 5.16) was a semi-mechanized sugar mill built in 1849. It was located in Cárdenas, the most rapidly expanding zone of the sugar frontier, and was about three kilometers from a station of the Cárdenas Railroad (Ferrocarril de Cárdenas). Monserrate illustrates the diverse response of the Cuban planters to technological change and the interplay of space and technology. Throughout the 1830s and 1840s, as steam engines and grinding mills became larger, more powerful, and more efficient, semi-mechanized ingenios had begun to appear. Milling capacity increased enormously, but there was no commensurate change in the technique for boiling the syrup. As we have seen, planters were able to process greater volumes of syrup by increasing the number of trains of open-kettle boilers. The number of trains and the number and arrange-

Figure 5.16. *Ingenio Monserrate. Cantero and Laplante,* Los ingenios, *1857.*

ment of kettles in each train varied from plantation to plantation. By the 1840s, when Monserrate was built, vacuum pans were available. However, they represented a very large investment, and not all planters were convinced that they were practical. The owners of Monserrate adopted advanced milling technology and expanded the scale of production. They installed a thirty-five-horsepower high-pressure horizontal steam engine manufactured at the foundry at West Point, New York. The engine drove two grinding mills. In order to make full use of the mill, 1,175 acres were planted in cane. However, open kettles were still used to convert the greatly increased quantity of syrup into crystallized sugar.

Laplante's lithograph documents the architectural changes and new spatial configuration that accompanied the restructuring of production and were characteristic of the semi-mechanized mill. Cantero noted that all of the buildings at Monserrate were of exceptionally large dimensions. The milling and boiling were combined in a single T-shaped building, which facilitated closer integration of the two operations. The mill was perpendicular to the furnaces. Its elongated structure expedited delivery of large quantities of cane and removal of the cane trash (bagasse). The large chimney on the far side of the refinery served the steam-powered mill. The three chimneys at the front of the refinery were for the mill's four Jamaica trains and two half trains. To the right of the mill, an enclosed barracks (*barracón*) with a single entrance replaced the slave cabins. The bell tower in front of the barracks regulated the activities of the plantation. In the foreground, the sheds stored bagasse to fuel the boiling house. To the left of the mill stood an enormous curing house (*casa de purga*), where the final crystallization of the sugar was completed.

It would be misleading to regard Monserrate and other mills in its class as examples of incomplete modernization. Rather, they provided an original solution to the problems presented by the horizontal steam mill and represent a distinct path of development. They achieved economies of scale and increases in output that allowed them to surpass the competitors in the old sugar colonies and dominate world sugar production by the 1830s. Such mills remained viable as major centers of production, even as fully mechanized mills made their appearance, and they were by far the most numerous type of sugar mill in Cuba. In 1860, there were 889 semi-mechanized mills with an average output of 445 metric tons of sugar.[24]

Laplante's lithograph of Ingenio Amistad (figure 5.17) calls attention to the diverse responses of Cuban planters to the pressures of the world sugar market, the need to increase yields, and technological innovation. Here, a water-powered mill was effectively used in conjunction with the most advanced refining technology. Amistad was founded as part of the initial expansion of the sugar frontier at the end of the eighteenth century and was located about two kilometers east of the town of Güines. Located along the Güines (Mayabeque) River, it was associated with the subsequently abandoned project of building a canal. One of the few Cuban mills to employ waterpower, its adoption of this source of energy represents an early example of technical innovation. Laplante's image highlights the integrated mill and boiling house and emphasizes the aqueduct carrying water to move the mill wheel. The waterwheel generated an estimated forty English horsepower and powered a horizontal grinding mill. The use of water as the motive source of the mill represented a great economy in fuel and animals. The mill could process enough cane that by the mid-nineteenth century two vacuum pans were used to refine the sugar. Nonetheless, the owner decided to specialize in the production of lower-quality muscovado sugar as well as rum. Amistad had an elaborate system utilizing the most up-to-date machinery to remove the impurities from the syrup and filter it. A variety of steam-powered pumps and other devices automatically moved the syrup from one stage of the process to the next. In 1849, it was the first mill in Cuba to use centrifuges to separate the molasses from the crystallized sugar, and it eventually had ten such machines. Six steam generators provided the power for these devices as well as the vacuum pans. In the early 1850s, the factory building was remodeled and the machinery rearranged to provide better control and integration of the production process. Cantero noted the lightness and strength of the new zinc roof, one of the first in Cuba, that was installed as part of the remodeling.

Laplante executed both exterior and interior views of the Flor de Cuba mill in Cárdenas near a trunk line of the Júcaro railroad. One of Cuba's giant mills, Flor de Cuba was fully mechanized and had a labor force of 550 slaves and Chinese contract workers. It cultivated 1,350 acres of Otaiti cane and annually produced about 3,000 tons of sugarcane. It was also in the process of experimenting with a new variety of Cristalina cane in order to increase the yield.

Laplantes's exterior view (figure 5.18) documents the monumental scale of operations and close spatial integration of the production processes that characterized fully mechanized mills. The residential and manufacturing nucleus (*batey*) was dominated by the factory building to the right of the road running through the compound, the great house and tower to the left of the road, the curing houses located behind them, and the slave barracks located behind the

Figure 5.17. *Ingenio Amistad. Cantero and Laplante,* Los ingenios, *1857.*

Figure 5.18. *Ingenio Flor de Cuba (exterior). Cantero and Laplante,* Los ingenios, *1857.*

curing houses at the rear of the compound. In addition, the estate contained an infirmary and various storehouses and workshops. The mill and refinery measured 106 × 60 meters. The roof was constructed in such a way to allow steam to exit the building and to admit fresh air and light. The upper roof was covered with tiles, the lower roof was covered with zinc, and the walls were built with arches to let in in light and air. Across the street from the factory were two curing houses that measured 270 × 42 meters. The two buildings were 15 meters apart and were connected by an iron railway that ran the length of each. Parallel to the curing houses and behind them was the slave *barracón*. This rectangular structure measured 145 × 85 meters. In the center of the courtyard was a 23-meter-square building that contained the kitchen on the lower floor and could house up to 100 Chinese contract workers on the upper floor. The rooms on the wall across the road from the refinery faced outward from the *barracón*. This wall had a second story that housed the infirmary. Chinese workers also lived in the rooms beneath the infirmary, while the supervisory and technical staff resided in the more spacious rooms at the two extremities of this wall.[25]

Flor de Cuba was one of the most technologically advanced mills in Cuba. The organization of the interior (figure 5.19) was similar to that of Ingenio San Martín (figure 5.09). A high-pressure 53-horsepower steam engine manufactured by McOnie and Mirlees of Glasgow effectively delivered 100 horsepower. It powered two horizontal grinding mills whose cylinders measured six and a half feet across and thirty-four inches in diameter. After much experimentation, the owner of Flor de Cuba, Pablo de Arrieta, developed the idea of having the mills turn slowly and exert greater pressure on the cane stalks. They could process a much greater quantity of cane and extract 72 percent of the juice from the cane instead of the 55 percent that was common in conventional mills. After the juice was extracted from the cane, it was pumped up to a raised platform, where it was passed through a system of clarifiers and carbon filters to remove the impurities in it. The juice was then pumped directly to the triple-effect vacuum pans at the center-left of the image to be refined. After refining, the sugar was then passed to one of the eight centrifuges pictured at the far left of the image, where centrifugal force separated the molasses from crystallized sugar. The remaining syrup was piped to the distillery located at the lower left of the image to be made into rum. In 1860, Flor de Cuba produced over 3,000 metric tons of sugar, 85 percent of which was white sugar.[26]

The construction of Flor de Cuba and other fully mechanized mills marked the closing of the sugar frontier. The availability of new land was the condition of the transformation of the sugar plantation in Cuba. As mills mechanized and scale of operations increased, the sugar frontier extended eastward from Havana onto new lands where larger plantations could be established. By 1860, there were sixty-four fully mechanized mills with an average capacity of 1,174 metric tons. Together they accounted for 15 percent of Cuba's sugar production. The size of their operations, the amount of capital invested, and the cost of transportation made it impractical to extend sugar production farther into the countryside, even though forestland was still available to continue expansion to the east. At that point, planters became interested in agronomy, soil science, and the use of fertilizers to maintain the productivity of their lands.[27]

The sugar frontier was chronically short of labor. As it expanded eastward from Havana and more and larger mills were built, there was a growing de-

Figure 5.19. *Ingenio Flor de Cuba (interior). Cantero and Laplante,* Los ingenios, *1857.*

Table 5.01. Physical plant of selected *ingenios*.

Ingenio	*Mill Type*	*Refinery*	*Acres in Cane*	*Number of Slaves*	*Sugar (Metric Tons)*
Paroy Plantation Limonade, Saint-Domingue (1780s)	Water-powered mill	2 Jamaica trains	200	179	55 of semirefined sugar 36 of muscovado sugar
San José a La Angosta	18-hp steam engine	4 Jamaica trains	770	—	650
Amistad	40-hp water mill	2 vacuum pans	670	—	780
Monserrate	35-hp steam engine	4 Jamaica trains and 2 half trains	1,175	360	875
Flor de Cuba	53-hp steam engine	Triple-effect vacuum pan	1,350	550	3,000
Echeverría	Steam engine	5 Jamaica trains and plans to build one more	3,350 (combined)	989 (combined)	4,500 (combined)
San Martín	40-metric hp steam engine	2 sets of triple-effect vacuum pans			

mand for slave labor. This demand was first met by the African slave trade. By 1820, Spain signed treaties with Britain that abolished the slave trade but subverted its enforcement. The trade continued illegally until the 1850s, when it was finally brought to an end.[28] As the supply of enslaved African laborers diminished, Cuban planters turned to contract laborers from China and Yucatán. Large mechanized and semi-mechanized plantations had slave populations of between 350 and 600 persons. The size of the labor force, including slaves and contract workers from China or Yucatán, promoted architectural changes on the plantation. The slave barracks or *barracón* became a distinguishing feature of large mills (figures 5.20 and 5.21). It represented the increased regimentation of slave life and facilitated plantation management. Barracks created uniform living conditions and enhanced physical control over the large number of enslaved workers and coordination of their activities. The largest were en-

Figure 5.20. Barracón *at Ingenio San Martín. Photograph by L. F. A. Rossi, ca. 1886. Álbum de fotos del ingenio San Martín (F C Álbum 175). Biblioteca Nacional de Cuba José Martí, Havana.*

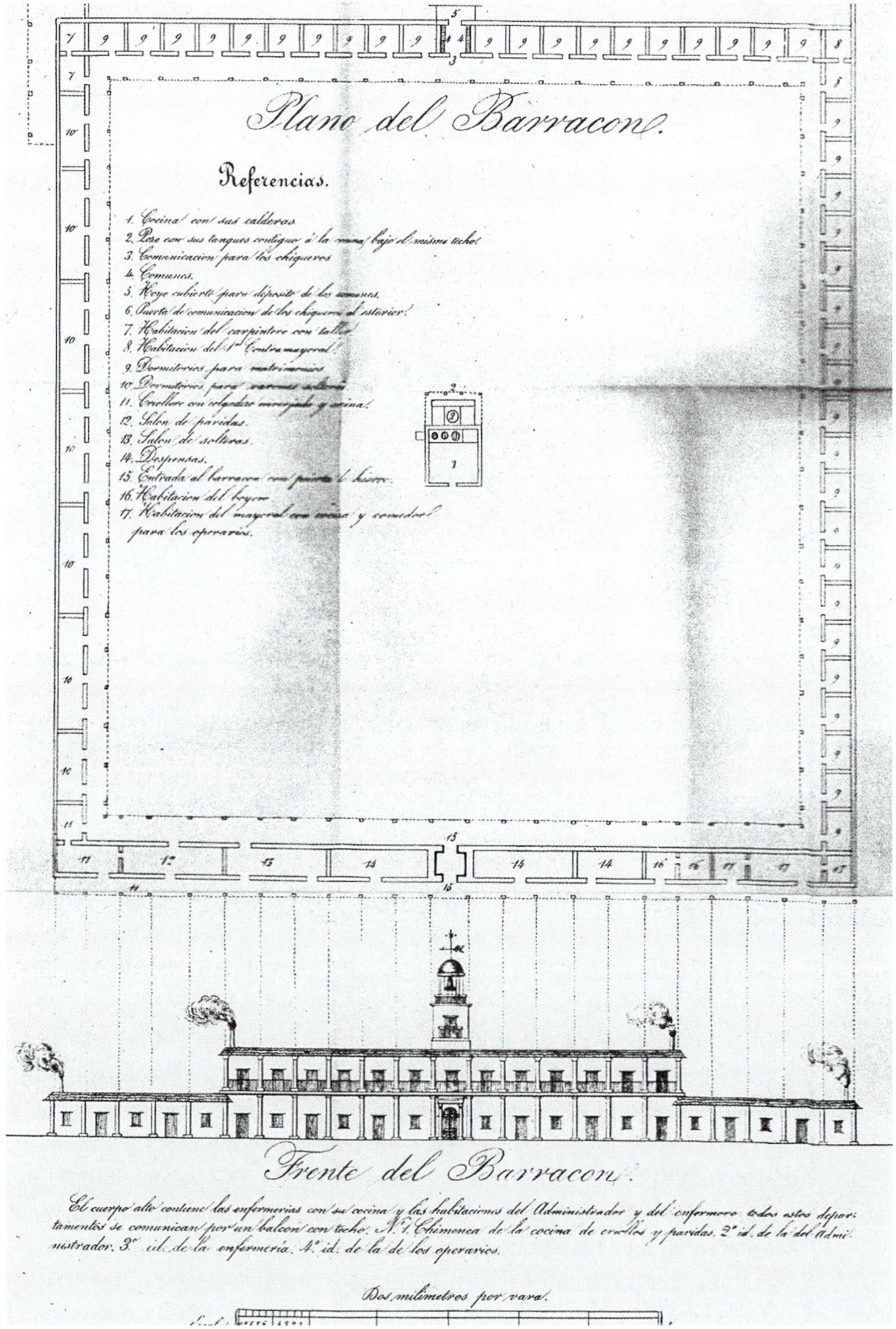

Figure 5.21. Barracón *plan. Fondo de agrimensores Serafín Sánchez Govín, Fundación Antonio Núñez Jiménez, Havana, Cuba.*

closed structures with a single entrance. This structure facilitated the assembly of the slave workforce and the assignment of tasks. The circulation of the gangs to workplaces throughout the plantation could be more easily controlled as they filed through the single entrance. The slaves lived in cubicles facing the inside of the square, where there was often a common kitchen as well as sanitation facilities. Children and Chinese workers were housed separately. Housing for supervisory personnel and craftsmen as well as storerooms and workshops were in a different part of the structure and opened to the exterior. The upper floor often held an infirmary. The monumental facade expressed the authority of thc master and often had a bell tower from which the activities of the plantation were regulated.

In the late 1850s, photography coexisted with the brief heyday of lithography as a means for the mass production of images. In both Cuba and Brazil, slavery persisted long enough for there to be a photographic record of it. The photographic images were subject to the technical limitations of early cameras and techniques. The documentary value of the images produced by pioneer photographers such as Charles DeForest Fredricks (Cuba) and Marc Ferrez and Christiano Junior (Brazil) may be contrasted with the detailed technical draftsmanship of Eduardo Laplante.

As the capacity of the sugar factory grew, more land had to be planted in cane. The distance from field to mill became greater, and the need to maintain the continuous flow of cane to the mill became an important consideration for planters. As fields grew larger, sections were meticulously measured. Detailed maps registered the elaborate geometry of the cane fields. Such maps served as means to calculate, plan, and regulate the disposition of land and labor, especially at harvesttime. The size of the sections was coordinated with the capacity of the mill and refinery. As the planting and harvest seasons lasted many months, planters could keep track of when fields were planted and when they would ripen so that the sections could be harvested sequentially and continuously. Diagonal lanes or *guardarrayas* were cut through the fields to provide a direct route to the mill (figure 5.22). These lanes facilitated the rapid circulation of the oxcarts and reduced the time required to carry the cut cane to the factory as the fields became more distant. Agricultural labor was not subject to technological innovation. The outward appearance of field labor did not change, but, with the increasing scale of operations, the labor of slaves was intensified and subjected to more rigorous time discipline, often expressed through new management strategies. The organization of agricultural space facilitated the control of nature and the subjection of enslaved workers to new rhythms of work and new cultures of control.

The oxcart (figure 5.23) was the strategic link between field and factory. In order to maintain continuity of production, the size of oxcarts was standardized. Cane stalks were cut to a uniform length, and the size of the load in each cart was also standardized. The cart served as the unit of measurement. The various phases of production were integrated with one another by calculations based upon the number of carts. The movement of carts was carefully planned and took on some of the characteristics of a conveyor belt. On some estates, groups

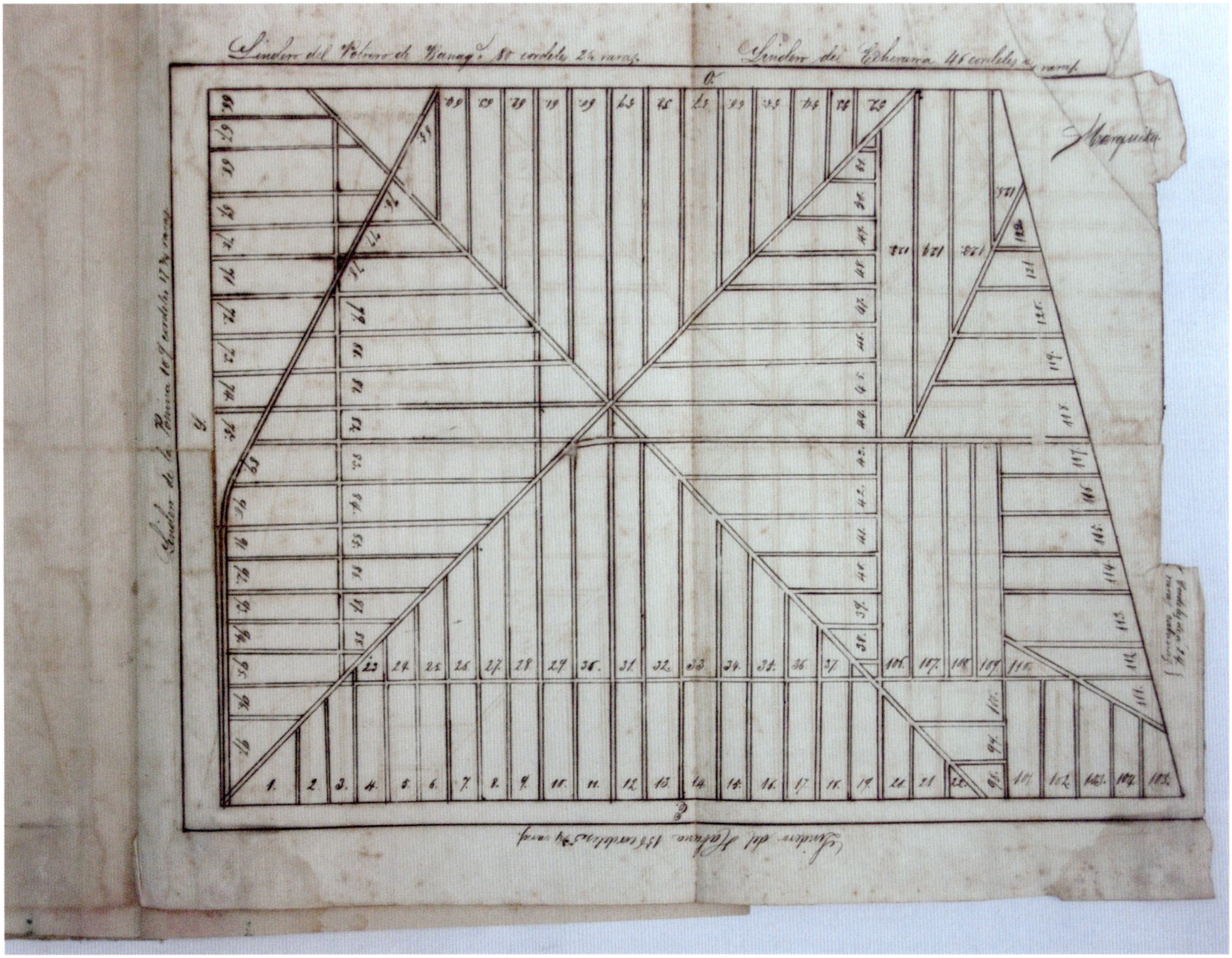

Figure 5.22. Guardarrayas. *Fondo de agrimensores Serafín Sánchez Govín, Fundación Antonio Núñez Jiménez, Havana, Cuba.*

of slaves were assigned to carts rather than to fields in order to ensure the continuous flow of cane to the mill.[29]

The map of La Recompensa (figure 5.24)—a plantation that had 1,610 acres planted in sugarcane and a labor force of 251 slaves, 79 Chinese contract workers, and 53 hired slave and free workers—provided an inventory of the plantation and facilitated the planning of its operations. The planter or manager could envision the entire operation of the estate in one view and establish visual control over the total agro-industrial complex throughout the course of the production cycle. La Recompensa was built in the interior of a former corral. Compared to the properties in figure 2.03, its irregular shape suggests that competition for access to fertile land, water, or transportation could affect the organization of property. The integration of fields and factory shaped the physical organization of the plantation. The manufacturing and residential nucleus was located at the center of the property to facilitate the efficient movement of slaves from their quarters to their jobs and rapid transportation of sugarcane from the fields to the mill during the harvest. The property was divided into four zones, and within each zone the fields were organized into carefully subdivided and arranged sections. The table at the bottom right of the map indicates the size of each section. The precise subdivision of the fields into uniform parcels and the elaborate system of roads that connected the fields to the mill permitted calculation of the quantity of cane available per day over the entire harvest season, the distance from field to mill, and the time necessary to transport it. On the basis of these calculations, activities in the fields were coordinated with those in the mill, and the daily tasks of the slave labor force throughout the agricultural year were determined. In contrast to the Paroy plantation, where livestock were left to graze on the wasteland, pastures (*potreros*) were clearly delineated and separate from the cane fields, and stock raising was a specialized activity on each estate. Designated pastures were necessary because the plantations were often contiguous with one another and required an enormous number of oxen and other livestock. The map further indicates the location of the station of the Cárdenas Railroad, which ran along the southeast corner of the property.

While Laplante's depiction of Ingenio Purísima Concepción (a) Echeverría (figure 5.25) focuses on the Echeverría estate, it shows its integration with the neighboring San Martín ingenio. Both plantations were owned by Doña Francisca Pedrosa y Herrera, and together they operated as a single unit. Laplante's image captures the dynamic character of the Cuban sugar industry. Prominent in the image is the line of oxcarts carrying cane from the fields to the mill, the internal railway connecting the two mills, and, on the left side of the image, the railroad carrying the finished product to the port. Laplante thus calls attention

Figure 5.23. *Sugarcane harvest. Photograph by Charles DeForest Fredricks, ca. 1857. Personal collection of Carlos Venegas.*

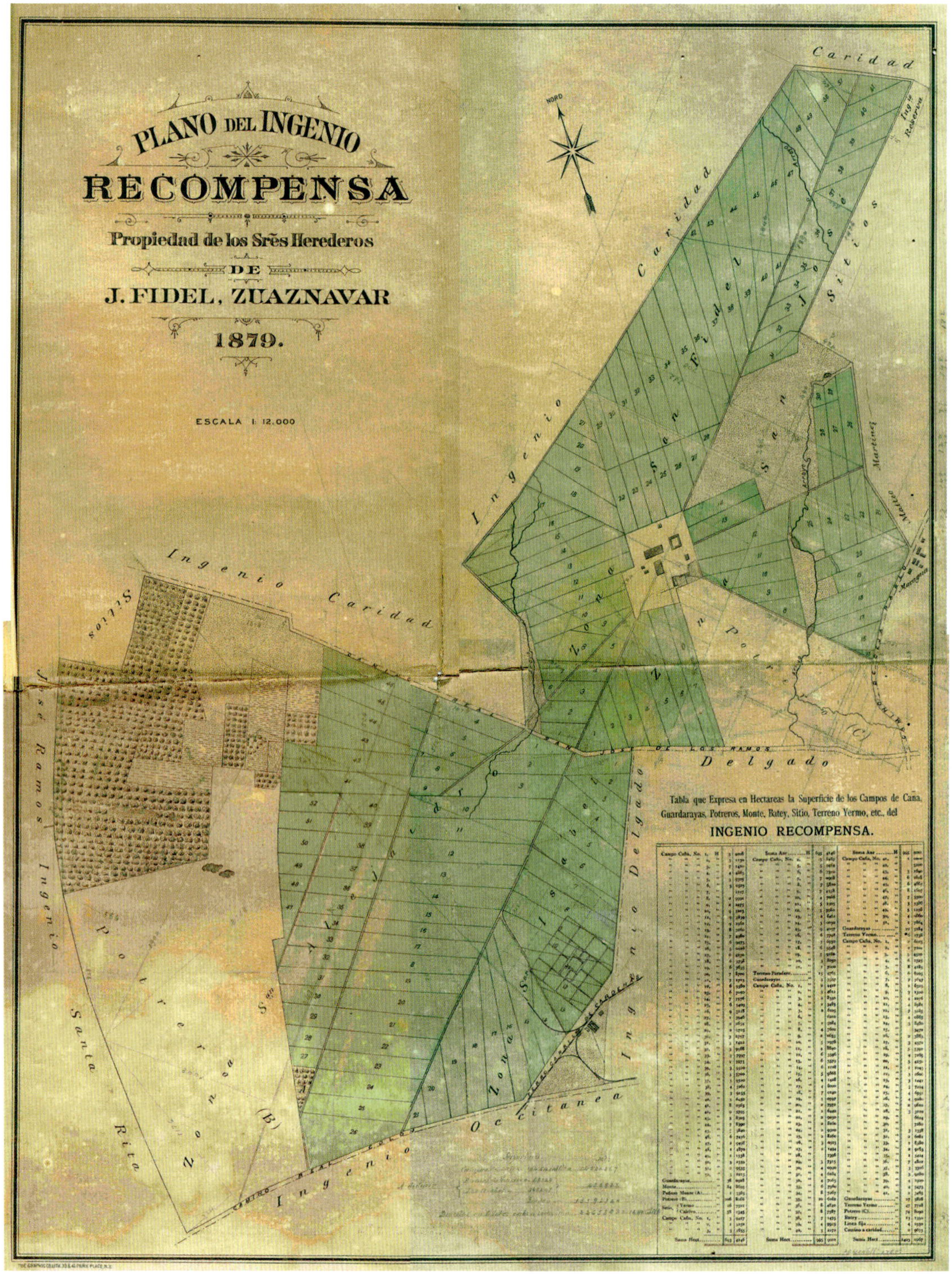

Figure 5.24. *Map of Ingenio La Recompensa. Fondo de agrimensores Serafín Sánchez Govín, Fundación Antonio Núñez Jiménez, Havana, Cuba.*

Figure 5.25. *Ingenio Purisima Concepción de Echeverría. Cantero and Laplante,* Los ingenios, *1857.*

to the continuous movement of huge volumes of material across extended distances, the integration of diverse activities, and the new conception of time and space that defined the agro-industrial landscape of the Cuban sugar frontier. Echeverría had a steam mill built in Glasgow, Scotland, and five Jamaica trains with plans to add a sixth in order to process the amount of cane from its fertile and extensive fields. An internal railroad pictured in the center of the image linked the refinery of the San Martín factory to the curing house. Although each mill could operate independently, the two-mile-long rail line allowed cane from Echeverría to easily be moved to the huge mill at San Martín, ensuring the continuity of production. San Martín had a forty-horsepower steam mill built by the French firm of Derosne and Cail and two sets of triple-effect vacuum pans. In addition to the rail line between the two plantations, San Martín had its own rail line that ran from the interior of the factory to the nearby railroad. The combined property of the two plantations had 3,350 acres in cane and a labor force of 989 slaves and Chinese contract laborers. It produced over 4,500 tons of sugar. Cantero commented that this immense and productive property was one of the giant mills whose immense stimulus to production inspired everyone.[30]

6
The Brazilian Coffee Fazenda

Although coffee was one of the most valuable products in world trade from the sixteenth century on, European colonial powers were slow to produce it. Coffee entered into European consumption in the seventeenth century, along with sugar, chocolate (cacao), and tea. These "drug crops" were stimulants and to one degree or another addictive. Sugar complemented the other three products, and their availability and popularity shaped new cultures of consumption in Europe. Yemen monopolized world coffee production up until the 1720s, when the Dutch introduced its cultivation to Indonesia. Soon after, the French followed suit in taking coffee production to Bourbon (Réunion). Unlike sugar, coffee is not a homogeneous product. The quality and taste of coffee varies with the conditions under which it is grown. Mocha and Java coffees are regarded as high-quality and are greatly sought after. In the 1720s, the Dutch and the French pioneered the adaptation of the coffee bush to the New World. Coffee was cultivated in Surinam, Martinique, and Guadeloupe and evolved into a plantation crop. However, the amount of coffee that reached European markets was modest and remained relatively stable at about 3,000 metric tons per year until the 1750s. After the Seven Years' War, coffee production climbed steadily, in large measure as a result of the explosion of coffee cultivation in Saint Domingue. By the 1790s, world coffee production reached about 64,000 metric tons, and Saint Domingue alone was responsible for almost half of that total.[1] Nonetheless, the coffee market remained relatively limited and was dominated by the luxury consumption of urban strata, particularly businessmen and intellectuals. Coffee was associated with sobriety and mental acuteness, and the coffeehouse provided an alternative to the tavern for these urban elites.[2]

Ideal conditions for coffee cultivation are found in a band about fifteen degrees on either side of the equator with an annual mean temperature between sixty-five and seventy-three degrees Fahrenheit. Coffee grows best on uplands, usually on mountainsides with an elevation of 1,500–4,500 feet above sea level. The vast lands of the Paraíba Valley in Brazil offered suitable though not ideal conditions for coffee cultivation. The coffee trees were planted from seedlings on the slopes of the "half orange" hills that faced the sun. The forest was cleared by a combination of cutting and burning. Burning produced an abundance of potash, which temporarily enriched the soil. The trees were planted in vertical rows up the slope with wide lanes between them, and regular weeding was

Figure 6.01. Coffea arabica. *Ellis,* Historical Account of Coffee. *Frontispiece.*

needed until trees reached maturity. Careful pruning was required to develop and maintain the productive capacity of the trees; left to themselves, the trees would grow to considerable height. But the tops were cut off and the trees were pruned to a height of six to eight feet. Instead of growing taller, the trees then spread out. This practice facilitated gathering the fruit.

Coffee trees begin to bear fruit in three to four years and by the sixth year reach their full yield. The average diameter of the trunk of a full-bearing tree is the size of man's wrist. Coffee trees produce a profusion of dark green, glossy leaves, and the fruit or berry forms on the woody stems, usually at the base of the leaves. The trees alternate between years of high yield and years of low yield. They may bear fruit for as many as thirty years, but on average they do so for about fifteen to twenty years.[3]

The ripe berry is red in color and resembles a large cranberry (figure 6.01). The coffee berry consists of five parts covering the bean. First is the outer skin, similar to that which covers a cranberry or cherry. Second is a soft pulp enclosed by and adhering to the outer skin. A third coating consists of a soft, glutinous substance, strongly saccharine in character. The fourth part is a sort of envelope called the parchment; it is tough and a bit thicker than the husk of wheat. It is yellowish-white in color and easily removed by friction. Finally, beneath the parchment is a thin gossamer film called the *pergaminho* in Brazil. In the Paraíba Valley the harvest began in April or May and continued until September. After picking, the beans were taken to the drying terrace, where they were dried in the sun. Once the berries were dry, the outer and inner shells were removed with a mortar and pestle or a simple shelling machine. The beans were then sorted, weighed, and stored until they were shipped to Rio de Janeiro.[4]

In 1798 Pierre-Joseph Laborie, a coffee planter from Saint Domingue, published his influential *Coffee Planter of Santo Domingo.* Like the Paroy sugar plantation in Saint Domingue during the same period, Laborie applied Enlightenment principles to the organization of the coffee plantation. Laborie's plan of the estate was laid out around the material requirements of coffee production. The measured, symmetrical, and geometrically uniform arrangement of space was designed to make efficient use of land and labor and to maximize output (figures 6.02 and 6.03). The layout allowed coffee to move easily and efficiently from one stage of production to the next. Coffee trees were planted in ordered rows. Coffee groves and drying terraces were proportional to one another in size and located in close proximity to one another. Buildings and other architectural elements were positioned in functional relation to one another. Gardens and pastures were conveniently located in clearly defined spaces without impinging on the principal crop. Laborie's plan for the rational organization of space combined

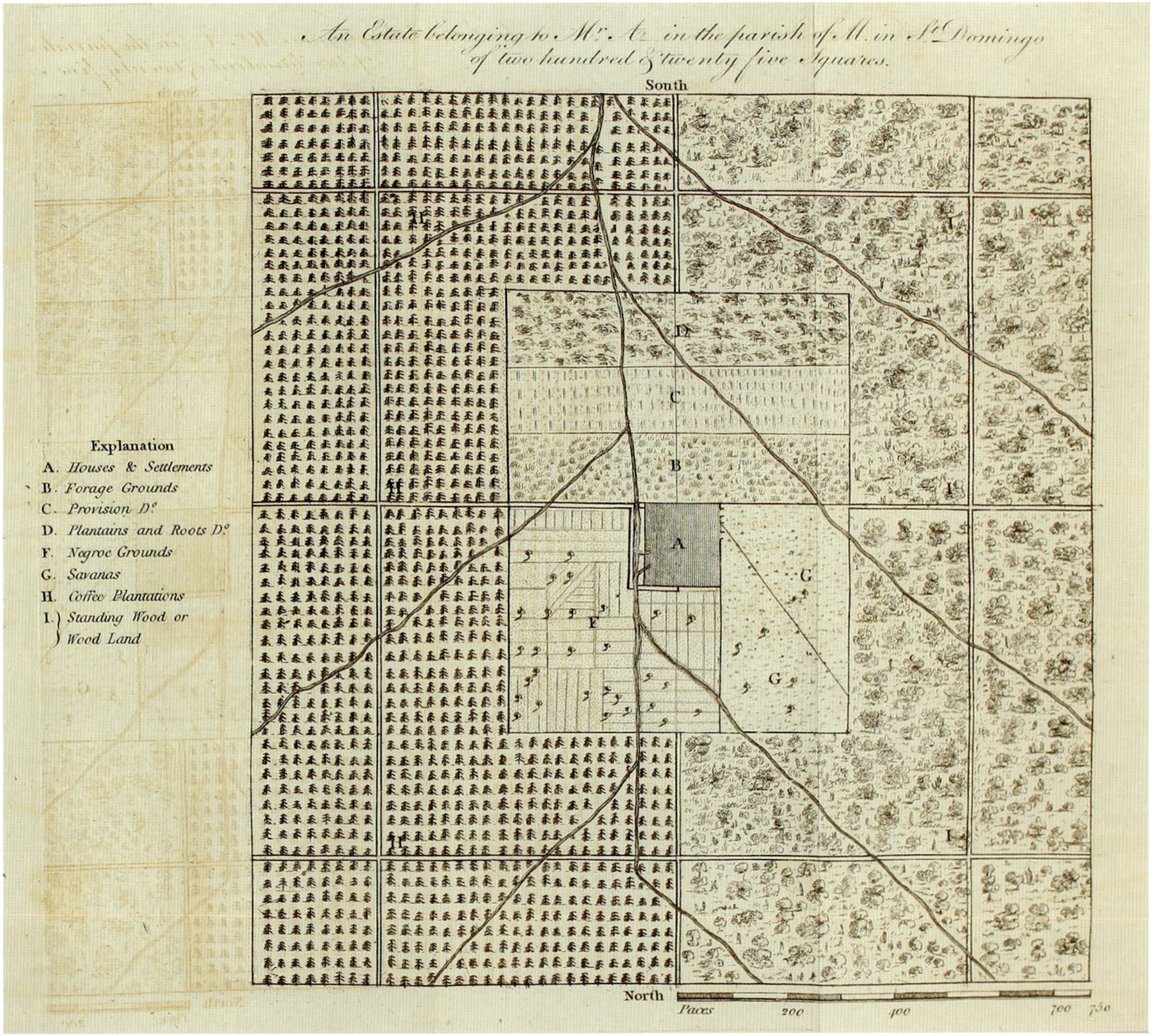

Figure 6.02. *Pierre-Joseph Laborie's model coffee plantation. Laborie,* Coffee Planter of Santo Domingo.

function, hierarchy, and control and established the material, spatial, and social integration of the plantation. Laborie's plan was an instrument of visual control over the landscape and management of land and labor. The landscape and built environment were constructed in conformity with the plan. Conversely, the plan enabled rational and calculable utilization of land and labor throughout the crop cycle.[5]

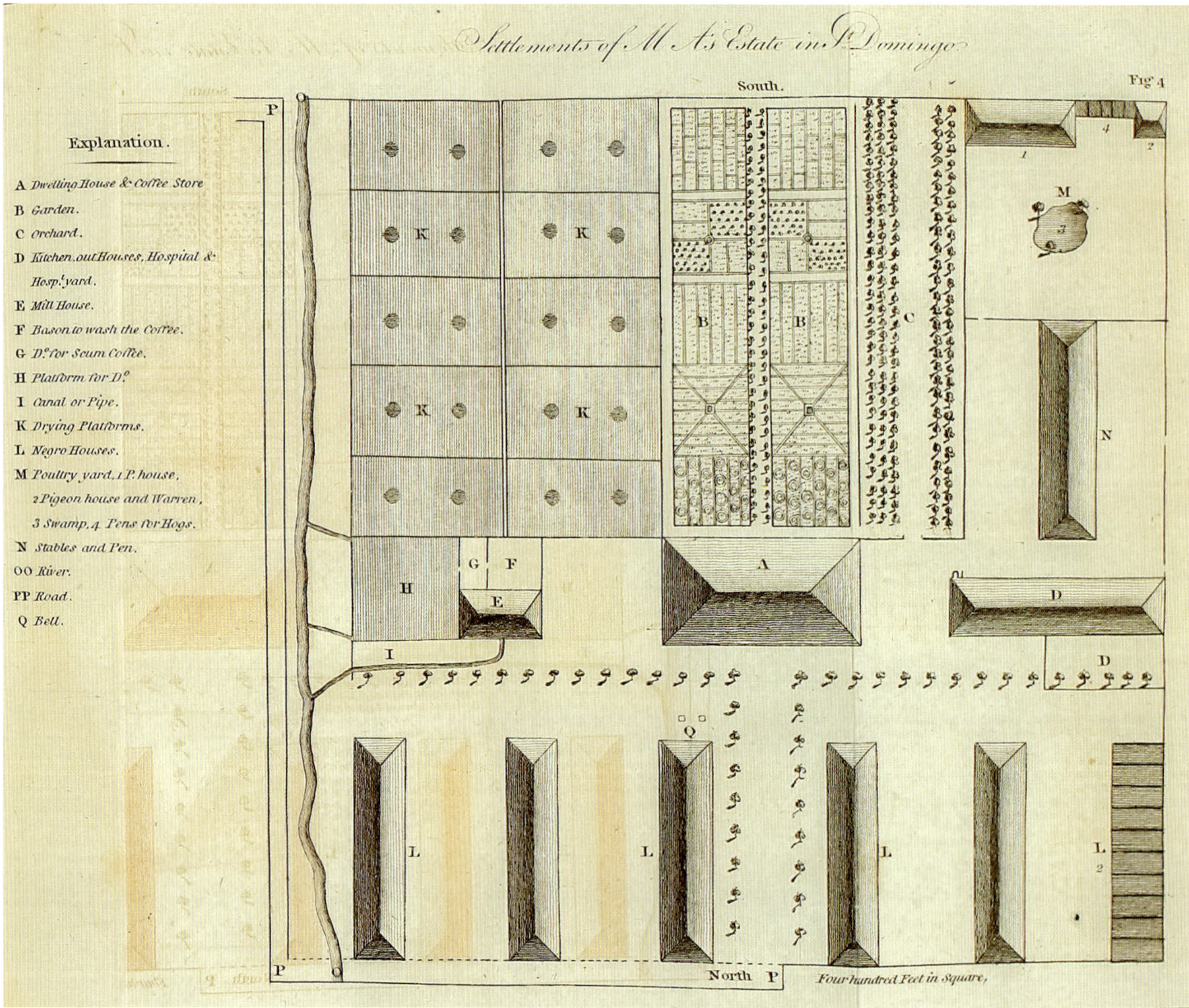

Figure 6.03. *Detail of Pierre-Joseph Laborie's model coffee plantation. Laborie,* Coffee Planter of Santo Domingo.

Laborie's manual also disseminated practices that had important consequences for coffee cultivation in the Americas. He determined that the distance between coffee trees should vary with altitude, temperature, and exposure to the sun. Plantings were denser in low-lying areas and more widely spaced at cooler high altitudes. Laborie also cut the tops of the trees so that they would grow no higher than the height of a standing man. Clusters of coffee trees were planted around the trunks of taller trees, whose branches formed a canopy over them and protected them from direct sun (figure 6.04). Laborie advocated careful

Figure 6.04. *Cafetal La Ermita (Cuba). Pierre Toussaint Frederic Mialhe,* La isla de Cuba pintoresca *(Habana: Lit. de la Real Sociedad Patriotica, 1838).*

weeding, the use of manure for fertilizer, and a system of quotas for the harvest. Because they were growing under the forest cover, the coffee trees in Laborie's plan required constant and active weeding. Shade-grown coffee yielded high-quality coffee. However, the individual beans on the same plant ripened at different times, and each bean had to be harvest individually. Harvesting was a slow task, as each bean had to be picked when it was ripe and the pickers had to return to the same plant several times. The average planting in Saint Domingue was 15,000 bushes per *alqueire* (4.84 hectares). At harvesttime, Laborie organized a system of quotas. Each slave was responsible for carefully picking about 150 liters of coffee beans a day. Once the quota was completed, the slave was given the rest of the day off.[6] Laborie's manual was extremely influential. Not only was his model of plantation organization widely adopted in Saint Domingue, but it spread throughout the Caribbean and Brazil, often carried by refugees from the Haitian Revolution. The manual itself was translated into Portuguese and Spanish and was an important guide for coffee planters throughout the hemisphere.[7]

The coffee fazenda of the Paraíba Valley introduced a spatial revolution in coffee production. Not mechanization but the material and social organization of the landscape, animated by the collective force of the slave laborers, created the conditions for the mass production of coffee. Key innovations included the increased scale of operations, planting coffee trees in the sun rather than in the shade, and extremely wide spacing between the rows of trees and between the trees in each row. These were adaptations to the environment of the Paraíba Valley. They promoted an unparalleled increase in productivity and total output. In 1789, Saint Domingue, then the world's largest coffee producer, employed about 158,000 slaves in coffee production and produced 32,000 metric tons of coffee. In contrast, in the Bananal District in the Valley of Paraíba in 1854, 8,100 metric tons of coffee were harvested with only 7,662 slaves—that is, with a labor force more than twenty times smaller than that of Saint Domingue, the planters of Bananal produced about one-fourth of the quantity of coffee.[8] The decisive factor in this dramatic increase in productivity was the restructuring of the spatial economy of Brazilian coffee fazendas.

Planters in the Paraíba Valley pioneered new ways of organizing nature and slave labor on an unprecedented scale in order to reinvent coffee as an item of mass production and mass consumption. Emphasis on extensive cultivation and production of large quantities of low-quality coffee necessitated both an increase in scale and the spatial and architectural reorganization of the plantation in order to process the great volume of material. Georg Grimm's painting *Fazenda Bom Retiro* (figure 6.05) shows the characteristic features of a large coffee plantation in the Paraíba Valley. Typical of Brazilian plantation landscape paintings of the time, immediate references to slaves or to the processes of coffee production are absent. The focus, rather, is on the architectural ensemble of the plantation and the social representation of the property and the proprietor as a unity. The built environment, itself constructed as a representation, is converted into the support for pictorial representation.

The built environment of the coffee fazenda combined economic efficiency, social control, and symbolic power around the material requirements of coffee production. The center of activity was the coffee drying terrace. The drying terrace, or *terreiro*, was the social and symbolic focal point of the plantation. It was both the site of processing the coffee and the residence of the slaves, and the entire architectural ensemble of the plantation was organized around it. Thus, in contrast to the slave barracks in Cuba, which were intended simply as a space of confinement, surveillance, and control, the slave barracks in the Paraíba Valley were integrated into the work space. Together with storehouses and work buildings, they commonly formed a rectangular compound around the drying terrace. These buildings had to be near the terrace not only because close proximity made it easier to move the bulky product but also because the coffee beans had to be protected in case of rain. This nucleus of the plantation functionally integrated the work processes, established social hierarchies, and facilitated control over the slave population.

The overseer's residence was separate from the big house and close to the slave quarters and the productive activities of the estate. In Grimm's painting, it is built into the structure enclosing the drying terrace (on the far right side of the wall facing the viewer), but it faced outward rather than inward. The single door giving access to the compound facilitated control over the movement of the slaves. Roads radiated out from the drying terrace to the fields. Thus, the circulation of the slaves to and from the fields and other work spaces was regulated by the spatial configuration of the plantation. Finally, the residence of the master and his family, or the *casa grande*, often formed part of the enclosure, facilitating control of the plantation and its enslaved population. The big house was the symbolic and administrative center of the plantation. It embodied the authority and prestige of the planter and his family. In Grimm's image, the social entrance to the house faces away from the terrace, and a wall divides the social life of the planter's family from the work space and the residence of the slaves.[9]

In Marc Ferrez's photograph of Fazenda Santo Antonio do Paiol in the town of Valença (figure 6.06), the same features are adapted to the local topography. Here the slave barracks, storehouses, and work buildings form a triangle around the drying terrace, while the big house is on top of the hill from which the photo was taken.

Property boundaries in the Paraíba Valley were poorly delineated. Once vast lands of the valley were opened to settlement, smallholders and squatters gravitated toward public lands and unoccupied land on the margins of the coffee estates. By the 1830s, the consolidation of the plantation system reached the point that some planters resolved to survey the land in order to establish undisputed legal title to it.[10] The survey map of the Bom Sucesso plantation (figure 6.07) is one of the few maps of a Brazilian coffee fazenda. It was produced in order to ascertain boundaries when the property was divided and sold in 1848. The map played an important role in regularizing property boundaries and establishing the economic and social order among landholders near the town of Bananal and in establishing the claims of plantation owners against smallholders and squatters. Significant buildings are carefully drawn on the map, and their rela-

Figure 6.05. Fazenda Bom Retiro. *Georg Grimm, 1881. Private collection.*

Figure 6.06. *Fazenda Santo Antônio do Paiol, Valença, Rio de Janeiro. Marc Ferrez, n.d. Instituto Moreira Salles, Rio de Janeiro, Brazil. http://201.73.128.131:8080/portals/#/detailpage/19213.*

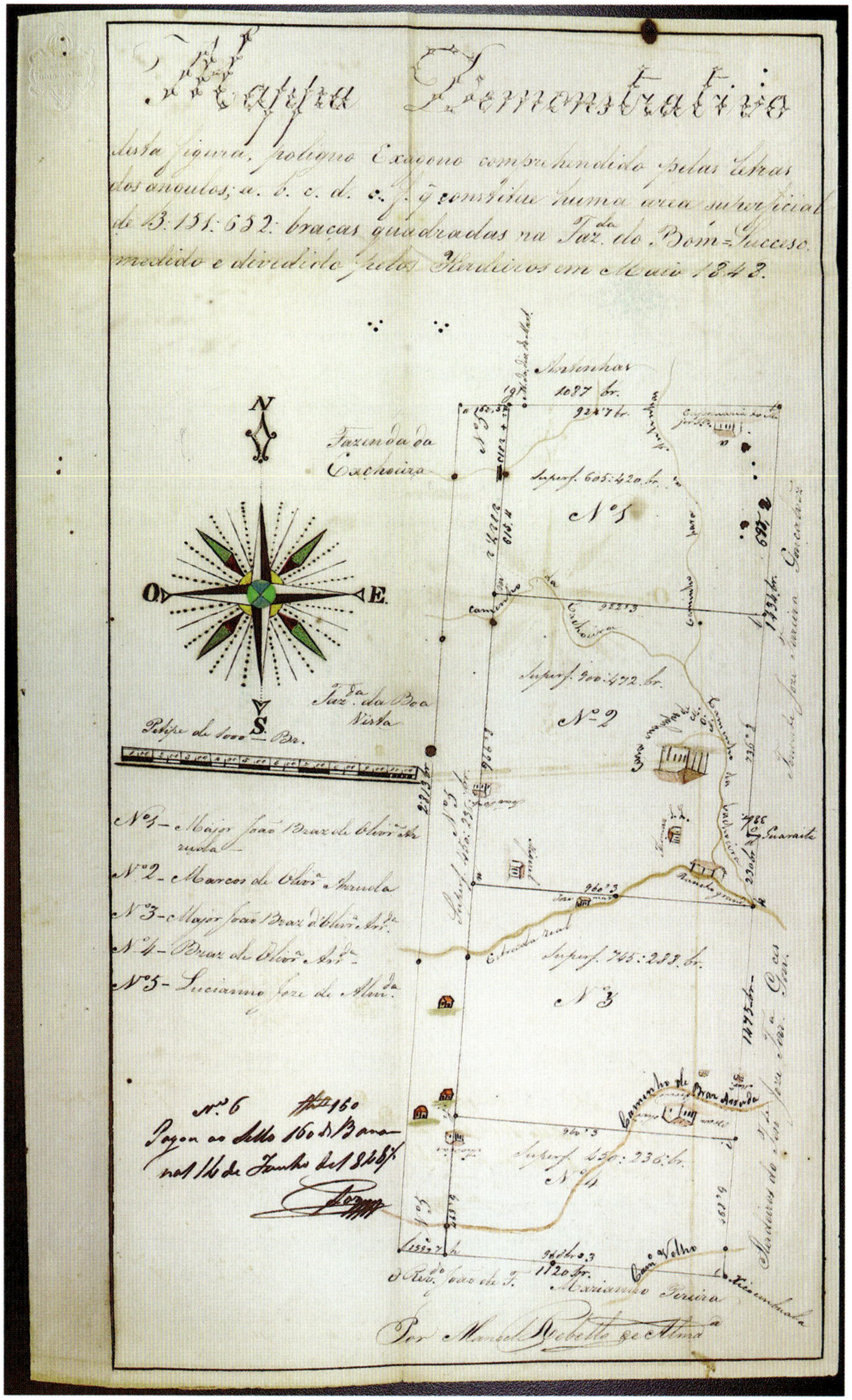

Figure 6.07. *Mapa do processo de medição amigável da fazenda do Bom Sucesso, Bananal-SP, 1848. Box 54, n. 979. Museu Histórico e Pedagógico Major Dias Novais, Cruzeiro, São Paulo, Brazil.*

tion to the roads connecting the plantations with one another and to the main road to Rio de Janeiro are indicated. However, it gives no precise layout or measurement of the fields. Perhaps the most noteworthy feature of the map are the small cabins found along the property boundaries. These cabins were occupied by *agregados*, often freed persons who were dependents of the owner. They were allowed to occupy a plot of land at the discretion of the landowner where they could build a cabin and plant a garden. The position of these dwellings at the margins of the estate established effective occupation of the land. It was the responsibility of the *agregados* to maintain the security of the property and protect it from incursions by squatters or other planters—and, of course, they were one more barrier against runaway slaves.[11]

Because photography made its appearance before the end of slavery, there is a photographic record of slavery in the Paraíba Valley. Marc Ferrez (1843–1923) was perhaps the outstanding photographer of nineteenth-century Brazil. Ferrez opened a studio in Rio de Janeiro in 1865 and attracted the interest of Emperor Dom Pedro II, himself fascinated with the new medium. With the financial support of the emperor, Ferrez was able to travel throughout Brazil. He produced an extraordinary body of work that included landscapes, natural features, ethnographic images, and maritime photography, in addition to documenting the urban development of Rio de Janeiro. Around 1885, in the midst of the crisis of slavery, he produced a series of photographs of Paraíba Valley coffee plantations. Ferrez's photographs document the essential social and spatial elements that characterize the slave coffee plantation in the Paraíba Valley.[12]

Enslaved laborers were the animating force behind plantation production. Ferrez's portrait of a community of enslaved workers represents the slave gang from the planter's point of view (figure 6.08). The group is assembled on the coffee drying ground in front of the slave barracks, or *senzala*, under the supervision of the driver. The driver is in a position of command at the head of the group and wears a coat, hat, and shoes to indicate his station and authority over the slave gang. (The size of the barracks suggests that the group in the photograph might be only a portion of the slaves resident on the estate.) The enslaved are portrayed as "hands" (*braços*) carrying agricultural tools. The tools suggest the symbolic nature of this photograph. The workers are carrying both the hoes used for planting and weeding and baskets used in the harvest. The photo includes children, mothers, and fathers, but the family units are dissolved into the collectivity without being clearly identifiable.

The organization and management of the slaves' activities was of paramount importance to planters. Slave gangs in the Paraíba Valley were much larger than the gangs in earlier coffee zones. A large coffee plantation could have from 250

Figure 6.08. *Slaves and barracks, Marc Ferrez, ca. 1885. Museu Afro Brasil, São Paulo.*

to as many as 500 slaves. With the increased scale of coffee production, slave housing changed from individual cabins to rectilinear barracks that were usually subdivided into windowless cubicles for slaves with partners and undivided rooms for single men or women. Morning and evening roll call, the assignment of the day's tasks, and distribution of tools usually took place on the drying terrace in front of the barracks. The central location of the terrace also facilitated

Figure 6.09. *Going to the fields. Marc Ferrez, ca. 1885. Museu Afro Brasil, São Paulo.*

the collective movement of the slave gangs. It was the point of assembly before they were marched out to the various tasks throughout the plantation (figure 6.09). Ferrez's camera captures the character of life in the slave barracks: command, discipline, and strict coordination of time and the circulation of workers.

Preparing the land for cultivation was the first step in establishing a coffee fazenda. The presence of certain trees and plants was regarded as a good indicator of the suitability of land for coffee and determined which parts of the forest were chosen to clear for planting. Clearing the hillsides for cultivation was a specialized and extremely dangerous task. Before the work began, the fazenda's carpenter selected prime hardwoods for use in construction. Next, vines and underbrush were removed to clear the way for the axmen, who cut partway through tree trunks at waist-level or higher. When the tree was weakened, a watchman signaled them to move up the slope to another tree. The trees remained tied to one another by the dense growth of lianas at the upper level. When all the trees on the slope had been prepared in this way, experienced cutters at the top of the hill selected a tree that they judged would bring down all the ones below it and cut it down. This set off an avalanche of giant tropical trees with a roar that could be heard for miles. The crowns and branches of the fallen trees were trimmed to hasten drying. Trees previously designated by the carpenter were sawed into boards on the spot and hauled away by oxcart. The other fallen trees were left to dry out until just before the arrival of the rainy season, when they were burned. The ash from the fire was considered good fertilizer for the coffee seedlings. The field was littered with high stumps and partially burned logs that were left where they were. Their presence made planting more difficult, and the uphill-downhill orientation of the logs exacerbated erosion on the slope. The destruction of the forest and its replacement by rows of coffee trees was regarded by many as an act of civilizing untamed nature.[13]

Marc Ferrez's photograph of the coffee harvest (figure 6.10) shows the coffee trees planted in vertical rows on the hillsides. The vertical plantings were the product of local experience. Plows could not be used on the hillsides, and planting and weeding was done by hand with hoes. The number of coffee trees allocated to each slave and consequently the area planted increased constantly over the course of the nineteenth century. In the complex of plantations belonging to Manuel do Aguiar Vallim in Bananal, the average number of trees picked per worker per year reached 5,000 in the 1870s.[14] The rows were spaced widely apart, as were the trees in each row, in order to give easy access to the coffee trees and to simplify weeding and harvesting. The spaces between the rows and between trees were much greater than what had been recommended by Laborie. The widely spaced rows and symmetrically ordered landscape facilitated visual control of the landscape and management of the slave gangs. The gangs were made up of small groups of twenty to twenty-five men and women. Each group was under the supervision of a slave driver. The overseer is visible near the center of the photograph, wearing a hat and coat to symbolize his rank and authority. In the image, the slaves are dispersed throughout the area being photographed for reasons of composition and because of the technical limits of

Figure 6.10. *Coffee harvest. Marc Ferrez, ca. 1885. Museu Afro Brasil, São Paulo.*

nineteenth-century photography. In practice, the slaves worked in a line that moved up the hill from bottom to top, accompanied by drivers. Each slave was assigned the bushes on one side of the lane. The overseer stood at the bottom of the hill and could easily manage the progress of the gang.[15]

The method of planting in Brazil led to coffee berries ripening at the same time. At harvesttime, each slave was assigned a daily quota of coffee to pick, but the quota did not determine the limit of the working day. If the slaves picked

Figure 6.11. *Picking coffee. Marc Ferrez, ca. 1885. Museu Afro Brasil, São Paulo.*

more than the quota, they were rewarded with a small amount of cash, but never free time. If they picked less than the quota, they were physically punished. Field hands moved along the rows, indiscriminately stripping the branches of the plant into wide baskets tied around their waists (figure 6.11). Sifting later separated the leaves and twigs from the coffee berries. The berries were then inspected and placed in large baskets to be taken to the drying terrace. In the foreground of figure 6.11 is the trunk of a tree that remains from clearing the hillside.[16]

Fields were far from the slave quarters. Figure 6.12, a photograph taken by Christiano Junior, shows the midday meal being prepared in the fields in order to minimize the interruption to the workday. It is possible to identify the overseer, with his hat, coat, and boots, and the slave driver, who is also wearing a hat. Food crops were planted between the widely spaced rows of coffee trees during

Figure 6.12. *Cooking in the field. Christiano Junior, ca. 1865. Museu Afro Brasil, São Paulo.*

Figure 6.13. *Winnowing beans. Christiano Junior, ca. 1865. Museu Afro Brasil, São Paulo.*

the first three years after the latter were planted. Figure 6.13 shows beans being harvested for consumption on the plantation.

In the Paraíba Valley, the coffee harvest took place during the dry season, from or May May to September. Consequently, once they were picked, the coffee berries could be dried in the open air rather than in ovens. The number and size of the drying terraces indicated the scale of production on any given plantation. Marc Ferrez's striking photograph of coffee drying suggests the enormous amount of coffee that was produced by large plantations in the Paraíba Valley

Figure 6.14. *Slaves on a coffee drying terrace. Marc Ferrez, ca. 1882. Instituto Moreira Salles, Rio de Janeiro, Brazil. http://201.73.128.131:8080/portals/#/detailpage/7069.*

(figure 6.14). After the berries were picked, leaves, dirt, and overripe berries were removed. The berries were washed in a tank of water. The overripe berries sank to the bottom of the vat and were separated from the ripe ones. The berries were then spread out on the drying terrace to dry in the sun. Figure 6.15, a photograph by Christiano Junior from the 1860s, shows a line of slaves filing through the single entrance of the central compound of the plantation carry-

Figure 6.15. *Overseer and slaves on a drying terrace. Christiano Junior, ca. 1860s. Museu Afro Brasil, São Paulo.*

ing baskets of coffee on their heads, which they deposited on the drying terrace, under the supervision of the overseer. (The overseer of the drying terrace was distinct from the overseer of the fields.) As indicated by the slave at the bottom of the image, the berries were constantly turned with wide wooden rakes for several days until they were dry. The terraces were made of beaten earth until the 1860s, when they began to be covered with brick or later macadam.

The processes of removing the hull and the inner parchment from the inner bean and sorting the beans according to quality were the most tedious and labor-intensive aspects of coffee production. These tasks were a bottleneck in the production process. Once the berries were dry, the outer shell and inner parchment were removed by pounding them with a mortar and pestle, a technique common in West and Central Africa. Care had to be taken not to break the beans. By midcentury, simple water-powered shelling machines (*engenho de pilões*), such as that portrayed by J. B. Wiegandt in figure 6.16, were adopted on many large plantations. With this technology, adapted from the Peruvian mining industry, a rotating axle lifted vertically placed wooden beams, which were released and fell on the coffee beans. The outer shell was broken and the beans fell through a grate into a receptacle below. The beans were then taken to the storehouse, or *tulha*, where they were sorted, weighed, and stored until they were shipped to Rio de Janeiro for sale. Coffee could be stored for two to three years, which allowed planters to adjust their sale to market conditions. Information about the state of the coffee market circulated with the mule trains and itinerant merchants and dealers. The coffee was sold in small lots over time, which allowed planters to protect themselves from short-term fluctuations in price.[17] Figures 6.17 and 6.18 show the coffee being weighed and stored in preparation for shipment to overseas markets. Sorting, grading, and weighing the beans were key steps in determining the price of coffee.

By the 1860s, processing and sorting the coffee beans became mechanized. Machines such as the Lidgerwood coffee-hulling machine (figures 6.19, 6.20, 6.21, 6.22) removed the outer hull and pulp and the inner parchment and polished and sorted the beans in a continuous process. A system of conveyors carried the coffee beans through a series of rotating drums that sequentially performed these operations, which were powered by water or steam. The adoption of the machine increased the exploitation of the slave labor force. It could process a greater quantity of coffee more rapidly and enabled slaves to be transferred to work in the fields. Although functional, the installation of this machine at Fazenda Flores do Paraíso also represents the machine as spectacle. The elaborate balustrade and columns create a theatrical setting for the machine and its operation. Cultural refinement was inscribed in the heart of the

Figure 6.16. Coffee-Sheller. *J. B. Wiegandt, woodcut. Herbert Smith,* Brazil: The Amazons and the Coast *(New York: C. Scribner's Sons, 1878), 524.*

Figure 6.17. Coffee Warehouse. *J. B. Wiegandt, woodcut. Herbert Smith,* Brazil: The Amazons and the Coast *(New York: C. Scribner's Sons, 1878), 535.*

Figure 6.18. Weighing Coffee. *J. B. Wiegandt, woodcut. Herbert Smith,* Brazil: The Amazons and the Coast *(New York: C. Scribner's Sons, 1878), 538.*

Figure 6.19. *Lidgerwood coffee-hulling machine, Fazenda Flores do Paraíso, Rio das Flores, Rio de Janeiro. Photograph by Cristiano Mascaro. Collection of Sergio Sahione Fadel, Rio de Janeiro, Brazil.*

Figure 6.20. *Detail of Lidgerwood coffee-hulling machine, Fazenda Flores do Paraíso, Rio das Flores, Rio de Janeiro. Photograph by Grupo Bocaina.*

Figure 6.21. *Detail of Lidgerwood coffee-hulling machine, Fazenda Flores do Paraíso, Rio das Flores, Rio de Janeiro. Photograph by Grupo Bocaina.*

Figure 6.22. *Detail of Lidgerwood coffee-hulling machine, Fazenda Flores do Paraíso, Rio das Flores, Rio de Janeiro. Photograph by Grupo Bocaina.*

Figure 6.23. Fazenda Montalto. *Nicolau Antonio Facchinetti, oil on canvas, 1881. Collection of Sérgio Sahione Fadel, Rio de Janeiro, Brazil.*

productive process and master-slave relations. Visitors to the plantation were frequent, and the combination of science, art, and property in the presentation of the machine enhanced the prestige and power of the owner.

Nicolau Antonio Facchinetti's 1881 painting of Fazenda Montalto (figure 6.23) is one in a series of oils that document the environmental destruction caused by coffee cultivation in the Paraíba Valley. The soil of the valley was shallow and moderately fertile and was further enriched by the biomass of the forest. The removal of the forest cover and its replacement by coffee monoculture deprived the soil of vital nutrients, while the practice of planting the coffee trees in vertical rows on the hillsides resulted in massive erosion during the rainy season. Rather than replanting old groves when yields began to decline, planters moved on to new lands. As coffee cultivation declined in the Paraíba Valley, agriculture was no longer feasible, and lands were given over to cattle raising. The constant grazing of cattle on the hillsides compacted the soil and made it even more unproductive.[18]

Conclusion

GEOMETRIES OF EXPLOITATION

This book has reconstructed the landscapes of the new commodity frontiers in the lower Mississippi valley, Cuba, and Brazil during the nineteenth century through the examination of a variety of visual sources. It focuses on the materiality of the working landscape and the slave labor process and on the production of plantation space. Two questions underlie this project. How does visual documentation help us to understand these landscapes? And what can such landscapes tell us about the history of the new commodity frontiers of the second slavery?

From its inception, the concept of landscape has been marked by a dualism. On the one hand, a highly interpretive approach to landscape derives from art and art history. Here, landscape appears as a subjective category that is treated as a well-defined and limited object—a representation, a view, a way of seeing—that conforms to cultural and aesthetic criteria. On the other hand, geographers and others have attempted to develop an objective concept of landscape in order to analyze the physical and material landscape. This approach to landscape tends to be descriptive and functional. However, despite geographers' intentions, it has proved difficult to establish this usage as a purely objective category. The material ordering of landscape cannot be conceptualized independent of the personal judgment of an observer. This tension is evident even in Carl Sauer's attempt to establish landscape as the foundational category of an empirically grounded geographic science.[1]

This apparently irreconcilable opposition is the result of a common assumption about landscape shared by both sides of this culture-material binary. Each in its own way treats landscape as an external, passive, and given reality that stands outside of a detached observer, whether the observer be a cultivated connoisseur or an objective scientist. By prioritizing different aspects of the same conception, these two approaches continually reproduce this dualism.

We do not question that images are representations and that there is a politics of representation. However, we insist that it is necessary to explore the relation between the visual image and the neglected space beyond the representation. Visual representation and culture are mediated by nature, material life, social relations, and, above all, labor at the same time that nature, material life, social relations, and labor are laden with culture and meaning. The images that have been examined here are parts of a definite visual practice. They break with

Figure C.01. *Ingenio Dolores Abreu, Remedios, Cuba. Photograph by Grupo Bocaina.*

conventional notions of picturesque nature that characterize the art historical concept of landscape and portray an overtly industrial and commercial landscape. The nature that they portray is the produced "second nature" of agrarian capitalism. They are concerned with rational, objective, and documentary depictions and measurement, calculation, the relation of means to ends, and the application of science to production. Each of the diverse genres of landscape representation that is used in this study documents the production, organization, management, and representation of the material and social relations of plantation space—and played a role in those activities. Maps and plans extended visual control of the landscape beyond what the eye could see. They made intelligible the productive landscape. Such representations were necessary links between conception and execution. They permitted planned, purposive activity and were instrumental in structuring the social-material environment. They materially and economically integrated commodity frontiers and allowed calculation of time and distance. On a smaller scale, plantation maps delineated property boundaries and cataloged productive resources. They enabled planters to plan and efficiently structure the spatial economy of the plantation. When the planned landscape conformed to the map, the map served as an invaluable instrument for managing land and labor throughout the crop cycle. Further, maps and the landscapes they represented were not merely functional. Their symbolic, cultural, and even aesthetic values shaped the perception, meaning, and experience of the landscape. Other types of images served other purposes. Justo Cantero and Eduardo Laplante's account of the Cuban sugar mill appeared as a travel album through the industrialized countryside of Cuba's sugar frontier. At the same time, its detailed and precise depictions of machinery and production processes had much in common with a commercial or industrial brochure.[2] Even images that more closely conformed to the conventions of landscape aesthetics were deeply implicated in the social and material practices of the plantation zones. They, as well as the landscapes they represented, were vehicles for the display of prestige, power, and wealth that was crucial to the establishment of the social and racial hierarchies upon which plantation slavery depended. Perhaps more importantly, their representational strategies naturalized and legitimized the second nature of capitalist agriculture and slave labor. Understood in this way, visual representations at once documented and produced the spatial configurations that characterized the new slave commodity frontiers. The diversity of kinds of images and the meanings they convey are testimony to the complexity of landscape as a material-social-cultural relation.

Landscapes are irreducibly local and particular. They are necessarily tied to specific locations. However, it would be misleading to treat these locations as discrete, self-enclosed zones with their own internal histories. They are not the result of fateful choices by powerful local elites or conflicts between contending local groups. Rather, they are the products of systemic world-economic processes and are formed through complex global-local interactions. The new zones of slave commodity production were premised on and contributed to the economic and material expansion of the capitalist world-economy. Particular regional environments were selected, appropriated, and restructured through the interaction of diverse but interrelated economic and political forces and relations that operated across diverse spatial temporal scales. The interaction and combination of these forces and relations configured these geographically extensive territories. In each zone, nature and slave labor relations were restructured around the material requirements for the production of each crop—cotton in the U.S. South, sugar in Cuba, and coffee in Brazil—to create distinct spatial economies and particular local landscapes. The extensive introduction of monocrop agriculture, the massive influx of enslaved laborers, the construction of transportation networks, and the formation of markets and credit flows created new global commodity circuits that integrated these zones into the world-economic division of labor. Thus, commodity production and slave relations necessarily developed *through* space rather than *in* space. In each commodity frontier, nature and labor were mobilized for the mass production of key commodities of the material culture of modernity and master-slave relations and slave labor were reconstituted in historically specific ways. The new commodity frontiers of the second slavery were no less capitalist factories than the mills of Manchester. Far from being a superstructural or marginal element, the construction of plantation landscapes was a fundamental aspect of the remaking of slavery and the expansion of the capitalist world-economy during the nineteenth century.

Notes

Introduction

1. Castro and Schnoor, *Resgate*, 49–50; Marquese, "Vale do Paraíba cafeeiro."

2. Marquese, "Vale do Paraíba cafeeiro."

3. See, for example, Cosgrove, *Social Formation*, esp. 20–27. See also Vlach, *Planter's Prospect*; and Harris, *Nature of Authority*, 36–37.

4. See Bermingham, *Landscape and Ideology*.

5. Dean, *With Broadax and Firebrand*, 168–212.

6. Green, "Looking at the Landscape," 31–42; Green, *Spectacle of Nature*, 2–14.

7. R. Williams, *Country and the City*, 120.

8. Meinig, *Interpretation of Ordinary Landscapes*.

9. J. W. Moore, "Sugar and the Expansion of the Early Modern World-Economy" and "Madeira, Sugar, and the Conquest of Nature," 1–24.

10. Eric Williams's classic *Capitalism and Slavery*, first published in 1944, is the cornerstone of scholarship on the problem of the relation of capitalism and slavery. It has continued to stimulate inquiry and generate debate up until the present, including Drescher, *Econocide*; Solow and Engerman, *British Capitalism and Caribbean Slavery*; Ryden, *West Indian Slavery and British Abolition*; Palmer, *Legacy of Eric Williams*; E. Williams, *Economic Aspect of the Abolition of the West Indian Slave Trade*; and *Review*'s special issue "Rediscovering Eric Williams."

11. The concept of the second slavery was first formulated in Tomich, "'Second Slavery.'" The original essay generated a growing body of international scholarship that extended and refined the concept and contributed to the reinterpretation of nineteenth-century slavery. The response included not only conferences, seminars, and panels at various congresses but also a number of publications. Among these are Schmidt-Nowara, *Empire and Antislavery*; Marquese, *Feitores do corpo*; Salles, *E o vale era o escravo*; Zeuske, "Comparing or interlinking?"; Kaye, "Second Slavery"; Marquese, Berbel and Parron, *Escravidão e política*; Parron, *Política da escravidão*; Marques, *United States and the Transatlantic Slave Trade*; Blackburn, *American Crucible*; Dal Lago, *American Slavery*; Chalhoub, *Força da escravidão*; Johnson, *River of Dark Dreams*; Baptist, *Half Has Never Been Told*; and Muaze and Salles, *Vale do Paraíba*. Growing interest in this perspective led to the formation of the International Research Seminar on the Second Slavery, which organized a series of conferences and produced a number of edited volumes dedicated to the theme. These included Tomich and Zeuske, "Second Slavery"; Tomich, da Cunha, and Gomes, "Re-thinking the Plantation"; Tomich, *New Frontiers of Slavery*; Piqueras, *Trabajo libre*; Tomich, *Politics of the Second Slavery*; Laviña and Zeuske, *Second Slavery*; Marquese and Salles, *Escravidão e capitalismo histórico*; Tomich, *Atlantic Transformations*; and Tomich and Lovejoy, *Atlantic and Africa*.

12. Benítez-Rojo, *Repeating Island*.

13. See Crichlow, *Globalization*.

14. Cosgrove, *Social Formation*, 19.

15. Green, "Looking at the Landscape," 32–34.

16. Kossoy, *Fotografia e história*, 35–47.

17. Barrell, *Dark Side of the Landscape*.

18. See Mitchell, *Lie of the Land*, 16–20.

19. For a contrasting approach, compare Mirzoef, *Right to Look*; and Casid, *Sowing Empire*.

Part I

1. Massey, "Politics and Space/Time"; Massey, *Space, Place, and Gender*; Lefebvre, *Production of Space*.

2. Tomich, *Through the Prism of Slavery*, 56–71.

3. J. W. Moore, "Sugar and the Expansion of the Early Modern World-Economy"; J. W. Moore, "Madeira, Sugar, and the Conquest of Nature."

4. Godinho, "Complexo histórico-geográfico."

5. Bunker and Ciccantell, *Globalization*, 3, 12.

6. A. Castro, *7 ensaios*, 1:41–66, 2:60–61.

7. Bunker and Ciccantell, *Globalization*, 2–12.

8. Trans-Atlantic Slave Trade Data Base, https://www.slavevoyages.org.

9. Tadman, *Speculators and Slaves*, 12.

10. Slenes, "Brazilian Internal Slave Trade."

11. Tomich, *Through the Prism of Slavery*, esp. 56–71; Marquese, *Feitores do corpo*.

12. Higman, "Spatial Economy."

13. Massey, *Space, Place, and Gender*, 146–56.

Chapter 1

1. Hobsbawm, *Industry and Empire*, 34–79; Beckert, *Empire of Cotton*, 3–273.

2. Grey, *History of Agriculture*, 2:691; Bruchey, *Cotton*, 107–17; Johnson, *River of Dark Dreams*, 10–11.

3. Hilliard, *Atlas*, 31–34, 38, 41–44.

4. Gudmestad, *Steamboats*, 117–31; Johnson, *River of Dark Dreams*, 88–90.

5. Hilliard, *Atlas*, 7, 11.

6. Bacot et al., *Marie Adrien Persac*, 58, 12.

7. Hilliard, *Atlas*, 7, 11; Morris *Big Muddy*, 116–18.

8. Ingraham, *South-West by a Yankee*, 2:19.

9. Rothstein, "Natchez Nabobs," 98–101; J. H. Moore, *Emergence of the Cotton Kingdom*, 117; James, *Antebellum Natchez*, 149–60.

10. Brazy, *American Planter*, 27; Miller and Miller, *Great Houses of Natchez*, 7.

11. Wayne, *Reshaping of Plantation Society*, 6–9.

12. Wayne, 6–9; James, Antebellum Natchez, 147–49.

13. La Tourrette, *A Plantation Map of the State of Louisiana, by John La Tourette, Southern Map-maker Prospectus* n.d.

14. Gudmestad, *Steamboats*, 143–45, 147–48, 156–57; Johnson, *River of Dark Dreams*, 6, 256.

15. Gudmestad, *Steamboats*, 141–43; Johnson, *River of Dark Dreams*, 78–79.

16. Bunker and Ciccantell, *Globalization*.

17. Gudmestad, *Steamboats*, 147–50.

18. Johnson, *River of Dark Dreams*, 87.

19. Johnson, 91.

20. Gudmestad, *Steamboats*, 142–43; Johnson, *River of Dark Dreams*, 91–93.

21. Gudmestad, *Steamboats*, 105–8, 146–47; Johnson, *River of Dark Dreams*, 93–94.

22. Gudmestad, *Steamboats*, 144; Johnson, *River of Dark Dreams*, 84–86.

23. Bacot et al., *Marie Adrien Persac*, 64, 13–14; Meinig, *Shaping of America*, 20.

24. J. H. Moore, *Agriculture in Ante-bellum Mississippi*, 55.

25. Johnson, *River of Dark Dreams*, 256–62.

Chapter 2

1. Funes Monzote, *From Rainforest to Cane Field*, 20–21; Funes Monzote, "Especialización azucarera."

2. Funes Monzote, *From Rainforest to Cane Field*, 17.

3. Funes Monzote, 62.

4. Funes Monzote, 18–19.

5. Arango y Parreño, *Discurso sobre la agricultura*.

6. Funes Monzote, *From Rainforest to Cane Field*, 4–28.

7. Funes Monzote, 84–85.

8. Funes Monzote, 83–126.

9. Alpers, *Art of Describing*, 138.

10. Alpers, 136–37, 147.

11. Funes Monzote, *From Rainforest to Cane Field*, 83–126.

12. Funes Monzote, 128–30; Funes Monzote and Tomich, "Naturaleza, tecnología y esclavitud"; Zanetti and García, *Sugar and Railroads*, 18–56.

13. Alpers, *Art of Describing*, 138.

14. Bunker and Ciccantell, *Globalization*, 1–32, 99–135.

15. Schmidt-Nowara, *Empire and Antislavery*.

16. Bergad, *Cuban Rural Society*, 56.

17. Venegas, *Cuba y sus pueblos*, 46–48; Venegas, "Habana y su region."

18. Cantero and Laplante, *Los Ingenios*, 123–26. All citations are to the 2005 edition.

19. Moreno Fraginals, *Ingenio*, 196–99.

20. Gayle and Gayle, *Cast-Iron Architecture*, 195–98; Giedion, *Space, Time and Architecture*, 193–98.

Chapter 3

1. Marrero, *Cuba*, 114.

2. Bergad, *Escravidão e história econômica*, 1–25; Luna and Klein, *Slavery and the Economy of São Paulo*, 28–52.

3. Marquese and Tomich, "Slavery in the Valley of Paraíba."

4. Florentino, *Em costas negras*, 74.

5. Luna and Klein, *Slavery and the Economy of São Paulo*, 58–59.

6. Marquese and Tomich, "Slavery in the Valley of Paraíba."

7. Marquese and Tomich, "Slavery in the Valley of Paraíba."

8. Topik, "Integration of the World Coffee Market."

9. Marquese, "African Diaspora."

10. Stein, *Vassouras*, 4–7.

11. Stein, 9–17; Motta, *Corpo escravo*, 34–40.

12. Marquese and Tomich, "Slavery in the Valley of Paraíba."

13. Alegrio, *Os Clemente Pinto*.

14. Dean, *With Broadax and Firebrand*, 181–88; Marquese, "African Diaspora."

15. Saint Hilaire, *Segunda viagem*, 101; Aguiar, *Pequena memória sobre a plantação*, 11; Taunay, *Manual do agricultor brasileiro*, 130; Marquese, "Capitalism, Slavery and the Brazilian Coffee Economy."

16. A. Castro, *7 ensaios*, 2:50.

17. Lenharo, *As tropas da moderação*.

18. Klein, "Supply of Mules"; Marquese and Tomich, "Slavery in the Valley of Paraíba."

19. Ribeiro, "'Leading Commission-House of Rio de Janeiro.'"

Part II

1. Bunker and Ciccantell, *Globalization*, 5.

2. Warman, *Corn and Capitalism*, 12–20.

3. Higman, "Spatial Economy."

4. Bunker and Ciccantell, *Globalization*, 1–32.

5. Scott, *Seeing Like a State*, 13–15.

6. Marquese, *Feitores do corpo*, 259–382.

Chapter 4

1. Bruchey, *Cotton*, 173.

2. Wailes, *Report on the Agriculture*, 139–40.

3. Chaplin, *Anxious Pursuit*, 220–24.

4. J. H. Moore, *Agriculture in Ante-bellum Mississippi*, 28–29; Lakwate, *Inventing the Cotton Gin*, 2.

5. Wailes, *Report on the Agriculture*, 143; J. H. Moore, *Agriculture in Ante-bellum Mississippi*, 33.

6. Olmstead and Rhode, *Creating Abundance*.

7. Johnson, *River of Dark Dreams*, 8.

8. Baptist, *Half Has Never Been Told*, 124–44; Johnson, *River of Dark Dreams*, 151–52; J. H. Moore, *Agriculture in Ante-bellum Mississippi*, 34–36, 280.

9. Kaye, *Making Places*, 21–50; Wayne, *Reshaping of Plantation Society*.

10. Johnson, *River of Dark Dreams*, 152–54; Olmstead, *Cotton Kingdom*, 416–17.

11. J. H. Moore, *Agriculture in Ante-bellum Mississippi*, 40.

12. Wayne, *Reshaping of Plantation Society*.

13. Thompson, *Plantation*, 26–32.

14. Bruchey, *Cotton*, 171; Jordan, *Tumult and Silence*, 42.

15. Bruchey, *Cotton*, 171; J. H. Moore, *Agriculture in Ante-bellum Mississippi*, 43–45.

16. Jordan, *Tumult and Silence*, 43–44; J. H. Moore, *Agriculture in Ante-bellum Mississippi*, 43–45; Bruchey, *Cotton*, 171.

17. Berlin, *Generations of Captivity*, 176.

18. J. H. Moore, *Agriculture in Ante-bellum Mississippi*, 43; Bruchey, *Cotton*, 174.

19. Bruchey, *Cotton*, 174; Jordan, *Tumult and Silence*, 43–44.

20. Wailes, *Report on the Agriculture*, 157–64; Lakwate, *Inventing the Cotton Gin*, 47–52, 77–78.

21. J. H. Moore, *Agriculture in Ante-bellum Mississippi*, 21–22.

22. Wailes, *Report on the Agriculture*, 167–70; Lakwate, *Inventing the Cotton Gin*, 77–78.

23. J. H. Moore, *Agriculture in Ante-bellum Mississippi*, 23–24, 47–49; Lakwate, *Inventing the Cotton Gin*, 78, 141–42; Wailes, *Report on the Agriculture*, 167–72.

24. J. H. Moore, *Agriculture in Ante-bellum Mississippi*, 23–24, 47–49; Lakwate, *Inventing the Cotton Gin*, 73, 78, 141–42, 146–47; Wailes, *Report on the Agriculture*, 167–72, 179–80; Bruchey, *Cotton*, 171, 175.

25. Wailes, *Report on the Agriculture*, 174–74; J. H. Moore, *Agriculture in Ante-bellum Mississippi*, 48–49; Bruchey, *Cotton*, 175.

26. J. H. Moore, *Agriculture in Ante-bellum Mississippi*, 53.

27. J. H. Moore, 51–53.

28. Wailes, *Report on the Agriculture*, 173–80; J. H. Moore, *Agriculture in Ante-bellum Mississippi*, 52–54; Bruchey, *Cotton*, 175.

29. Tadman, *Speculators and Slaves*, 12.

30. Berlin, *Generations of Captivity*, 163–75; Kaye, *Making Places*, 26.

31. Berlin, *Generations of Captivity*, 149–151, 176–79.

32. Berlin, 150, 177–78.

33. Jordan, *Tumult and Silence*, 37–38.

34. Northrup, *Twelve Years a Slave*, 162–68.

35. Johnson, *River of Dark Dreams*, 245–46; Baptist, *Half Has Never Been Told*, 131–36.

36. J. H. Moore, *Agriculture in Ante-bellum Mississippi*, 43–46; Bruchey, *Cotton*, 174.

37. Stephenson, "Quarter-Century of a Mississippi Plantation," 355–56.

38. Johnson, *River of Dark Dreams*, 245; Scott, *Seeing Like a State*, 12–15.

39. Scott, *Seeing Like a State*, 11–15.

40. Johnson, *River of Dark Dreams*, 244–45.

41. Rothstein, "Natchez Nabobs"; James, *Antebellum Natchez*, 149–60.

42. Brazy, *American Planter*, 21.

43. Jordan, *Tumult and Silence*, 40–41.

Chapter 5

1. Galloway, *Sugar Cane Industry*, 11–15.

2. Mintz, *Sweetness and Power*, 21–23; Tomich, "Material Process," 291–93; Tomich, *Slavery in the Circuit of Sugar*, 196–99.

3. Tomich, *Slavery in the Circuit of Sugar*, 196–99.

4. Watt, *West Indies*, 384–89; Tomich, "Material Process," 293–99; Moreno Fraginals, *Ingenio*, 173.

5. Moreno Fraginals, *Ingenio*, 159–62.

6. Tomich, *Slavery in the Circuit of Sugar*, 216–17.

7. Tomich, "Material Process," 293–99; Moreno Fraginals, *Ingenio*, 173.

8. Moreno Fraginals, *Ingenio*, 178–80; Tomich, *Slavery in the Circuit of Sugar*, 246–48.

9. Tomich, *Through the Prism of Slavery*.

10. Tomich, "Material Process," 291–99; Tomich, *Through the Prism of Slavery*.

11. Tomich, "Material Process," 291–93.

12. Moreno Fraginals, *El Ingenio*, 675–76; Lapique Becali, *Notas bibliográficas*, 131; Kutzinski, *Sugar's Secrets*, 45–54.; Lapique, "Notas bibliográficas," 131.

13. Venegas, "Libro de los ingenios," 91; Lapique, "Notas bibliográficas," 131–32.

14. Eduardo Laplante and Luis Marquier, "A la Real Junta de Fomento," in Cantero and Laplante, *Los Ingenios*.

15. Venegas, "Libro de los ingenios"; Tomich, "Anomalies, Clues, and Neglected Transcripts," 228–38.

16. Cantero and Laplante, *Los ingenios*, 278–81.

17. Cantero and Laplante, 242–53.

18. Cantero and Laplante, 242–53.

19. Cantero and Laplante, 140–43.

20. Cantero and Laplante, 218–22.

21. Cantero and Laplante, 272–75.

22. Cantero and Laplante, 176–79.

23. Cantero and Laplante, 254–57; Moreno Fraginals, *Ingenio*, 173–77; Satchell, *Sugar, Slavery, and Technical Change*, 91–95, 132–64.

24. Moreno Fraginals, *Ingenio*, 146–49.

25. Cantero and Laplante, *Los ingenios*, 242–53.

26. Cantero and Laplante, 242–53.

27. Funes Monzote and Tomich, "Naturaleza, tecnología y esclavitud"; Moreno Fraginals, *Ingenio*, 146–49.

28. Murray, *Odious Commerce*.

29. Tomich, "Invention of the Cuban Sugar Mill."

30. Cantero and Laplante, *Los ingenios*, 194–97, 236–39.

Chapter 6

1. Trouillot, "Motion in the System," 337.

2. Schivelbusch, *Tastes of Paradise*, 15–84.

3. Thurber, *Coffee*, 4–8; Marquese "African Diaspora."

4. Stein, *Vassouras*, 33–36; Dean, *With Broadax and Firebrand*, 180–86.

5. Marquese, "Laborie en traducción," 185–215.

6. Marquese, "Vale do Paraíba cafeeiro," 107–9.

7. Marquese, "Laborie en traducción," 185–215.

8. Marquese, "Vale do Paraíba cafeeiro," 107–9.

9. Marquese, "Paisagem da cafeicultura."

10. Stein, *Vassouras*, 11–20.

11. Marquese, "African Diaspora."

12. Muaze, "Escravidão no Vale do Paraíba."

13. Stein, *Vassouras*, 31–33; Marquese, "Paisagem da cafeicultura."

14. Fragoso and Rios, "Um empresário brasileiro do oitocentos," 200–206.

15. Marquese, "Vale do Paraíba cafeeiro," 107–9.

16. Marquese, 107–9; Stein, *Vassouras*, 33–36.

17. Stein, *Vassouras*, 36–38.

18. Marquese, "Paisagem da cafeicultura"; Dean, *With Broadax and Firebrand*, 188–90.

Conclusion

1. Sauer, "Morphology of Landscape," 323.

2. Venegas, "Libro de los ingenios," esp. 92–94.

Bibliography

Aguiar, Pe. João Joaquim Ferreira de. *Pequena memória sobre a plantação, cultura e colheita do café*. Rio de Janeiro: Imprensa Americana de L. P. da Costa, 1836.

Alegrio, Leila Vilela. *Os Clemente Pinto: Importantes cafeicultores do sertão do leste fluminense*. Rio de Janeiro: Letra Capital, 2015.

Alpers, Svetlana. *The Art of Describing: Dutch Art in the Seventeenth Century*. Chicago: University of Chicago Press, 1983.

Arango y Parreño, Francisco. *Discurso sobre la agricultura de la Habana y medios de fomentarla*. In *Obras de D. Francisco Arango y Parraño*, 1:115–239. Havana: Dirección de Cultura. Ministerio de Educación, 1952.

Bacot, H. Parrott, Barbara SoRelle Bacot, Sally Kittredge Reeves, John Magill, and John H. Lawrence. *Marie Adrien Persac: Louisiana Artist*. Baton Rouge: Louisiana State University Press, 2000.

Baptist, Edward E. *The Half Has Never Been Told: Slavery and the Making of American Capitalism*. New York: Basic Books, 2014.

Barrell, John. *The Dark Side of the Landscape: The Rural Poor in English Painting, 1730–1840*. Cambridge, UK: Cambridge University Press, 1980.

Beckert, Sven. *Empire of Cotton: A Global History*. New York: Alfred A. Knopf, 2014.

Benítez-Rojo, Antonio. *The Repeating Island: The Caribbean and the Postmodern Perspective*. Durham, N.C.: Duke University Press, 1992.

Bergad, Laird W. *Cuban Rural Society in the Nineteenth Century: The Social and Economic History of Monoculture in Matanzas*. Princeton, N.J.: Princeton University Press, 1990.

———. *Escravidão e história econômica: Demografia de Minas Gerais, 1720–1888*. Portuguese translation. Bauru, SP: EDUSC, 2004.

Berger, John. *Ways of Seeing*. Harmondsworth, UK: Penguin Books, 1972.

Berlin, Ira. *Generations of Captivity: A History of African-American Slaves*. Cambridge, Mass.: Belknap Press of Harvard University Press, 2003.

Bermingham, Ann. *Landscape and Ideology: The English Rustic Tradition, 1740–1860*. Berkeley: University of California Press, 1986.

Blackburn, Robin. *The American Crucible: Slavery, Emancipation and Human Rights*. London: Verso, 2011.

Brazy, Martha Jane. *An American Planter: Stephen Duncan of Antebellum Natchez and New York*. Baton Rouge: Louisiana State University Press, 2006.

Bruchey, Stuart, ed. *Cotton and the Growth of the American Economy: 1790–1860: Sources and Readings*. New York: Harcourt, Brace and World, 1967.

Bunker, Stephen G., and Paul S. Ciccantell. *Globalization and the Race for Resources*. Baltimore: Johns Hopkins University Press, 2005.

Cantero, Justo G., and Eduardo Laplante. *Los ingenios: Collección de vistas de los principales ingenios de azúcar de la isla de Cuba*. Havana: Litográfia de Luis Marquier, 1857.

———. *Los ingenios: Collección de vistas de los principales ingenios de azúcar de la isla de Cuba*. Edited by Luís Miguel García Mora and Antonio Santamaría García. Madrid: Doce Calles, 2005.

Casid, Jill H. *Sowing Empire: Landscape and Colonization*. Minneapolis: University of Minnesota Press, 2005.

Castro, Antonio Barros de. *7 ensaios sobre a*

economia brasileira. 2 vols. Rio de Janeiro: Forense Universitaria, 1980.

Castro, Hebe Maria Mattos de, and Eduardo Schnoor. *Resgate uma janela para o oitocentos*. Rio de Janeiro: Topbooks, 1995.

Chalhoub, Sidney. *A força da escravidão: Ilegalidade e costume no Brasil oitocentista*. São Paulo: Companhia das Letras, 2012.

Chaplin, Joyce E. *An Anxious Pursuit: Agricultural Innovation and Modernity in the Lower South, 1730–1815*. Chapel Hill: University of North Carolina Press, 1993.

Cosgrove, Denis E. *Social Formation and Symbolic Landscape*. Madison: University of Wisconsin Press, 1998.

Crichlow, Michaeline A. *Globalization and the Post-Creole Imagination: Notes on Fleeing the Plantation*. Durham, N.C.: Duke University Press, 2009.

Dal Lago, Enrico. *American Slavery, Atlantic Slavery, and Beyond: The U.S. "Peculiar Institution" in International Perspective*. Boulder, Colo.: Paradigm Publishers, 2012.

Dean, Warren. *With Broadax and Firebrand: The Destruction of the Brazilian Atlantic Rainforest*. Berkeley: University of California Press, 1995.

Drescher, Seymour. *Econocide: British Slavery in the Era of Abolition*. Pittsburgh: University of Pittsburgh Press, 1977.

Ellis, John. *An Historical Account of Coffee with an Engraving, and Botanical Description of the Tree*. First published in London, 1774. Cambridge, UK: Cambridge University Press, 2013.

Florentino, Manolo Garcia. *Em costas negras: Uma história do tráfico atlântico de escravos entre a África e o Rio de Janeiro (séculos XVIII e XIX)*. Rio de Janeiro: Arquivo Nacional, 1995.

Fragoso, João Luis, and Ana Maria Lugão Rios. "Um empresário brasileiro do oitocentos." In *Resgate uma janela para o oitocentos*, edited by Hebe Maria Mattos de Castro and Eduardo Schnoor, 197–224. Rio de Janeiro: Topbooks, 1995.

Funes Monzote, Reinaldo. "Especialización azucarera y crisis de la ganadería en Cuba, 1790–1868." *Historia Agraria* 57 (2012): 105–34.

———. *From Rainforest to Cane Field in Cuba: An Environmental History since 1492*. Chapel Hill: University of North Carolina Press, 2008.

Funes Monzote, Reinaldo, and Dale Tomich. "Naturaleza, tecnología y esclavitud en Cuba: Frontera azucarera y revolución industrial." In *Trabajo libre y coactivo en sociedades de plantación*, edited by José Antonio Piqueras, 75–117. México: Siglo XXI, 2009.

Galloway, J. H. *The Sugar Cane Industry: An Historical Geography from Its Origins to 1914*. Cambridge, UK: Cambridge University Press, 1989.

Gayle, Margot, and Carol Gayle. *Cast-Iron Architecture in America: The Significance of James Bogardus*. New York: W. W. Norton, 1998.

Giedion, Siegfried. *Space, Time and Architecture: The Growth of a New Tradition*. Cambridge, Mass.: Harvard University Press, 1956.

Godinho, Vitorino Magalhães. "Complexo histórico-geográfico." In *Dicionário de história de Portugal*, II, edited by João Serrão, 130–35. Porto, Port.: Iniciativas Editoriais, 1961.

Green, Nicholas, "Looking at the Landscape: Class Formation and the Visual." In *The Anthropology of Landscape: Perspectives on Place and Space*, edited by Eric Hirsch and Michael O'Hanlon, 31–42. Oxford: Clarendon Press, 1995.

———. *The Spectacle of Nature: Landscape and Bourgeois Culture in Nineteenth-Century France*. Manchester: Manchester University Press, 1990.

Grey, Lewis C. *History of Agriculture in the Southern United States to 1860*. 2 vols. Washington, D.C.: Carnegie Institution, 1933.

Gudmestad, Robert. *Steamboats and the Rise of the Cotton Kingdom*. Baton Rouge: Louisiana State University Press, 2011.

Harris, Dianne. *The Nature of Authority: Villa Culture, Landscape, and Representation in Eighteenth-Century Italy*. University Park: Pennsylvania State University Press, 2003.

Higman, Barry W. *Jamaica Surveyed: Plantation Maps and Plans of the Eighteenth and Nineteenth Centuries*. Kingston, Jam.: University of the West Indies Press, 1988.

———. "The Spatial Economy of Jamaican Sugar Plantations: Cartographic Evidence from the Eighteenth and Nineteenth Centuries." *Journal of Historical Geography* 13, no. 1 (1987): 17–39.

Hilliard, Sam Bowers. *Atlas of Antebellum Southern Agriculture*. Baton Rouge: Louisiana State University Press, 1984.

Hobsbawm, E. J. *Industry and Empire*. London: Penguin Books, 1969.

Humboldt, Alejandro de. *Ensayo político sobre la Isla de Cuba*. Edited by Miguel Ángel Puig, Consuelo Naranjo Orovio, and Armando García González. Madrid: Ediciones Doce Calles, 1998.

Ingraham, Joseph Holt. *The South-West by a Yankee*. 2 vols. New York: Harper and Brothers, 1835. Reprint, Readex Microprint, 1966.

James, D. Clayton. *Antebellum Natchez*. Baton Rouge: Louisiana State University Press, 1968.

Johnson, Walter. *River of Dark Dreams:*

Slavery and Empire in the Cotton Kingdom. Cambridge Mass.: Belknap Press, 2013.
Jordan, Winthrop D. *Tumult and Silence at Second Creek: An Inquiry into a Civil War Slave Conspiracy.* Baton Rouge: Louisiana State University Press, 1993.
Kaye, Anthony. *Making Places: Slave Neighborhoods in the Old South.* Chapel Hill: University of North Carolina Press, 2007.
———. "The Second Slavery: Modernity in the Nineteenth-Century South and the Atlantic World." *Journal of Southern History* 73, no. 3 (2009): 627–50.
Klein, Herbert. "The Supply of Mules to Central Brazil: The Sorocaba Market, 1825–1880." *Agricultural History* 64, no. 4 (1990): 1–25.
Kossoy, Boris. *Fotografia e história.* São Paulo: Ateliê Editorial, 2001.
Kutzinski, Vera M. *Sugar's Secrets: Race and the Erotics of Cuban Nationalism.* Charlottesville: University of Virginia Press, 1993.
Laborie, Pierre-Joseph. *The Coffee Planter of Santo Domingo.* London: T. Cadell and W. Davies, 1798.
Lakwate, Angela. *Inventing the Cotton Gin: Machine and Myth in Antebellum America.* Baltimore: Johns Hopkins University Press, 2003.
Lapique Becali, Zoila. "Notas bibliográficas sobre el libro de *Los Ingenios.*" *Revista de la Biblioteca Nacional José Martí,* September–December 1970, 131–39.
La Tourrette, John. *A Plantation Map of the State of Louisiana, by John La Tourette, Southern Map-maker Prospectus.* n.d. Pdf. https://www.loc.gov/item/rbpe.02501100/.
Laviña, Javier, and Michael Zeuske, eds. *The Second Slavery: Mass Slaveries and Modernity in the Americas and in the Atlantic Basin.* Berlin and Zürich: LIT Verlag, 2014.
Lefebvre, Henri. *The Production of Space.* Oxford: Blackwell, 1991.
Lenharo, Alcir. 1992. *As tropas da moderação: O abastecimento da Corte na formação política do Brasil, 1808–1842.* Rio de Janeiro: Prefeitura do Rio de Janeiro (SMCTE), 1979.
Luna, Francisco Vidal, and Herbert S. Klein. *Slavery and the Economy of São Paulo, 1750–1850.* Stanford, Calif.: Stanford University Press, 2005.
Marques, Leonardo. *The United States and the Transatlantic Slave Trade to the Americas, 1786–1867.* New Haven, Conn.: Yale University Press, 2016.
Marquese, Rafael de Bivar. "African Diaspora, Slavery and the Paraíba Valley Coffee Plantation Landscape." *Review (Fernand Braudel Center)* 31, no. 2 (2008): 195–216.
———. "Capitalism, Slavery and the Brazilian Coffee Economy." In *The Legacy of Eric Williams: Caribbean Scholar and Statesman,* edited by Colin A. Palmer, 190–223. Mona, Jam.: University of the West Indies Press, 2015.
———. *Feitores do corpo, missionários da mente: Senhores, letrados e o controle dos escravos nas Américas, 1660–1860.* São Paulo: Companhia das Letras, 2004.
———. "Laborie en traducción: La construcción de la caficultura cubana y brasileña desde una perspectiva comparada, 1790–1840." In *Plantación, espacios agrarios y esclavitud en la Cuba colonial,* edited by José Antonio Piqueras, 185–215. Castelló de Plana, Spain: Publicacions de la Universitat Jaume I, 2017.
———. "A paisagem da cafeicultura na crise da escravidão." *Revista do Instituto de Estudos Brasileiros* 44 (2007): 55–76.
———. "O Vale do Paraíba cafeeiro e o regime visual da segunda escravidão: O caso da fazenda Resgate." *Anais do Museu Paulista* 18, no. 1 (January–July 2010): 83–128.
Marquese, Rafael, Márcia Berbel, and Tâmis Parron. *Escravidão e política: Brasil e Cuba, c. 1790–1850.* São Paulo: Hucitec, 2010.
Marquese, Rafael, and Ricardo Salles, eds. *Escravidão e capitalismo histórico no século XIX: Cuba, Brasil, Estados Unidos.* Rio de Janeiro: Civilização Brasileira, 2016.
Marquese, Rafael de Bivar, and Dale Tomich. "Slavery in the Valley of Paraíba and the Formation of the World Coffee Market in the Nineteenth Century." In *Atlantic Transformations: Empire, Politics, and Slavery during the Nineteenth Century,* edited by Dale W. Tomich, 193–223. Albany: State University of New York Press, 2019.
Marrero, Levi. *Cuba: Economia y Sociedad.* Vol. 11. Madrid: Editorial Playor, 1985.
Massey, Doreen. "Politics and Space/Time." *New Left Review* 196 (1992): 65–84.
———. *Space, Place, and Gender.* Minneapolis: University of Minnesota Press, 1994.
Meinig, D. W., ed. *The Interpretation of Ordinary Landscapes.* New York: Oxford University Press, 1979.
———. *The Shaping of America: A Geographical Perspective on 500 Years of History.* Vol. 2, *Continental America, 1800–1867.* New Haven, Conn.: Yale University Press, 1993.
Miller, Mary Warren, and Ronald W. Miller. *The Great Houses of Natchez.* Jackson: University of Mississippi Press, 1986.
Mintz, Sidney W. *Sweetness and Power: The Place of Sugar in Modern History.* New York: Penguin Books, 1985.
———. *Tasting Food, Tasting Freedom: Excursions into Eating, Culture, and the Past.* Boston: Beacon Press, 1996.
Mirzoef, Nicholas. *The Right to Look:*

A Counterhistory of Visuality. Durham, N.C.: Duke University Press, 2011.

Mitchell, Don. *The Lie of the Land: Migrant Workers and the California Landscape*. Minneapolis: University of Minnesota Press, 1996.

Mitchell, W. J. T. *Landscape and Power*. Chicago: University of Chicago Press, 2002.

Moore, Jason W. "Madeira, Sugar, and the Conquest of Nature in the 'First' Sixteenth Century, Part II: From Regional Crisis to Commodity Frontier, 1506–1530." *Review (Fernand Braudel Center)* 33, no. 1 (2010): 1–24.

———. "Sugar and the Expansion of the Early Modern World-Economy: Commodity Frontiers, Ecological Transformation, and Industrialization." *Review (Fernand Braudel Center)* 23, no. 3 (2000): 409–33.

Moore, John Hebron. *Agriculture in Antebellum Mississippi*. Columbia: University of South Carolina Press, 2010.

———. *The Emergence of the Cotton Kingdom in the Old Southwest: Mississippi, 1770–1860*. Baton Rouge: Louisiana State University Press, 1988.

Moreno Fraginals, Manuel. *El Ingenio: Complejo económico social cubano del azúcar*. Barcelona: Editorial Crítica, 2001.

Morris, Christopher. *The Big Muddy: An Environmental History of the Mississippi and Its Peoples from Hernando De Soto to Hurricane Katrina*. Oxford: Oxford University Press, 2012.

Motta, José Flávio. *Corpo escravo, vontades livres: Posse de cativeros e família escrava em Bananal (1801–1829)*. São Paulo: Annablume, n.d.

Muaze, Mariana. "A escravidão no Vale do Paraíba pelas lentes do fotógrafo Marc Ferrez (1880–1885.)" In *Dimensões e fronteiras do Estado brasileiro no oitocentos*, edited by Jose Murilho de Carvalho and Lúcia Maria Bastos Pereira de Neves, 163–82. Rio de Janeiro: Eduerj, 2014.

Muaze, Mariana, and Ricardo Salles, eds. *O Vale do Paraíba e o Império do Brasil nos quadros da segunda escravidão*. Rio de Janeiro: 7 Letras, 2015.

Murray, David. *Odious Commerce: Britain, Spain and the Abolition of the Cuban Slave Trade*. Cambridge, UK: Cambridge University Press, 1980.

Northrup, Solomon. *Twelve Years a Slave*. Auburn, N.Y.: Derby and Miller, 1853.

Olmstead, Alan L., and Paul W. Rhode. *Creating Abundance: Biological Innovation and American Agricultural Development*. New York: Cambridge University Press, 2008.

Olmsted, Frederic Law. *The Cotton Kingdom: A Traveller's Observations on Cotton and Slavery in the American Slave States*. Boston: Da Capo Press, 1996.

Palmer, Colin, ed. *The Legacy of Eric Williams: Caribbean Scholar and Statesman*. Mona, Jam.: University of the West Indies Press, 2015.

Parron, Tâmis. *A política da escravidão no Império do Brasil, 1826–1865*. Rio de Janeiro: Civilização Brasileira, 2011.

Piqueras, José Antonio, ed. *Esclavitud y capitalismo histórico en el siglo XIX: Brazil, Cuba y Estados Unidos*. Santiago de Cuba: Editorial del Caribe, 2016.

———. *Trabajo libre y coactivo en sociedades de plantación*. Madrid: Siglo XXI, 2009.

"Rediscovering Eric Williams: The Intellectual History of *Capitalism and Slavery*." Special issue, *Review (Fernand Braudel Center)* 35, no. 2 (2012).

Ribeiro, Alan dos Santos. "'The Leading Commission-House of Rio de Janeiro': A firma Maxwell, Wright & Co. no comércio do Império do Brasil (c. 1827–c. 1850)." Master's thesis, Niterói/RJ, Universidade Federal Fluminense, 2014.

Rothstein, Morton, "The Natchez Nabobs: Kinship and Friendship in an Economic Elite." In *Toward a New View of America: Essays in Honor of Arthur C. Cole*, edited by Hans L. Trefousse, 97–112. New York: Franklin, 1977.

Ryden, David Beck. *West Indian Slavery and British Abolition, 1783–1807*. Cambridge, UK: Cambridge University Press, 2009.

Saint Hilaire, Auguste de. *Segunda viagem do Rio de Janeiro a Minas Gerais e a São Paulo, 1822*. Belo Horizonte: Itatiaia Editor, 1974.

Salles, Ricardo. *E o vale era o escravo: Vassouras, século XIX. Senhores e escravos no coração do Império*. Rio de Janeiro: Civilização Brasileira, 2008.

Satchell, Veront. *Sugar, Slavery, and Technical Change: Jamaica, 1760–1830*. Saarbrücken, Ger.: VDM Publishing, 2010.

Sauer, Carl O. "The Morphology of Landscape." In *Land and Life: A Selection from the Writings of Carl Ortwin Sauer*, edited by John Leighly, 315–50. Berkeley: University of California Press, 1974.

Schivelbusch, Wolfgang. *Tastes of Paradise: A Social History of Spices, Stimulants, and Intoxicants*. New York: Vintage Books, 1993.

Schmidt-Nowara, Christopher. *Empire and Antislavery: Spain, Cuba, and Puerto Rico, 1833–1874*. Pittsburgh: University of Pittsburgh Press, 1999.

Schulten, Susan. *Mapping the Nation: History and Cartography in Nineteenth-Century America*. Chicago: University of Chicago Press, 2012.

Scott, James C. *Seeing Like a State: How Certain Schemes to Improve the Human Condition Have Failed*. New Haven, Conn.: Yale University Press, 1998.

Slenes, Robert W. "The Brazilian Internal Slave Trade, 1850–1888: Regional Economies, Slave Experience, and the Politics of a Peculiar Market." In *The Chattel Principle: Internal Slave Trades in the Americas*, edited by Walter Johnson, 327–33. New Haven, Conn.: Yale University Press, 2004.

Solow, Barbara L., and Stanley L. Engerman, eds. *British Capitalism and Caribbean Slavery: The Legacy of Eric Williams*. Cambridge, UK: Cambridge University Press, 1987.

Stein, Stanley J. *Vassouras: A Brazilian Coffee County, 1850–1900*. Princeton, N.J.: Princeton University Press, 1985.

Stephenson, Wendell Holmes. "A Quarter-Century of a Mississippi Plantation: Eli J. Capell of 'Pleasant Hill.'" *Mississippi Valley Historical Review* 23, no. 3 (1936): 355–74.

Tadman, Michael. *Speculators and Slaves: Masters, Traders and Slaves in the Old South*. Madison: University of Wisconsin Press, 1989.

Taunay, Carlos Augusto. *Manual do agricultor brasileiro*. Edited by Rafael de Bivar Marquese. 1839. São Paulo: Companhia das Letras, 2001.

Thompson, Edgar T. *The Plantation*. Edited by Sidney W. Mintz and George Baca. Durham, N.C.: Duke University Press, 2010.

Thurber, Francis Beatty. *Coffee, from Plantation to Cup: A Brief History of Coffee Production and Consumption, with an Appendix Containing Letters Written during a Trip to the Coffee Plantations of the East and through the Coffee Consuming Countries of Europe*. New York: American Grocer Publishing Association, 1884.

Tomich, Dale. "Anomalies, Clues, and Neglected Transcripts: Microhistories and Representations of the Cuban Sugar Frontier, 1820–1860." In *Small Worlds: Method, Meaning, and Narrative in Microhistory*, edited by James F. Brooks, Christopher R. N. DeCorse, and John Walton, 225–45. Santa Fe, N.Mex.: School for Advanced Research Press, 2008.

——, ed. *Atlantic Transformations: Empire, Politics, and Slavery during the Nineteenth Century*. Albany: State University of New York Press, 2020.

——. "The Invention of the Cuban Sugar Mill: Space, Time and Labor Management, 1820–1860." In *Francisco Arango y la invención de la Cuba azucarera*, edited by María Dolores González-Ripoll Navarro and Izaskun Álvarez Cuartero, 133–49. Salamanca: Ediciones Universidad de Salamanca, 2010.

——. "Material Process and Industrial Architecture: Innovation on the Cuban Sugar Frontier, 1818–1857." In *Nature, Raw Material and Political Economy*, edited by Paul Ciccantell, David A. Smith, and Gay Seidman, 287–307. Amsterdam: Elsevier, 2005.

——, ed. *New Frontiers of Slavery*. Albany: State University of New York Press, 2016.

——, ed. *The Politics of the Second Slavery*. Albany: State University of New York Press, 2016.

——. "Rethinking the Plantation: Concepts and Histories." *Review (Fernand Braudel Center)* 24, nos. 1–2 (2011): 15–39.

——. "The 'Second Slavery': Bonded Labor and the Transformation of the Nineteenth-Century World Economy." In *Rethinking the Nineteenth Century: Movements and Contradictions*, edited by Francisco O. Ramirez, 103–17. Westport, Conn.: Greenwood Press, 1988.

——, ed. *Slavery and Historical Capitalism during the Nineteenth Century*. Lanham, Md.: Lexington Books, 2017.

——. *Slavery in the Circuit of Sugar: Martinique and the World-Economy, 1830–1848*. Albany: State University of New York Press, 2016.

——. *Through the Prism of Slavery: Labor, Capital, and World Economy*. Lanham, Md.: Rowman and Littlefield, 2004.

——. "The Wealth of Empire: Francisco Arango y Parreño, Political Economy, and the Second Slavery in Cuba." *Comparative Studies in Society and History* 45, no. 1 (2003): 4–28.

Tomich, Dale, Olívia Maria Gomes da Cunha, and Flávio dos Santos Gomes, eds. "Re-thinking the Plantation: Histories, Anthropologies, Archeologies." Special double issue, *Review (Fernand Braudel Center)* 34, nos. 1–2 (2013).

Tomich, Dale, and Paul Lovejoy, eds. *The Atlantic and Africa: The Second Slavery and Beyond*. Albany: State University of New York Press, in press.

Tomich, Dale, and Michael Zeuske, eds. "The Second Slavery: Mass Slavery, World Economy and Comparative Microhistories." Special double issue, *Review (Fernand Braudel Center)* 31, nos. 2–3 (2008).

Tompkins, Daniel Augustus. *Cotton Mill, Commercial Features: A Text-Book for the Use of Textile Schools and Investors. With Tables Showing Cost of Machinery and Equipments for Mills Making Cotton Yarns and Plain Cotton Cloths*. Charlotte, N.C., 1899.

Topik, Steven. "The Integration of the World Coffee Market." In *The Global Coffee Economy in Africa, Asia, and Latin America, 1500–1989*, edited by W. G. Clarence-Smith and Steven Topik, 21–49. Cambridge, UK: Cambridge University Press, 2003.

Trans-Atlantic Slave Trade Data Base. https://www.slavevoyages.org.

Trouillot, Michel-Rolph. "Motion in the

System: Coffee, Color, and Slavery in Eighteenth-Century Saint Domingue." *Review (Fernand Braudel Center)* 5, no. 3 (1982): 331–88.

Venegas Fornias, Carlos. *Cuba y sus pueblos: Censos y mapas de los siglos XVIII y XIX.* La Habana: Centro de Investigación y Desarrollo de la Cultura Cubana Juan Marinello, 2002.

———. "La Habana y su región: Un proyeto de organización espacial de la plantación esclavista." *Revista de las Indias* 56, no. 207 (1996): 333–65.

———. "El Libro de los ingenios." In *Agua, trabajo y azúcar: Actas del Sexto Seminario Internacional sobre la Caña de Azúcar, Motril, 19–23 de sep. de 1994*, edited by Antonio Malpica, 87–99. Grenada, Spain: Diputación Provincial de Granada, 1996.

Vlach, John Michael. *The Planter's Prospect: Privilege and Slavery in Plantation Paintings.* Chapel Hill: University of North Carolina Press, 2002.

Wailes, Benjamin L. C. *Report on the Agriculture and Geology of Mississippi: Embracing a Sketch of the Social and Natural History of the State.* Jackson, Miss.: E. Barksdale, State Printer, 1854.

Warman, Arturo. *Corn and Capitalism: How a Botanical Bastard Grew to Global Dominance.* Chapel Hill: University of North Carolina Press, 2003.

Watt, David. *The West Indies: Patterns of Development, Culture and Environmental Change since 1492.* Cambridge, UK: Cambridge University Press, 1987.

Wayne, Michael. *The Reshaping of Plantation Society: The Natchez District, 1860–1880.* Baton Rouge: Louisiana State University Press, 1983.

Williams, Eric. *Capitalism and Slavery.* First published, 1944. Chapel Hill: University of North Carolina Press, 2014.

———. *The Economic Aspect of the Abolition of the West Indian Slave Trade and Slavery.* Edited by Dale Tomich. Lanham, Md.: Rowman and Littlefield, 2014.

Williams, Raymond. *The Country and the City.* New York: Oxford University Press, 1973.

Zanetti, Oscar, and Alejandro García. *Sugar and Railroads: A Cuban History, 1837–1959.* Chapel Hill: University of North Carolina Press, 1998.

Zeuske, Michael. "Comparing or Interlinking? Economic Comparisons of Early Nineteenth-Century Slave Systems in the Americas in Historical Perspective." In *Slave Systems: Ancient and Modern*, edited by Enrico dal Lago and Constantina Katsari, 148–83. Cambridge, UK: Cambridge University Press, 2008.

Index